HIGHWAY 61

HIGHWAY 61

Crossroads on the Blues Highway

DEREK BRIGHT

The History Press

Dedicated to my mother, brother Ian and grandson Oliver

All photographs are the work of Richard Brown. The photographic work of Richard Brown can be found at www.arjaybeephotography.co.uk

Front cover image: The Crossroads, Clarksdale. (beccasaucier.wordpress.com)

First published 2014

The History Press
The Mill, Brimscombe Port
Stroud, Gloucestershire, GL5 2QG
www.thehistorypress.co.uk

British Library Cataloguing in Publication Data.
A catalogue record for this book is available from the British Library.

ISBN 978 0 7524 8924 7

Typesetting and origination by The History Press
Printed in Great Britain

CONTENTS

ACKNOWLEDGEMENTS

The author would like to thank the following people for their help, time and encouragement during the research and production of this book.

In particular I would like to acknowledge the support and friendship of Susanna Ernst and Frank Suerth, who gave so much of their time as well as their enthusiasm and passion for the history of Chicago, and without whom much of this book could not have been written.

I would also like to thank those that have shared the journey down Highway 61 with me and have in various ways contributed towards shaping this book. These include Phil Sugden, who undertook the road trip to the Mississippi Delta with me in 2007; my eldest son Jack Bright, who undertook the journey to Chicago and Memphis with me in 2013; and my good friend Richard Brown, photographer, whom I undertook the journey from Chicago to New Orleans with in 2012, upon which this book is based. I am grateful for both his time and patience during the course of our journey, and for his style and expertise, reflected in the numerous photographs that support the text.

I am also indebted to the many kind people we met along the way, who took the time to discuss the themes explored in the book and responded to my enquiries during the course of researching and writing the book. These include: Marc Borms, Luc Borms, Peggy Brown, Brad Cobb, Keith Dixon, David S. Dreyer, Joe Edwards, Bridgette Gray, John Gray, Paul Garon, Bruce Iglauer, Steve LaVere, Bill Lester, Bill Luckett, Carol Marble, Malcolm Mills, James Moss, De Shunn O'Bray, Steve Pasek, William Patton, 'Sunshine' Sonny Payne, Frank Ratliff, Mickey Rogers, Caneal Rule, Willie Seaberry, Mike Stephenson, Roger Stolle, Don Wilcock and Darrell White.

I am immensely grateful to Johnny Green for kindly contributing the foreword in his own inimitable style, as well as his encouragement and advice during the course of writing the book, which kept me focussed on the journey ahead and stopped me exploring too many by-ways.

Also deserving of my thanks is my wife, Mandy Lowe, who devoted a holiday to undertaking the initial proofread and spent days getting the manuscript into a semblance of order. Thanks must also go to Viv Hotten for his help and constructive criticism on the draft manuscript.

Finally I would like to thank all the blues musicians both alive and dead, who are the subject matter of this book and who have, through their art, immeasurably enhanced my life in so many ways.

FOREWORD

by Johnny Green

What could possibly persuade a bright British boy to wind up on Main Street, USA, an exile in Mississippi? Why, an odyssey, of course, to discover not only the birth of the blues but to quench his own burning sense of injustice.

Derek Bright is a driven man on these subjects. So he's made the blindingly obvious move. He's swung the hired motor down Highway 61 in search of, well, the source of it all. This book continues his theme of inner yearning, a pilgrimage, if you will.

I am entranced. Bright has rewound the tape. This book allows the reader to open the passenger door, climb into the front (preferably bench) seat next to our driver, guide 'n' courier and peer through the windscreen. All the time, Derek tunes the car radio to the very best black music that America has to offer. It is some purposeful road trip.

Yet, you may wonder, what insight does an Englishman have to offer about the blues? The lineage of rediscovery is solid. Ask Keith Richards. English musicians have been flagging up the blues right back to the birth of rock 'n' roll. Lonnie Donegan adapted the genre into homespun skiffle in the 1950s, turning on a generation. The Stones took it all back home, like coals to Newcastle, in the 1960s. Wilko Johnson, in the seventies, referenced Dr Feelgood's music as being 'from the Thames Delta'. During these decades, many great blues men, such as Muddy Waters, had to play in the UK for recognition when they couldn't get a decent gig in their own homeland.

The blues was always there for us. When The Clash first toured the USA in 1979, our support of choice was Bo Diddley. The white punk rockers in the crowd barely knew him. We stood on the side of the stage every night mesmerised like gauche schoolboys and sat at his feet like acolytes on the tour bus. Re-education to his beat was the essential order of the day.

I, like many another youth, learnt in the clubs and the back rooms of pubs from the white acts. I first heard Alexis Korner playin' bottleneck guitar, singin' gruffly with Victor Brox on pocket cornet in the dingy basement of Les Cousins, off the Charing Cross Road in the mid 1960s. It was a revelation, not a history lesson. John Mayall's Bluesbreakers, featuring Eric Clapton, came to a boozer in my provincial town and blew the place apart with 'Double Crossin' Time'. The flood gates opened for Peter Green with Fleetwood Mac and so, so many others. It took an excavation of specialist record shops in London to unearth Robert Johnson's *King of the Delta Blues Singers* …

I was inspired. The tunes directly linked up with my growing radicalism. First time I hit Chicago, I went out on a bar crawl with Joe Strummer. Through good fortune and local guidance, we ended up in some dodgy joint to celebrate ecstatically the birthday of Sunnyland Slim. We criss-crossed that route east–west, west–east. Bright goes for the jugular, north–south, back to roots, defiantly peering around the next corner.

But it ain't just musical style. Derek comes from a fine tradition of political struggle that makes perfect sense within the blues framework. He never forgets the long battle for emancipation and equality within this supposed sophistication of civilisation. For those of us yet to make this trip into a still-so-relevant psycho-geographical culture, he is our eyes, ears and conscience.

'A change is gonna come?'

Plenty of folk are still waiting and, in the meantime, still singing their songs of woe 'n' joy.

Johnny Green
Road Manager, The Clash
December 2013

INTRODUCTION

There are two great American road trips. One is immortalised by Nat King Cole's version of the Bobby Troup song 'Route 66'. The highway crosses America from east to west and for many once symbolised the promise of new frontiers and ever-expanding possibilities of the American Dream. For others the route is the epitome of the rock 'n' roll road trip, sassy and chrome-plated.

There is, however, another great highway that cuts across the United States. Designated for much of its length as the 'Great River Road', Highway 61 runs south for 1,400 miles from Wyoming, Minnesota, to New Orleans and the Gulf of Mexico. It doesn't stray far from the banks of the Mississippi River as it drills down into the heart of America's troubled past. It passes south through towns steeped with the history of modern America; towns inextricably linked with cotton and slavery, civil war and the struggle for civil rights. Alongside these histories one can find the story of America's most important indigenous musical form, the blues.

Highway 61, also known as the 'Blues Highway', is followed by those in search of the music created by the black population of the American South. Blues pilgrims are drawn there in search of authenticity in the landscape and its people that is the essence of the blues. As blues harmonica player Sugar Blue said, it is 'from this crucible the blues was born, screaming to the heavens that I will be free, I will be me'.[1] Yet today, the music holds limited interest for America's black population, but through imitation and incorporation has an immense following worldwide from a largely white male audience of blues enthusiasts.

Just as Route 66 offered the promise of a new start for impoverished white farming communities of the Southern plains in the 1930s, Highway 61 offered escape from the South for thousands of African Americans. However, the quid pro quo wasn't by any means rosy. For most blacks a new life meant poorly paid manual employment in burgeoning industrial cities of the North and Midwest and new forms of urban discrimination and segregation. The African American writer Richard Wright captured the sense of anticipation; he describes how he had sat 'in a Jim Crow coach, speeding northward, making the first lap of my journey to a land where I could live with a little less fear'.[2]

It's estimated that between 1920 and 1960 the black population of Chicago increased by 703,179 and the largest group of migrants was African Americans from the South.[3] This black diaspora brought forms of music that – like the people who created it – would adapt to the new environment of the Northern cities.

Towards the end of the period of mass migration north, Bob Dylan and Mike Bloomfield went electric, rockin' up the blues to the disdain of a primarily white folk audience at the 1965 Newport Folk Festival. According to Greil Marcus, 'backstage Pete Seeger and the great ethnomusicologist Alan Lomax attempted to cut the band's power cables with an axe'.[4] Ironically, Muddy Waters sang 'the blues had a baby and they called it rock 'n' roll', and an amplified Bob Dylan sang about Abe's sacrifice and the killing done down on Highway 61.

Five years earlier Muddy Waters had brought electric Chicago blues to a white audience at the 1960 Newport Jazz Festival. An event described by Robert Gordon as the day Muddy established his personal acquaintance with white America with a performance that 'played raucous, hard-grinding Chicago blues, his band like a tractor driving up a hill'.[5]

For most blues fans, their route to the music probably didn't start with an epiphenomenal exposure to a Chicago blues artist of the likes of Muddy Waters, Howlin' Wolf or Little Walter, or even one of the numerous rediscovered country blues guitarists during the first blues revival. For most of us it was along lines similar to that suggested by blues historian Elijah Wald: from 'the Rolling Stones via Chuck Berry and Muddy Waters'.[6] The path, incidentally, rewarded numerous white rock bands and record companies with financial returns unimaginable to the music's originators. As blues historian Paul Oliver concluded in The Story of the Blues, 'black bluesmen who escaped the "chitlin circuit" to perform for the college and concert circuits may have been better paid than before, but none made the fortunes that some of their admirers who extended the blues into the rock and pop world acquired'.[7]

Parallels between the journey taken by blues fans to the Mississippi Delta and religious pilgrimage are striking, particularly because so many references to the Delta are conferred with religious connotations. According to the

Mississippi Delta Tourism Association, the region is where music meets the soul, and the Mississippi Blues Commission invites visitors to come to the birthplace of the blues, pay homage to the musicians and walk where they walked. Steve Cheseborough's invaluable guide, *Blues Traveling*, has the subtitle *The Holy Sites of Delta Blues*.

In the opening sequences of Jim Jarmusch's *Mystery Train* the two central characters, Mitzuko and Jun, arrive in Memphis, Tennessee, to the faint sound of church bells. This gives way to a soundtrack of blues guitar as the pilgrims search for Graceland. Both the camera and Mitzuko make reference to the fact that their journey takes them along Chaucer Street. As the young pilgrims debate the respective merits of Carl Perkins and Elvis Presley en route to the shrine of the king, they stop to pay homage at Sam Phillips's legendary Sun Studios.

Modern-day pilgrims visiting Sun Studios are invited to touch the microphone used by Presley, and a cross on the floor marks the spot where Elvis stood one July night in 1954 to record his version of Arthur Crudup's 'That's All Right'. The studio's website declares, 'if music was a religion, then Memphis would be Jerusalem and Sun Studios its most holy shrine.'[8] When a young Bob Dylan arrived at Sun Studios, he knelt and kissed the spot where Elvis had stood. The historian Marybeth Hamilton, speaking at Warwick University in 2000, referred to the blues revivalists who journeyed to the Mississippi Delta in the early 1960s as pilgrims 'absorbed in the romance that they had woven around the music'.[9] Typically young, white, male and enthusiastic, fans of this generation had a profound effect on the legacy of the music: they cemented a particular interpretation of what constituted authentic blues. Eric Clapton described his own discovery of the blues as similar to a religious journey: 'It was as if I had been prepared to receive Robert Johnson, almost like a religious experience that started out with hearing Chuck Berry, and then at each stage went further and deeper until I was ready for him.'[10] Despite a sign requesting visitors to desist from removing splinters of wood from Muddy Waters's sharecropper's cabin, blues pilgrims continued to strip wood from the shack as a form of relic.

What I observed on my first blues pilgrimage didn't always sit neatly with my expectations. First, it became apparent that not only did most of the African Americans I met have little interest in blues, but neither did they share a similar historical narrative of the blues to the one which I, as a white blues pilgrim, sought when visiting their locale. This observation was reinforced by an absence of African Americans at local blues festivals, despite being held in towns with predominantly black populations, irrespective of whether such events were accessible to those with limited sources of disposable income.

On my first blues pilgrimage, in 2007, I pulled off of Highway 49 into Tutwiler, Mississippi, a small town that holds an iconic place in blues history. Tutwiler's population is a mere 1,400, of whom 87 per cent are African American. My travelling companion asked directions from a couple of men of similar age to ourselves who had their heads buried under the bonnet of an old car. When he explained we were looking for the grave of the legendary harmonica player Sonny Boy Williamson, his question was met by a genuine look of bemusement. Neither of the men was aware that Williamson was buried at the edge of their town. As we bade our farewells, an elderly man appeared from the side of the clapboard house and asked what we wanted. He directed us back along the road we'd just come to Williamson's grave, where we found it complete with harmonica and coins left by blues pilgrims who'd visited before us.

A few years later I ran this experience past a prominent member of the Tutwiler community, who suggested that many people in the town would not have been aware of Williamson's popularity and as such would be unaware of the significance of the grave to anyone outside of the town.

I subsequently undertook two more trips to the South because I wanted to retrace the first, alert to criticism of how my own blues narrative had been constructed. What I found on those subsequent trips heightened my experience as a blues pilgrim rather than diminished it.

Notes

1. Reich, Howard, 'A Heated Discussion on Race, Gender and the Blues', *Chicago Tribune*, 20 May 2012.
2. Wright, Richard, *Black Boy*, Longman, 1970, p.181.
3. Rowe, Mike, *Chicago Blues: The City and the Music*, Da Capo, 1975.
4. Marcus, Greil, *Invisible Republic*, Picador, 1996, p.12.
5. Gordon, Robert, *Can't Be Satisfied: The Life and Times of Muddy Waters*, Pimlico, 2003, p.167.
6. Wald, Elijah, *Escaping the Delta: Robert Johnson and the Invention of the Blues*, Amistad, 2005, p.128.
7. Oliver, Paul, *The Story of the Blues: The Making of Black Music*, Pimlico, 1997, p.194.
8. www.sunstudio.com/plan-your-tour.
9. Hamilton, Marybeth, 'The Blues, the Folk and African-American History', *Transactions of the Royal Historical Society*, 11, 2001, p.32.
10. Adelt, Ulrich, *Blues Music in the Sixties: A Story of Black and White*, Rutgers University Press, 2010, p.63, and Clapton, Eric, 'Discovering Robert Johnson', liner notes from *Robert Johnson: The Complete Recordings*, CBS, 1990, p.26.

Frank had the look of a saintly artisan, due to his long white beard and outwardly calm demeanour. His weathered face and thick, knitted jumper suggested someone both contemplative and practical. Susanna, Frank's partner, exuded Chicagoan enthusiasm and an outgoing, friendly nature. Neither Richard nor I had met Frank or Susanna prior to arriving on their doorstep.

As the trip to Chicago had drawn nearer, we had had difficulties planning our itinerary. Finding opportunities to visit historical blues sites as well as catching some live blues in our limited time in the country was proving challenging. Just weeks prior to our trip, Susanna's aunt visited England to undertake a pilgrimage to Canterbury and chose my company to organise her walk. We'd got around to talking about my forthcoming trip down Highway 61, at which point Josephine volunteered she had a niece in Chicago who'd visited many of the clubs located in the South Side, albeit in her youth. So that's how Richard and I found ourselves sitting on the steps of a house in north-west Chicago.

Frank and Susanna's family history reflected the pattern of European immigration to Chicago. Frank described himself as a seventh-generation Chicagoan of Irish descent. His family originally emigrated from Ireland to the United States in 1854, as had thousands of Irish Catholic families in the years immediately following the Great Famine of 1845–48. It was upon the labour of Irish immigrants such as Frank's ancestors that much of Chicago's wealth had been built. By 1850 a fifth of Chicago's population hailed from Ireland, attracted by the opportunity of work in the city's steel mills and stockyards. Many of these new immigrants settled in the densely populated enclaves of the city's South Side, in overcrowded housing close to the stockyards in an area known as Back of the Yards. Also referred to as 'Packingtown', this neighbourhood of impoverished housing covered approximately 2½ square miles and by 1920 was estimated to be home to 75,000 people.[1]

Between 1890 and 1920 a second wave of immigrants followed the Irish. Large numbers of Polish peasants seeking escape from economic hardships in Europe found work in the factories, mills and stockyards and established a strong Polish cultural identity. Susanna explained that her own ancestors were Poles who had arrived in Chicago in 1907. Over a period of thirty years from 1890, Chicago's Polish population increased by 125,000 and it has been estimated that by 1920 three-quarters of Packingtown's dwellers hailed from east of the Danube.[2] Like the Irish who had preceded the Poles, many of the new arrivals found employment in the stockyards, albeit often on an extremely casual basis.

During the First World War a third group of migrants began arriving in Chicago in search of work and a better life. These newcomers differed in three fundamental ways. Firstly, they were American, coming up from America's Southern states. Secondly, very many of these migrants were likely to have descended from people who had not come to America by choice: the likelihood, certainly for most African Americans living south of the Mason-Dixon line, was that their great-grandparents would have been slaves. Thirdly, apart from a few brief years immediately following the Civil War, these migrants had lived under Jim Crow laws, which reinforced a system of white supremacy and black inferiority. A system of segregation that:

> was a world framed by 'white' and 'coloured' – emblems meant not only to separate but to denote superior or inferior status. The expenditure in funds and effort to maintain this form of racial charade was prodigious. Separate water fountains, rest rooms, entrances, seating, eating facilities, schools, and even days to shop were among the more obvious manifestations of segregation. But signs were not the only physical reminders of separation. The unpaved streets, unpainted houses, absence of sewers, running water, and electricity, as well as the filthiness of spate accommodations provided under the rubric colored, spoke volumes about place in the South. These reminders spelled inferiority and humiliation on a daily basis.[3]

An increased demand for labour to maintain industrial output, due to higher European demand and labour shortages arising from the war in Europe, presented black Americans with opportunities for employment in urban centres like Chicago. Of course, in the wake of a new wave of migrants follows diversity in customs and culture. Francis Davis suggests in his *History of the Blues* that as 'late as the 1950s there were stretches of the South Side that resembled Mississippi, with chickens raised in back-yard pens and hand-lettered signs on grocery stores advertising fresh fish'.[4] As with all migrant communities, they incorporated parts of their past as they embraced a new future and this included the down-home music that was blues.

In the first sixty years of the twentieth century Chicago's black population increased from 30,150 to 812,637, an increase from just under 2 per cent to nearly a quarter of the city's total population.[5] It's hardly surprising that the lives and work of many musicians who established themselves in Chicago reflected the experience of black Americans in a new urban environment. The lyrics of Eddie Boyd's classic 'Five Long Years', recorded in Chicago and released by JOB in 1952, refers to time spent working in a steel mill. Boyd had left Mississippi to escape Jim Crow laws and discrimination.

By 1930 more black Americans were arriving in Chicago from Mississippi than from any other Southern state.[6] Mike Rowe's study of Chicago blues suggests that the Illinois Central Railroad was a dominant factor, allowing ease of migration from Mississippi. His estimate, based on the 1950 US Census, shows that within a thirty-year period America's black population experienced a huge demographic shift from the South to the North, and between 1940

Vacant lot, corner of Forty-Seventh Street and South Vincennes Avenue.

and 1950, half of the 154,000 migrants to Chicago originated from Mississippi. This marked a transformation from a predominantly rural population to one in which, by 1970, 80 per cent of African Americans lived in cities.[7] It was in the city of Chicago that black musicians from the South moulded a new type of urban music that became known as Chicago blues.

African Americans arriving in Chicago had limited areas of the city where they could find accommodation. Irrespective of the promise of more freedom than in the South, segregation still manifested itself in a number of forms, in terms of where one lived and what jobs one could undertake. Initially, African Americans had been kept to an area known as the 'black belt', which ran down the eastern side of 'Back of the Yards' and, as Rick Halpern's study makes clear, 'Chicago was a strictly segregated city in the early twentieth century. Practically its entire black population was crammed into a narrow finger of land wedged between Bridgeport and Wabash Avenue. Thus, outside of the workplace, whites and blacks had virtually no occasion for social intercourse.'[8] Nicholas Lemann describes Illinois Central Station as being the Ellis Island of black migration to Chicago, and how on arrival 'if you'd been told to expect it, that you could detect the pungent aroma of the stockyards, which were only a few miles off to the south-west – the smell of abundant hard work that paid much better than picking cotton.'[9]

As our plane approached O'Hare and descended over the skyscraper-lined shore of Lake Michigan, I reflected on just how little I knew about the city. The few facts that I could recall had come from Upton Sinclair's The Jungle. This book provided me with an insight into the squalor of Chicago's Packingtown and the ease with which human lives could be wasted in the pursuit of profit. How, I wondered, could anyone not fail to be moved to the cause of the workers' struggle having read Sinclair's description of the day-to-day dangers faced by workers in Chicago's slaughterhouses and packing plants:

Worst of any, however, were the fertilizer men, and those who served in the cooking rooms. These people could not be shown to the visitor – for the odour of a fertilizer man would scare any ordinary visitor at a hundred yards, and as for the other men, who worked in tank rooms full of steam, and in some of which there were open vats near the level of the floor, their peculiar trouble was that they fell into the vats; and when they were fished out, there was never enough of them left to be worth exhibiting, sometimes they would be overlooked for days, till all but the bones of them had gone out to the world as Durham's Pure Leaf Lard![10]

Sinclair's appeal to reason on behalf of the packing-house workers of America failed in favour of support for Roosevelt's Pure Food and Drug Act, with its stated intention to reform food hygiene. Sinclair later reflected that he had 'aimed at the public's heart and by accident had hit it in the stomach'.[11]

Nevertheless, Upton Sinclair enlightened me to the meaning of Led Zeppelin's 'Lemon Song', as I now knew that a 'killing floor' was where the business of slaughtering and dismembering livestock was conducted. In his study of black and white workers in Chicago's packinghouses, aptly entitled Down on the Killing Floor, Rick Halpern explains just how significant the stockyards were in the lives of Chicago's African American newcomers:

In 1914, thirty-seven establishments utilized 26,408 workers. In 1919, before demobilisation had taken its toll, 45,695 packinghouse workers earned a living in Chicago's forty-six plants. Beneath this expansion lay a demographic shift, the most important contour of which was a climb in the proportion of blacks from 3 to 25 percent of the labor force. In some of the larger plants African Americans accounted for more than 30 percent of the total figure. Indeed, the meatpacking industry was the single most important source of employment for blacks in Chicago. By the end of the decade one out of every two black men who held jobs in manufacturing was employed in the stockyards.[12]

It is not surprising therefore that the stockyards are to be found in the original lyrics of the blues songs that began to reflect this new urban environment. Songs such as by Skip James's 'Hard Times Killing Floor Blues', Howlin Wolf's 'Killing Floor' and Floyd Jones's 'Stockyard Blues'. Jones's songs reflect the hardship and struggle faced daily by workers in the stockyards; the lyrics of the 1947 'Stockyard Blues' make direct reference to a labour dispute:

Well I left home this morning, boy, y'know about half-past nine
I passed the stockyards y'know, the boys were still on the picket line
Y'know I need to earn a dollar
Y'know I need to earn a dollar
The cost of living have gone so high, now then I don't know what to do.[13]

Floyd Jones was no doubt referring to the United Packinghouse Workers of America (UPWA) strike of the previous year. Rick Halpern's study of black and white workers in Chicago's packinghouses claims Jones was an Armour packinghouse worker. Irrespective of Floyd's packinghouse credentials, he would have seen at close hand the everyday struggles of those living in the Back of the Yards. In his second record, 'Hard Times', Jones (who blues historian Mike Rowe describes as 'a serious and thoughtful man') sings about the union and the company negotiations and delivers the line 'slow production – we'll give you four days a week'.[14]

An article published in the Chicago Defender in 1939 captured both the tensions and the aspirations for unity amongst the three ethnic groups working in the Chicago stockyards:

Chicago: 'Windy City' and the blues capital of the world.

Today, because the PWOC (Packinghouse Workers Organizing Committee) planted the seed of unity in the stony soil of Packingtown, Negroes walk freely and in safety. Any public place which refused them service would be quickly put out of business by a boycott of the white union members. On the very streets where danger once lurked at every corner for Negroes, colored men stop for long chats about baseball with Polish and Irish workers.[15]

Howlin' Wolf's 'Killing Floor' was recorded at Chess Studios, Chicago, in August 1964 in a session that has been described as 'one of the best in the history of Chicago blues'.[16] Segrest and Hoffman, in their biography of Wolf, make the connection that the term 'killing floor' had already been used by Son House in his 'Dry Spell Blues'. The lyric 'If I followed my second mind' was probably taken from the 1941 Son House song 'Camp Hollers'.[17]

David Grazian, in his post-modern assault on the authenticity of Chicago's blues clubs, suggests that the city's 'identification as America's so-called "Home of the Blues" or "Blues Capital of the World" is actually a relatively recent invention'.[18] Grazian argues that it was only when blues started moving into the up-and-coming North Side clubs that the city started to incorporate the blues legacy into its self-image. Certainly, the city's blues legacy is emphasised less on the South Side.

I was expecting to find in Chicago a history that may have been reinvented, reconfigured and eventually transported to safer and more commercially viable spaces. The blues had come to me through the interpretation of a few white

Chicago Blues Festival, Grant Park.

males from London and the Home Counties of England, who had themselves been smitten with a sound that originated outside of their own cultural domain. The source of the blues that had so moved me was the product of the 1960s blues revival, yet commentators like Paul Garon, one of the founders of *Living Blues* magazine, warns:

> Had it not been created through the genius of an oppressed people, its language and speech would not have contained the same demands. Before the blues revival of the 1960s, it was taken for granted that blues contained an eloquent protest, but during the blues revival, professional pessimists, hailing themselves as realists, declared that such protest could not be detected in blues lyrics. This after decades of scholarship had uncovered the hidden meanings and the rebelliousness 'coded' in spirituals, and decades after the findings were totally accepted.[19]

I was a growing more aware that there were many lenses through which the blues pilgrim perceives the story of the blues. As such, I was conscious that what I found on my journey would not only be based upon my own evaluation, but to a great extent would also be pieced together from the historical narratives of others.

Our plan was to spend nocturnal hours sampling the blues in Chicago clubs; daylight hours would be spent visiting historic sites connected with the musicians who'd crafted a new urban sound in the 1940s and '50s. Susanna and Frank lent us an old car in which we could explore the poorer neighbourhoods of Chicago's South Side. Richard Knight warns in *Blues Highway* that tourists stick out in the South Side and recommends that to avoid attention visitors should restrict cruising down in a flash or obviously rented car.[20] Though, as Susanna pointed out, the South Side is made up of many varied neighbourhoods; she reminded us that President Obama has a family house in an extremely desirable South Side neighbourhood.

Traffic was heavy on the Kennedy Expressway from O'Hare as we passed through Chicago's northern neighbourhoods, and the clustered outline of downtown Chicago's skyscrapers grew in magnitude. The Willis Tower – now America's tallest building, formerly known as the Sears Roebuck Tower – serves as a frame of reference, peaking as it does above the surrounding buildings of the Chicago skyline. Since 2009 the tower has taken its name from London-based insurer Willis Insurance Holdings. The tower's former name has an historic association with the mail order catalogue Sears, which offered a means for many poor black musicians living in the South to purchase inexpensive guitars such as Silvertones and Stellas. The instruments were delivered to rural Southern railroad depots via the Illinois Central Railroad; some commentators have even suggested that the combination of W.C. Handy, the Sears, Roebuck & Co. and the Illinois Central Railway were the three components that gave rise to the blues.

As we approached the South Side I pondered the warning I'd read in one guidebook, which cautioned that 'today the South Side remains a rundown and sometimes dangerous neighbourhood. The West Side is worse.'[21] The weekend prior to our arrival the media reported at least six men had been killed and another twenty-three wounded in shootings. Maybe not so extraordinary when one considers that unemployment in the worst areas of the city runs at 30 per cent and it's said that in some neighborhoods there are more guns than computers.

Frank drove west down Forty-Seventh Street for a mile or so, into the area that half a century earlier had been the vibrant heart of Bronzeville, the city's black metropolis. We were looking for the fabled 708 Club, located on Forty-Seventh, which in the mid 1950s had been one of the South Side's pulsating arteries.[22] The 708 Club was popular with artists when the South Side blues clubs were at their height because it was larger than many of the bars that hosted music. By the late 1940s the 708 had become one of the South Side's key venues and many considered it to be the premier blues club in the city.[23] Originally the building was one of three liquor stores owned by Leonard Chess, who relinquished control of the 708 prior to it becoming a blues venue.

An account by the singer Billy Boy Arnold described how in the late 1950s the 708 Club had a front window through which passers-by could check out the music, and that when Earl Hooker played 'the lure of his music was so strong that often thirty people or more would jam the sidewalk and occasionally back up traffic!'[24] Robert Gordon's biography of Muddy Waters tells how the success of his first record, 'I Can't Be Satisfied' in April 1948, drew bigger crowds. On a Sunday Muddy would play at Silvio's on the West Side in the afternoon and then set up for an evening session at one of the South Side clubs like Romeo's Place, the Squeeze Club, Browns Village or the 708 Club, which Gordon describes 'as a fancier place, despite the exposed plumbing pipes that ran throughout'.[25]

By the 1950s Howlin' Wolf was ranking alongside Muddy Waters as one of the top acts of the Chicago blues scene. Wolf's shows were explosive affairs full of emotional showmanship and many of his antics were precursors to the exhibitionism later imitated by rock 'n' roll artists to connect with their audiences. Wolf would drag and crawl on all fours, thumping the floor in a display of emotional desperation and then cut a swathe through the revellers and leap onto the bar. These were riotous shows, according to Jody Williams, guitarist with Wolf for two years: 'Wolf's style was more flamboyant – more like a street riot than a church service.' He also described how on one occasion Wolf walked out of the 708 Club in the middle of a number still 'whoopin' and hollerin' with his harmonica and singing – and the police run him back there! Oh that place was jumpin'! They loved him!'[26]

By the early 1950s the Chicago blues bars were regularly booking four- or five-piece amplified bands fronted by Howlin' Wolf; Muddy Waters; a slide

The 708 Club, 708 Forty-Seventh Street.

guitarist from Belzoni, Mississippi, named Elmore James; and Sonny Boy Williamson II (Rice Miller), a harp player from Helena, Arkansas.

Paul Oliver compares the styles of Wolf and Muddy Waters and suggests 'Wolf's aggressive music was less subtle than Muddy Waters's but it was a matter of degree'.[27] The apparent antagonism that existed between Muddy Waters and Howlin' Wolf was not dissimilar to the rivalry between the Beatles and the Rolling Stones, which a decade or so later would be hyped up for marketing purposes.

The differences in Wolf's and Waters's musical styles and stage personas came to be associated with the areas of Chicago where they made their respective homes, with Muddy moving to a respectable and imposing red-brick house at 4339 South Lake Park following the success of 'Hoochie

Coochie Man' in 1954, whereas Wolf, considered to have the more aggressive style of blues and brash stage presence, moved into a tougher West Side neighbourhood. In addition to their rivalry, an ongoing antagonism persisted between the two most prominent artists on Chicago's club scene. Music writer Robert Palmer's take on the difference between Wolf and Waters in his seminal history of the blues was more direct when he wrote 'Muddy was superstud, the Hoochie Coochie Man; Wolf was a feral beast'.[28]

Neither artist was above poaching musicians from the other's band. Wolf even filed a grievance against Muddy Waters with the musicians' union for loss of earnings at Silvio's, having been promised the opportunity to cover gigs while Muddy's band were out of town on tour. Despite such public differences, Wolf was one of Waters's first lodgers at 4339 South Lake Park Avenue on his arrival in Chicago.[29] Moreover, as saxophonist Eddie Shaw suggests in Segrest and Hoffman's biography of Howlin' Wolf, the competition was 'partly a put-on: good for business'. The authors make the point that 'onstage, Wolf and Muddy played up their rivalry; offstage, they sometimes drank and dined together' and that by the 1960s and early '70s 'both men had mellowed and could commiserate over their common fate as ageing bluesmen'.[30]

Buddy Guy's first encounter with Muddy Waters took place on a cold winter's night in 1958, on the street directly outside the 708 Club. Guy talks of the 708 being 'one of the hottest clubs on the South Side'.[31] In Guy's autobiography he recalls the cold of Chicago's biting winters and how he'd not eaten for two days. He was about to concede to hunger and return to Louisiana when he was asked by a stranger if he could play the guitar he carried on his back. The chance meeting subsequently led to the young Buddy Guy being introduced to Otis Rush at the 708 and invited to fill in while Rush stood down for a couple of numbers. Otis Rush, like so many other Chicago musicians, had come up from Mississippi in the late 1940s and found work in the stockyards, where he also found his first drummer, Mike Netton.[32]

Buddy Guy has described that performance, his first time in front of a Chicago blues audience, as being possessed by the spirit of Guitar Slim. He covered 'Things I Used to Do' and jumped into the crowd, playing his Stratocaster over his head and behind his back, pulling out tricks of showmanship he'd seen Guitar Slim work an audience with in Baton Rouge five years earlier.[33]

Word of the 708 audience's appreciative reaction to the youngster's stage antics reached Muddy Waters at his home, whereupon he was driven to the club by his long-term friend and driver, Andrew 'Bo' Bolton. The 708 Club's owner, Ben Gold, told Buddy Guy there was someone parked outside who wanted to meet him. According to whether you read Waters's or Guy's account, Buddy was invited to join Chicago's biggest blues star in either the back or the front of the station wagon. At this first meeting Waters talked to Guy about their shared experiences of the South, quizzing him about his musical influences; more importantly Muddy shared a baloney sandwich with the famished young guitarist, who hadn't eaten for days.

Bluesmen such as Wolf, Waters and Walters were joined by the next generation of black artists like Buddy Guy and Junior Wells, who were ripping through the Chicago clubs with an exciting sound of electrified blues.

Today a plastic banner hangs from the bus stop situated outside a boarded-up 708 Club informing visitors they're at the heart of what was once Chicago's 'Historic Black Metropolis'. Shuttered shopfronts and empty lots reflect little of the urban urgency familiar to the blues men and women in the days when Bronzeville was a bustling and thriving black neighbourhood. We walked back to the car. Maybe we'd parked where Muddy came to meet a young Buddy Guy.

I recalled that I'd heard Muddy Waters play live by chance when I was 20 years old. I'd turned up on the off-chance that I could walk in towards the end of the day's events and catch Chuck Berry. Waters was the act before Berry and I remember him talking to the audience about alcohol being one of the world's greatly underestimated drugs. A few years prior to this, Waters had started bleeding from his nose and eyes. His doctor advised him to steer clear of liquor, and so, thereafter, he drank only champagne, which Pinetop Perkins recalled being delivered to the basement at South Lake Park Avenue by the truckload.[34]

After leaving the club, we continued down Forty-Seventh. In my mind's eye I conjured an image of a sweat-soaked Wolf strutting along the bar of the 708, leaping into a packed throng of dancers, and then disappearing through the club's doors into the cool Chicago night air, still bellowing out vocals and frenziedly blowing the harp, before being run back into the club by the police.[35] Where did a man from the cotton fields of Mississippi learn those moves? We know that Charley Patton was living on Dockery plantation not far from Ruleville when Wolf was in his teens. It was Patton – a consummate showman, known for playing the guitar behind his head, throwing it into the air and thumping out a rhythm on the guitar's body – who taught Wolf the rudiments of guitar.

At the crossroads of Forty-Eighth and Indiana we looked for a flight of steps leading down to a basement of the building named Indiana Manor, the original site of blues bar Theresa's Lounge. The concrete steps offered temporary respite from the rigours of work in the stockyards to the west of Bronzeville, the steel mills to the south and the numerous factories and service industries dependent on local labour. The tavern's proprietor was Theresa Needham, a woman whose history was similar to many of her customers and the artists who frequented her bar. She'd migrated from Meridian, Mississippi, to Chicago sometime in the 1940s and by 1949 had established the tavern that became known as Theresa's Lounge.

Theresa's Lounge was where Buddy Guy and Junior Wells started playing together at open house jam sessions known as Blue Mondays.[36] The pair adopted an opening routine of starting by playing in the kitchen or the men's room, building a sense of anticipation amongst the audience, before bursting through the waiting crowd into the bar. This was another trick Buddy Guy copied from Guitar Slim.[37] The wooden hoarding sign that once stood at the top of the

cellar stairs, which announced 'Theresa's Lounge, featuring live entertainment, Fri–Sat–Sun–Mon' has long gone. However, the original stair rails and steel railings are still intact and can be seen inside the newer security railings.

Theresa ran a tight ship and was known for her dirty apron – it carried a pistol in one pocket and a billy club in the other.[38] She gave both Buddy Guy and Junior Wells openings early in their careers. Junior Wells fronted the house band at Theresa's and recorded songs which included 'Messin' with the Kid' and 'It Hurts me Too'.

Following the theft of his Gibson Les Paul one night, Buddy Guy appealed to Theresa Needham. She lent him $160 to buy a Stratocaster, enabling him to fulfil a recording engagement.[39] Guy and Wells eventually teamed up and maintained what became a tempestuous recording and touring partnership that lasted until the end of the 1970s, when they parted company. According to Buddy Guy, the relationship became strained by Junior's heavy drinking, together with his erratic and threatening behaviour, which often involved guns.[40] Their partnership also gives clues to the transition of blues in Chicago from an important part of African American culture to something of an anachronism and a reminder of life under Jim Crow laws in the South. Young blacks were looking to the future and for many blues was seen as a throwback to the past.

Charles Shaar Murray, in his exploration of Jimi Hendrix and post-war pop, argues that Guy and Wells represented 'the last generation of gifted young black musicians to see the blues as a viable outlet for their talents and ambitions. Which tells us, fairly accurately, just when the blues ceased to express what black America wanted to hear itself expressing.'[41]

Theresa's remained a regular hangout for many South Side blues artists and even in the 1960s, as the North Side blues bars aimed at white customers started to open, the neighbourhood bars in the South Side remained important venues for musicians like Muddy Waters, Howlin' Wolf and Little Walter. According to Bob Koester of Delmark Records, the ghetto bar 'was the base of operations. It was sort of a paid rehearsal. You played there week in and week out unless something better came along. And that was the understanding. With a better gig they leave with one hour's notice.'[42]

Fernando Jones, blues musician and educator, who grew up in Chicago's South Side, suggests that Theresa's was much more than a club and served the local black community as a social and cultural centre. He describes the buzz around Theresa's and the customers who frequented the bar in its heyday: 'On weekends, the "corner" was accented with fancy cars and all kinds of hep-cats sharply dressed. The ladies that came down there were regal. Conversations always flowed and everybody seemed to be famous for one reason or another.'[43]

The South Side blues bars were seen as dangerous; shooting and stabbings were not uncommon. The Chicago Defender reported one incident at Theresa's in which the bartender shot and killed a noisy customer, George Dillard, who'd been asked to 'quiet his talk', whereupon the customer 'allegedly drew a pistol, but was slain by the bartender, who said he used the gun kept behind the bar'.[44]

The artists who forged the Chicago blues in bars like Theresa's and the 708, in spite of gaining recognition well beyond the neighbourhoods of the South and West Sides, lived tough and chaotic lives, all too often sustained by alcohol (and, for some, drugs), where violence was never far away.

Pat Hare, Muddy Waters's guitarist, served time for homicide;[45] Howlin' Wolf, according to his pianist, Sunnyland Slim, is alleged to have cut off a man's head with a hoe;[46] Wolf's drummer, Sam Lay, lost a testicle when a pistol he carried in his pocket discharged while he was drumming for James Cotton;[47] the harp player Henry Strong, known as 'Pot', collapsed in the lobby of his apartment, having been stabbed through the lungs by his wife, and died in Waters's car before they reached hospital;[48] and at a New Year's Eve celebration Waters accidentally shot his driver, Bo, in the leg. In order to avoid adverse publicity, Bo was transferred to the basement and given strong liquor, which Otis Spann had been dispatched to collect.

These guys didn't need sophisticated publicity machines to turn them into outlaws. What they strove for were images of professionalism that concealed the chaotic and dysfunctional reality of their everyday lives. When the Rolling Stones performed with Muddy Waters at the South Side's Checkerboard Lounge in 1981, what we see is the juxtaposition of black with white, originator with imitator and reality with lifestyle myth.

The life of Marion Walter Jacobs – better known as Little Walter, Muddy Waters's one-time harmonica player – demonstrates the tragic downside of a tough Southern upbringing followed by a life in the Chicago ghettos.

Little Walter had self-destruct imbedded in his DNA and was an archetypal example of the artist as genius and misunderstood young man. Although he was dead by the age of 37, Little Walter gave the world a string of hits that outsold both Howlin' Wolf and Muddy Waters. He also left a road map to destruction for any misunderstood artist thereafter. Mike Rowe suggests: 'Little Walter needed the adulation of the crowds and the sympathy of friends; with it he was friendly and helpful as many will testify, and without he was lost; bitter and distrustful and lonely.'[49]

On a street near Theresa's Lounge, Walter eventually suffered a violent end to his own chaotic life. Junior Wells, describing the incident that led to Little Walter's death, said:

> a man throwed the dice and hit Walter in the butt with 'em and went to reach and get the money and Walter picked up the money. The man asked Walter for the money and Walter wouldn't give him the money and he took a hammer and hit Walter in the head with it.[50]

Irrespective of his troubled personality, Little Walter was one of the true great artists of the Chicago blues scene and his music remains influential to this day. Robert Palmer captured the extent of Little Walter's influence when he wrote, 'almost everybody that picks up a harmonica, in America or England or France or Scandinavia, will at some stage in his development emulate either Little Walter or a Little Walter imitator.'[51] With a stable of recordings that includes 'My Babe', 'You're So Fine', 'Key to the Highway', 'Boom Boom (Out Go the Lights)', 'One More Chance with You' and 'You'd Better Watch Yourself', Little Walter's back catalogue stands as a monumental source of inspiration, while his cupped hand method of playing has remained de rigueur for generations of aspiring harmonica players.

Between 1952 and 1957 the driving rhythm of Fred Below, originally Muddy Waters's drummer, features on most of Little Walter's recordings. The significance of Below's back beat is noted in Francis Davis's dedication at the front of his book *The History of the Blues,* which simply states, 'To Fred Below, the secret architect of rock 'n' roll'.[52] Below went on to make a number of hit records with many of the stars of the Chicago clubs, including Chuck Berry, Elmore James and Howlin' Wolf.

The staccato kick of Little Walter's 'You're So Fine' emanated from the car's CD player as we headed down Indiana Street and right onto Forty-Third. Bronzeville around this end of Forty-Third is a mix of recent developments interspersed with dilapidated businesses and housing, all of which seemed outnumbered by empty lots on each block. Grass and weeds triumphed over parking lots without offices and forecourts without shops, leaving a patchwork of urban fields. Susanna pointed to a vacant lot that stretched the length of a block, bordered on its far side by a three-storey red-brick building with rusting fire escapes and windows shuttered with corrugated iron. This was the site of the original Checkerboard Lounge, which had been used for the filming of the Stones performing with Muddy Waters, Buddy Guy and Junior Wells in 1981. It later relocated out of the South Side to its present location in the Hyde Park area of Chicago.

After about a mile Forty-Third ran into Muddy Waters Drive and we looked for the turning into South Lake Park Avenue. Waters had been living in a two-bedroom West Side apartment, which, according to his stepson Charles, necessitated his using a commode and washing in a small pan.[53] Following the success of 'Hoochie Coochie Man' in 1954, Waters purchased his two-storey red-brick house and would be a resident of Chicago's South Side for the next two decades.[54]

Life was on the up and, as Robert Gordon remarks, Muddy was now 'confirmed middle class'. The house was within walking distance of the new Chess offices at South Cottage Grove, and the spacious accommodation housed an extended family in the broadest sense, as South Lake Park Avenue became home to Muddy's family as well as band members. Otis Spann, Muddy's pianist, moved into the front room and Bo Bolton had the middle room in the basement. Upstairs, Waters's stepsons, Charles and Dennis, had separate bedrooms and other band members also rented rooms. Paul Oliver, the blues historian, and his wife were guests at Waters's house in 1960 and Oliver was amazed by the tenants he found living there: St Louis Jimmy; Muddy's harmonica player, James Cotton; and George 'Mojo' Buford, who took over harp after Cotton was shot five times while waiting for a bus.[55]

From where we parked we could see that all the windows of 4339 are now boarded up, and the house itself is bordered by a vacant lot. However, the front door retains two wrought-iron pink flamingos that Waters had made, which include his name and the door number. Despite the respectable appearance of the sizable houses in the tree-lined avenue, by the 1960s the street was close to a dividing point between rival South Side gangs. One of the gangs was the well-documented Blackstone Rangers, which could be seen 'walking around

the streets carrying guns, their mere presence making life much less pleasant for law-abiding people in Woodlawn'.[56] Like Muddy's South Lake Park Avenue house, many parts of Chicago's South Side look as though someone pulled the shutters down a quarter of a century ago and invested the money in another part of town.

Our next destination was South Michigan Avenue. We were on the lookout for a magnificent mural depicting the Great Migration, which adorns the side of the Elliott Donnelly Youth Center, and which I'd read about in *The Blues Highway*.

Parked under a rusting iron bridge carrying a section of the El's Green Line, we were able to gain good views of the larger of the two murals from an alley that ran between the youth centre and the El. Like other parts of Bronzeville, the area lacked the vibrancy of the once-thriving black metropolis. Grass competed with the few signs of economic growth for tenure of the vacant lots.

Pictures do not capture the scale and vividness of Marcus Akinlana's The Great Migration, which isn't surprising, as it covers 2,700sq.ft.[57] Within minutes of skirting the perimeter fence, De'Shunn Bray, one of the centre's trustees, came out and invited us in to take a closer look at the Elliott Donnelly Art Garden and meet Caneal Rule, a team co-ordinator at the centre. Caneal pointed to each of the figures illustrated in 'The Great Migration', which was painted in 1995, explaining how Akinlana sequentially depicts the Great Migration. Starting with life in the rural South, represented by a family working in the fields, followed by the hopes and dreams of a new future in Chicago, with the Illinois Central Railway delivering the migrants past towering city skyscrapers, where they eventually adapt to new jobs. The finale of the journey is illustrated by work in manufacturing jobs or on the killing floors of the Chicago stockyards. The river is probably the Ohio River, representing the border between slavery and freedom.

Hazel Rowley's biography of Richard Wright, the African American intellectual and writer, describes how he had heard of 'folk kneeling down to pray when their train crosses the river, kissing the ground and bursting into songs of deliverance – "The Flight out of Egypt" or "Bound for the Promised Land"'.[58]

Wright was born near Natchez, Mississippi in 1908, migrated to Chicago in 1927 and was appointed by the Relief Authorities as a supervisor at the centre known then as the South Side Boys Club, which became the Elliott Donnelly Center. His literary achievements are acclaimed worldwide, to the extent that in 2009 he was featured on a United States postage stamp.

Wright's understanding of the world was forged by his experience of life as an African American growing up in Mississippi, having been born on Rucker's

Muddy Waters's house, 4339 South Lake Park Avenue.

plantation near Natchez before living in other towns in the South, including Jackson and Greenwood. Wright eventually left Mississippi for Memphis at the age of 17, and like so many others, arrived in Chicago's South Side in search of new opportunities. Some of the people Wright met at the South Side Boys' Club inspired fictional characters in his novel *Native Son*. His biographer suggests this book illustrates the 'utter hypocrisy of white philanthropy', which was financed by money that 'had been amassed from the exorbitant rents paid by black people for their slum kitchenettes'.[59]

Wright's best-known novel is *Black Boy,* an autobiographical account of a young black man growing up in the Jim Crow South. Geoffrey Summerfield, in an introduction to *Black Boy*, stresses why this novel is important for anyone who wants to appreciate a little of what life growing up in the South at the time of the Great Migration would have been like. For blues pilgrims, Richard Wright is important first and foremost as an African American writer who directly experienced the period of history that produced the blues and recorded that experience in a literary form.

Journeying south down Highway 61, we met Wright's legacy time and time again. If blues was, as Paul Garon suggests, the subliminal or codified message of repressed African Americans who yearned for a qualitative change to their condition, then the writing of Richard Wright illuminated the conscious feeling of oppressed blacks and translated it into activity in his lifetime. In 1945 the African American novelist Ralph Ellison paid tribute to Wright's *Black Boy* in 'Richard Wright's Blues':

> Nowhere in America today is there social or political action based upon the solid realities of Negro life depicted in *Black Boy*; perhaps that is why, with its refusal to offer solutions, it is like the blues. Yet, in it thousands of Negroes will for the first time see their destiny in public print. Freed here of fear and the threat of violence, their lives have at last been organised, scaled down to possessable proportions. And in this lies Wright's most important achievement: he has converted the American Negro impulse towards self-annihilation and 'going-under-ground' into a will to confront the world, to evaluate his experience honestly and throw his findings unashamedly into the guilty conscience of America.[60]

De'Shunn was keen to show us inside the centre and the now empty swimming pool in need of repairs. She explained it was one of the only pools for young people in the neighbourhood. Wright refers to a pool in a boys' club on the South Side in his novel *Native Son*. De'Shunn said the centre was

'The Great Migration', a mural by Marcus Akinlana, Elliott Donnelly Youth Center.

Gate to the Chicago Union Stockyards, built 1879, West Exchange Avenue.

finding it difficult maintaining the funding to repair the pool, which at the time we visited was completely drained of water. I contacted De'Shunn when we got back to England, about three months after our trip, and she told me that sadly they were still fighting to save the pool.

After saying our goodbyes to everyone at the centre, we made our way up Wabash Avenue and into East Pershing Road to find the last remaining gate to what had once been the immense Union Stockyards. This white limestone gothic structure stands proud but isolated on an urban island of grass in the middle of West Exchange Avenue. We walked through the white stone gate to the memorial for the twenty-one firefighters who died in the great stockyard fire of 1910. A carved statue of the head of a solitary prizewinning steer stared out from above the arched gateway to the yards across Packingtown. Across the arch letters carved into the limestone blocks read 'Union Stock Yard – Chartered – 1865'.

Standing on the railroad track that runs past the front of the Union Stockyards gate I tried to visualise Back of the Yards slum housing and conjure up the stench of industrialised slaughter that had permeated the air until the closure of the yards in 1971. I thought of my dad, who'd had tuberculosis as a young man, and the disease-ridden housing portrayed by Upton Sinclair in *The Jungle*. This area of housing around the yards had one of the highest rates of tuberculosis in the country.[61] I'd read that in the 1930s Richard Wright had gathered a group of black stockyard workers at his friend's house and read them modernist literature. His audience was enthralled and responded by laughing and constantly interrupting Wright to make comments about the characters they identified with.[62]

The evening was drawing in and Chicago's blues clubs beckoned. However, we still had a couple of South Side sites with historic links with the Great Migration to fit in. Driving north along Indiana Avenue, we were on the lookout for the original offices of the *Chicago Defender*, the African American-owned newspaper established in 1905. It was the first black-owned newspaper to have a circulation of over 100,000 and a claimed readership of 500,000. Under African American ownership, it refused to use the word 'black' or 'Negro'; instead, it described its readers as 'the Race'. The paper reached far further than Chicago and was read by African Americans throughout the country. It had to be smuggled into the South by Pullman porters, where newspaper distributors refused to handle it.

With the outbreak of the First World War and the curtailment of immigration to the United States, the *Chicago Defender* commenced its Great Drive North campaign to encourage blacks in the South to migrate to 'freer air' in the

Office of the *Chicago Defender* newspaper, 3435 South Indiana Avenue.

Northern cities. An article in the *Defender* on 5 August 1916 offered a long list of reasons why African Americans should leave the South:

> the north pays more for its labour in manufacturing, mining and commerce and for this reason there will be just millions of our people leave the south, where was born slavery, lynching, segregation, prejudice, ostracism, concubinage, disfranchisement and 'Jim Crow' cars, and go north, where there is more freedom and greater opportunities to work, live, rear a family and become a citizen, respected and honoured because he has spilled blood in all its wars for the protection of its flag and people.[63]

A few months later the *Chicago Defender* carried an article that referred to the migration north as an 'exodus', arguing that 'maltreatment of the whites towards members of the Race is the sole cause of the exodus'. Moreover the article forecast that 'a million will leave with the Great Northern Drive, Tuesday, May 15'.[64]

Nevertheless, this transformation cannot only be seen in terms of the labour demands of Northern industry. The act of leaving the South is argued by some commentators to have been a conscious act of defiance on the part of many African Americans:

> Leaving had its own satisfaction by breaking the cycle of dependency on southern whites while at the same time challenging the prevailing white belief in benign race relations. During the 1930s, years when hard times everywhere should have restricted interregional mobility, the South experienced a net loss of a half million blacks to the North – even though the network of friends and relatives in the North had likely communicated the difficulties of Depression-era life in those locales. The North held symbolic value that transcended reality.[65]

As the evening drew in we made a final stop on Dr Martin Luther King Jr Drive, to see 'Salute to the Great Migration', the bronze statue sculpted in 1994 by Alison Saar. At first sight the figure appeared to be covered in fish scales or leaves but on closer inspection these were hundreds of worn shoe soles, which represented the arduous journey faced by travellers who made their way to Chicago from the Southern states. The figure faces north to symbolise the traveller's destination and his hand is raised in a greeting towards his new home. The worn suitcase he carries represents the journey together with the dreams and talents he brings with him to Chicago.

We'd spent over an hour on the Kennedy Expressway with what seemed like half of Chicago, crawling bumper to bumper back to Jefferson Park from the South Side. That evening it made a change to get out of the Chicago traffic and let the El whisk us downtown to find some live music. We left the El at the Loop, named for where the El's lines converge to encircle the downtown area,

Monument to the Great Northern Migration, by Alison Saar, Dr Martin Luther King Jr Drive and Twenty-Sixth.

and made our way to the Jazz Record Mart on East Illinois Street, where we'd arranged to meet Steve Pasek, who runs Chicago Blues tours.

The Jazz Record Mart claims to be the world's largest jazz and blues record store. It stays open till 8 p.m., so browsing through its extensive stock of CDs, vinyl records, books and magazines is a good way to end the day. Its owner, Bob Koester, was the founder of Delmark Records and a key player in the final years of the original Chicago blues scene. He went on to become not only central in the 1960s blues revival but someone who has continued to remain an energetic force in the contemporary blues story.

Koester arrived in Chicago in the summer of 1958, having established Delmark as a label in St Louis in 1953, the same year that Muddy Waters's 'Hoochie Coochie Man' peaked at number three in the Billboard R&B chart.[66] Koester argues that what set him apart from companies like Chess and previous blues recording studios was that when Delmark Records recorded Junior Wells' 'Hoodoo Man', it was the first studio Long Player or album to be made with a 'working electric Chicago blues band'.[67] Koester is important because Delmark was operating in the transitional period when blues moved from a primarily black audience to a much wider white audience. As such Delmark was recording the pianist Speckled Red[68] and Delta blues guitarist Big Joe Williams[69] at a time when other labels weren't interested. Koester was also responsible for rediscovering artists, such as Sleepy John Estes in 1961.[70] Many of Koester's employees went on to make significant contributions to the world of blues, such as Alligator Records boss Bruce Iglauer, who worked in the Jazz Record Mart when it was a storefront at 7 West Grand, with Delmark operating from the basement.

When we caught up with Bruce Iglauer the following day, he spoke about how he'd arrived in Chicago in 1969 on what he describes as his own blues pilgrimage, and got a job working for Koester at the Jazz Record Mart. Explaining its significance, Iglauer said that 'the Jazz Record Mart was a magic door because the blues clubs on the South and West side didn't exist as far as the daily newspapers and other media were concerned. They didn't exist because they were mainly neighbourhood bars and they couldn't afford advertising on black-orientated radio – so you had to know where they were or you had to find some way of hearing about these things.'[71]

Iglauer's story illuminates the period of transition from the decline of Chicago blues as a marketable commodity to the black community and its discovery as a musical form amongst an enthusiastic new young white audience:

Delmark was in the basement of the Jazz Record Mart and because recording opportunities for blues musicians were very limited – Chess had been sold; although it was still here it was not committed to blues anymore. Vee Jay was out of business and a lot of the little labels that had done 45s, had come and gone or were inactive. So pretty much the only opportunities for blues artists were cut an album for this Bob Koester guy and maybe get some gigs playing for hippies.[72]

The Jazz Record Mart became an important information exchange for the Chicago blues scene. Iglauer's recollection conveyed the sense of excitement shared by a group of primarily young white enthusiasts, who became the promulgators of what had become a diminishing and sidelined element of African American culture. He recalled how the musicians would drop by the store and let them know where they were playing and they'd put a notice up on a bulletin board or even tape scraps of paper to the wall saying 'Earl Hooker, Tuesday night at Peppers'.

Out of a small group of blues devotees came *Living Blues* magazine, which still declares itself as the magazine of the African American blues tradition. Iglauer was there at the beginning with Jim O'Neal, Amy van Singel, Paul Garon, Diane Allmen, Andre Souffront and Tim Zorn; as Iglauer says, it grew out of a key place: the Jazz Record Mart.

Iglauer, who came to blues from a folk background, had what he called his magic moment when he heard Mississippi Fred McDowell in 1966. When he found blues music he said 'it was like some parallel universe, some parallel America going on that almost wasn't touching the mainstream white America I grew up in'. He's still passionate when he recalls the America he grew up in as a young man and points out, 'I was a college student in the second half of the 1960s, born in '47, so the Civil Rights Movement was happening all around me and I was passionately pro-civil rights and I was passionately against the war in Vietnam.'[73] His observations betrayed an empathy that went beyond his love of blues; he adds, 'I didn't have to get up every day and be perceived first and foremost by anybody of any colour as a black person, because that is what happens to black people in this country.'[74]

When Iglauer discussed marketing Alligator's artists, I sensed a man who still hadn't tired of getting a message across. His own analogy was of someone operating in 'a world like an impenetrable jungle and I'm the guy with the machete. I'd keep hacking away in an attempt to get the attention of whatever media I can reach.' He was aware of his own energy when he said, 'I became the booking agent, the personal manager, sometimes the driver or the publicist or the song publisher. I did all these things because no one else was doing them for the artists.' He then turned to the radio campaigns adding, 'we service close to a thousand radio stations in the United States. Nobody else in the blues business services anything like that number. When I'm hacking through the jungle I'm always looking for supportive media.'[75]

Steve Pasek pulled up in a people carrier at the agreed meeting point outside the Jazz Record Mart. It's not only blues tours that occupied Steve, who as a songwriter and record producer described himself as someone dedicated to promoting Chicago blues. He puts bands out under his own small Chicago Blues label, including five Chainsaw Dupont albums. We squeezed into the back of Steve's minibus and set off towards Garfield Park on the West Side. The plan was to visit three venues between 9 p.m. and 2 a.m., giving us a cross-section of blues bars in the city.

Bruce Iglauer (right), founder of Alligator Records.

Our first stop was a relatively new venue, the Water Hole Lounge, situated on South Western Avenue. It sells itself as a small friendly bar with a free blues jukebox and offering live music some nights. On our arrival a couple of people from the bar came out to greet us and we were ushered through to a back bar, where we found Blu Willie T & da Mid-Nite Lovers just getting into their first set. A four-piece, Willie T's band was knocking out their own material interspersed with their take on some old blues standards with lap steel guitar and Willie T's own distinctive style of soloing. This wasn't the infamous set from hell by a long chalk, but it was traditional blues, which, Steve pointed out, is almost unheard of now in the West Side bars, where you would expect to hear a band delivering a soul blues set rather than traditional blues.

Mary came out of the kitchen bringing spicy Italian beef, which oozed so much grease and chili it permeated both the corn bread and the serviette in which it was served. Each mouthful was both a divine experience and reminder of one's own mortality. The food perfectly complemented the Water Hole's 'down at heel' feel and required nothing more than to be washed down with another cold beer and a dose of Willie T's blues. Whether this was an authentic experience I have no idea, and I guess that depends on one's definition of authenticity. Nevertheless, as Steve explained, the bar had functioned as a roadhouse for a number of decades prior to hosting live music and happens to be only a block away from Route 66. Willie T seemed to be going down as well with the locals as he was with visitors like ourselves, as we washed down the Italian beef with a final beer before making our farewells and climbing back into Steve's minibus.

Next stop was Nick's Beer Garden on North Milwaukee Avenue, just a couple of miles north from the Water Hole, in the Wicker Park area of the city. Once home to a large Polish community, and later a large Puerto Rican community, the area attracted substantial numbers of artists in the 1980s and finally underwent a period of gentrification that has given it a reputation as a haven for yuppies. The band Blue Road featured Gary Gand, who Steve explained was a veteran from the 1970s and who has made a name for himself in the musical equipment business. Nick's had a lively audience of primarily young white middle-class customers, who looked as though they would have been up for good time, as long as the band did the business, regardless of any particular musical genre.

The final bar of the evening was Rosa's Lounge, in the Near North-west Side. The club has been run by Tony Manguillo for thirty years and was rated by Richard Knight in *The Blues Highway* 'as the best blues club on the West Side'. Rosa's Friday night offering was Blind Boy Willie Williams, a South Side Chicago-based soul blues singer, whose career has spanned five decades and is known locally as the blind James Brown.

After we left Rosa's, Steve drove us back downtown and dropped us off in the Loop, where we could catch an El back to the suburbs. It was now two in the morning and while we'd been in the clubs Chicago's homeless had bedded down for the night. Camped out on grass borders between the neatly laid flowerbeds were rows of sleeping bags with the hoods drawn tightly down, the occupants of which were attempting to shut themselves off from the nocturnal activity of the city. I turned to Frank and enquired how many weeks before the weather would turn.

The composer of 'All Right Mama', Arthur 'Big Boy' Crudup, arrived in Chicago from Forest, Mississippi, and lived in a wooden crate under the El station at Thirty-Ninth Street, earning money by singing to passers-by.[76] Lester Melrose discovered Crudup singing on a Chicago street corner in 1941, and Crudup recorded 'That's All Right' for the RCA Bluebird label on 6 September 1946. Despite Elvis Presley's success with the song eight years later, Mike Rowe suggests that Arthur Crudup saw none of the money.[77]

The El trundled through northern Chicago until we reached our station. It was now raining and the wind had got up; puddles formed on the surface of the car park. A young black man leaned against the wall of the station's out-buildings, a few metres apart from a little group of homeless white people intently occupied with the bottle of spirits one of them held. I glanced down at the young man, stepping around his legs. The young man studied his forearm, which rested upon his leg. He appeared as though he was trying to make sense of what he saw. A dark patch had wet the pavement by his legs. As I took a second step to pass him I noticed the blood slowly pulsating from his wrist as he fidgeted with the cuff of his shirt.

Susanna made a call to the emergency services asking for police and an ambulance. Within a couple of minutes sirens dominated the night-time silence of the car park as flashing lights strobed the walls of the station's building. We walked away from the scene, putting umbrellas up as the rain got heavier.

The Chicago Bears were playing the St Louis Rams at midday. The streets around Maxwell Street Market were filled with the expectant anticipation of fathers and sons making their way to Soldier Field, the home of the Bears. Roads across the canal towards the ground had been temporarily cordoned off to two-way traffic and Chicago Police Department cars sat on the bridges funnelling a continuous stream of people toward the ground.

A Maxwell Street Polish, or a Kielbasa, as it's known in Poland, is the perfect market-day breakfast. We grabbed one from Jim's Original on South Union Avenue, which claims to be the original Polish sausage stand from Maxwell Street. We then walked up to the site of the old market, before its relocation to South Des Plaines Street, just a few hundred metres north on the Dan Ryan Expressway. One of the last of the Delta blues guitarists from the Robert Johnson era, David 'Honeyboy' Edwards, who died in 2011, recalled playing at Maxwell Street market: 'That hamburger stand on Maxwell and Halsted, sitting in the same spot now, (was) open every day. You got a polish sausage there for a dime, pork chop sandwich, get that for twenty cents, stacked all up with meat and onions. Get one to feed two people. We was making money.'[78]

Blind Willie Williams, Rosa's Lounge, 3420 West Armitage Avenue, Chicago.

Maxwell Street Market at its new location on South Des Plaines Street.

For blues pilgrims the site of the market is of great interest because this is where many Chicago blues artists first came to make what many have described as good money. At Maxwell Street Market they could find the largest street audience in the city. The street's historical role in the creation of modern urban blues features in the film *The Blues Brothers*, in the scene where John Lee Hooker plays 'Boom Boom'. Also known as 'Jew Town', it was here that musicians met on arrival from the South and formed networks that led to many of the musical partnerships that would establish them in the South and West Side bars and clubs.

Little Walter arrived in Chicago at the age of 17. His talented harp playing was recognised at the market by Big Bill Broonzy.[79] Other accounts have Jimmy Rogers hearing Walter playing at the market one Sunday morning from his flat nearby. Rogers rushed round to see who was making the sound and the two

A bronze Maxwell Street Market statue, Chicago.

subsequently teamed up to play the streets. Rogers eventually mentioned this new harp player to Muddy Waters and, as Glover, Dirks and Gaines state in their biography of Little Walter, 'with that, the stage was set for a partnership that would have an incalculable and permanent impact on the shape and sound of the blues'.[80]

Walter made his way to Chicago with David 'Honeyboy' Edwards, riding the freight trains up from Memphis. Paul Oliver described the area around the market as a 'desolate wasteland off Halstead, Peoria and Sangamon Streets' and how musicians would rent power lines from nearby houses to power their amplification.[81]

Eddie Taylor was another musician who came up from the South to Chicago in 1949 and started playing on Maxwell Street at weekends. It's said that when he was a youngster in the Delta he followed both Charley Patton and Robert Johnson to house parties, crawling under the shacks to listen to the guitarists.[82] Taylor was also a childhood friend of Jimmy Reed, who taught Reed to play guitar when they lived in Leland, Mississippi.[83] The pair teamed up again in Chicago and Reed recorded a string of hits with Vee Jay including 'You Don't Have to Go', 'Ain't that Lovin' You Baby', 'Big Boss Man' and 'Bright Lights Big City'. Mike Rowe suggests that Eddie Taylor's 'association with Jimmy Reed is one of the great partnerships in blues'.[84] Reed had health and alcohol issues and Eddie Taylor parted company with him on two occasions: once when he replaced Jimmy Rogers in Muddy Waters's band and later when he worked with Elmore James.[85]

It's said that Maxwell Street was one of the most integrated areas in what was and still is a deeply segregated city. The last half century has seen local struggles regarding property development, such as the construction of the Dan Ryan Expressway in 1957 and the expansion of the University of Illinois at Chicago (UIC) from 1967. The story of the Maxwell Street Coalition's fight to save the district from redevelopment is captured in Ranstrom's documentary *Cheat me Fair: The Story of Maxwell Street Market*, filmed in 1994 and premiered in 2007.

Walking down Maxwell Street today, one is met by bronze figurines depicting Chicagoans from the 1940s and '50s going about their business. These are the only indicators to remind visitors of the traders, shoppers and musicians that frequented what was North America's largest open-air market. Pushing through the football crowds still making their way to Soldier Field, we made our way to the new Maxwell Street on South Des Plaines Street. There's still a sense that the market has something to be discovered. This multi-ethnic mixing point is where Chicagoans come together looking for bargains on the flea market stalls. Puerto Ricans, Latinos, African Americans all rummaging

Chess Records, 2120 South Michigan Avenue.

through the stalls, stopping to eat from street vendors offering pulled pork, tamales, huarache (a fired masa bread), or tacos and quesadilla.

Within a couple of minutes perusing the market I stumbled across a stall-holder selling clothes, assorted knick-knacks and a pile of albums from the 1960s. At the bottom of the pile I found the Rolling Stones' second American album, *12 × 5*; it was released in 1964 and some of the tracks were recorded at Chess Studios. The US version includes the Stones' instrumental homage to Chess Studios, '2120 South Michigan Avenue', which was not included on the UK version of the album, *The Rolling Stones No. 2*.

'How much for the album?' I asked, expecting something close to $30. He asked for $8 and we agreed on $7.

The seemingly infinite throng of Bears fans along Roosevelt Road suddenly became a mere trickle as the game started at Soldier Field. We made our way along clear streets looking for number 2120 South Michigan Avenue. Chess moved to 2120 in 1957 and was sold to the General Recorded Tape (GRT) in 1969. But in the mid 1970s the final recording operations closed down, bringing to an end an era that captured some of the best of Chicago blues, with the likes of Muddy Waters, Howlin' Wolf, Jimmy Rogers, Little Walter, Willie Dixon and Sonny Boy Williamson II (Rice Miller), and pioneered the early days of rock 'n' roll with Chuck Berry and Bo Diddley.

Visitors to the studio today may well be greeted by Keith Dixon, Willie Dixon's grandson, as the Dixon family run the Blues Heaven Foundation. Keith walked us through the rooms where Willie Dixon and Chess's stable of Chicago blues stars had worked; showed us the offices of Phil and Leonard Chess, and walked us up the stairs used by the Stones when they met their Chicago blues heroes in 1964.

In many respects, for me, the visit to Chess brought to mind the heady days of Chicago blues as well as the crossover in the 1960s to white audiences. As Nelson George suggests, the 1960s was a decade in which the blues artists who found new audiences 'found themselves getting paid better than at any other time in their lengthy careers because they started reaching that elusive white audience'.[86] But what, I wondered, of the generation of African Americans that had come up from the South to transform their lives, just as the likes of Muddy Waters, Howlin' Wolf and Little Walter had transformed the music that came with them? These older black fans, according to George:

… rarely came to these temples of youth culture partly because they didn't feel comfortable among middle-class white teens and college students, and partly because they didn't know about the gigs; advertising, in the underground press and progressive rock radio (the media of ascendant rock culture), never reached them. To blacks who valued the blues, it seemed these cultural heroes had been kidnapped by the younger brothers and sisters of the folks who'd led Chuck Berry astray.[87]

Notes

1. Halpern, Rick, *Down on the Killing Floor: Black and White Workers in Chicago's Packinghouses, 1904–54,* University of Illinois Press, 1997, p.22.
2. Ibid., p.21.
3. Goldfield, R. David, *Black, White and Southern: Race Relations and Southern Culture 1940 to the Present*, Louisiana State University Press, 1990, p.11.
4. Davis, Francis, *The History of the Blues: The Roots, the Music, the People*, Da Capo, 2003, p.181.
5. Rowe, Mike, *Chicago Blues: The City and the Music*, Da Capo, 1975, p.35. Originally published in 1973 as *Chicago Breakdown*.
6. Ibid., p.35.
7. Davis, *History of the Blues*, p.135.
8. Halpern, *Down on the Killing Floor*, p.40.
9. Lemann, Nicholas, *The Promised Land: The Great Black Migration and How It Changed America*, Vintage Books, 1992, p.43.
10. Sinclair, Upton, 'What life means to me', *Cosmopolitan* 41:594, October 1906.
11. Sinclair, Upton, *The Jungle*, Presswick House, 2005, p.1,000.
12. Halpern, *Down of the Killing Floor*, p.47.
13. Snooky and Moody, 'Stockyard Blues', Marvel M-1312, vocal Jones, Floyd, Marvel Record Co., Chicago Hill, 1947. See also Rowe, *Chicago Blues*, p.59.
14. Ibid., pp.58, 60.
15. *Chicago Defender*, national edition, 23 September 1939, p.13.
16. Segrest, James and Hoffman, Mark, *Moanin' at Midnight: The Life and Times of Howlin' Wolf*, Thunder Mouth Press, 2005, p.204.
17. Ibid., p.205.
18. Grazian, David, *Blues Chicago: The Search for Authenticity in Urban Blues Clubs*, University of Chicago Press, 2003, p.187.
19. Garon, Paul, *Blues and the Poetic Spirit*, City Lights, 1996, pp.198–9.

20. Knight, Richard, *The Blues Highway: New Orleans to Chicago*, Trailblazer Publications, 2001, p.258.
21. Ibid., p.263.
22. Danchin, Sebastian, *Earl Hooker: Blues Master*, University Press of Mississippi, 2001, p.77.
23. Pruter, Robert, *Doowop: The Chicago Scene*, The Board of Trustees of the University of Illinois, 1996, p.15.
24. Danchin, *Earl Hooker*, p.99.
25. Gordon, Robert, *Can't Be Satisfied: The Life and Times of Muddy Waters*, Pimlico, 2003, p.95.
26. Segrest and Hoffman, *Moanin' at Midnight*, pp.109–10.
27. Oliver, Paul, *The Story of the Blues: The Making of Black Music*, Pimlico, 1997, p.182.
28. Palmer, Robert, *Deep Blues*, Viking Penguin, 1982, p.232.
29. Segrest and Hoffman, *Moanin' at Midnight*, p.104.
30. Ibid., p.240.
31. Ritz, David, with Guy, Buddy, *When I Left Home: My Story*, Da Capo, 2012, p.75.
32. Rowe, *Chicago Blues*, p.175.
33. Ritz, *When I Left Home*, pp.40–1, 73–80.
34. Gordon, *Can't Be Satisfied*, p.217.
35. Segrest and Hoffman, *Moanin' at Midnight*, pp.109–10.
36. Ritz, *When I Left Home*, p.164.
37. Ibid., p.40.
38. Ibid., p.98.
39. Ibid., p.99.
40. Ibid., pp.236–7.
41. Murray, Charles Shaar, *Cross Town Traffic, Jimi Hendrix and Post-War Pop*, Faber and Faber, 2001, p.163.
42. Merrill, Hugh, *The Blues Route*, William Morrow and Company, Inc., 1990, p.93.
43. Jones, Fernando, *I Was There When The Blues Was Red Hot*, Charisse Witherspoon Marketing Group, BKA, 2009, p.72.
44. *Chicago Defender*, daily edition, 18 April 1960, p.2.
45. Oliver, *Story of the Blues*, p.118.
46. Segrest and Hoffman, *Moanin' at Midnight*, p.31.
47. Ibid., p.175.
48. Gordon, *Can't Be Satisfied*, pp.131–2.
49. Rowe, *Chicago Blues*, p.92.
50. Glover, Tony, Dirks, Scott and Gaines, Ward, *Blues with a Feeling*, Routledge, 2002, p.272.
51. Palmer, *Deep Blues*, p.16.
52. Davis, *History of the Blues*.
53. Gordon, *Can't Be Satisfied*, p.126.
54. Ibid., pp.125.
55. Ibid., pp.171–3.
56. Lemann, *Promised Land*, p.102.
57. Knight, *Blues Highway*, p.267.
58. Rowley, Hazel, *Richard Wright: The Life and Times*, John Macrae/Owl Books, 2002, p.50.
59. Rowley, Hazel, *Richard Wright: The Life and Times*, John Macrae/Owl Books, 2002, p.91.
60. Ellison, Ralph, 'Richard Wright's Blues', *Antioch Review* 50:1/2, Winter to Spring, p.74, originally published *Antioch Review* 5:2, Summer 1945.
61. Ruggles, D. Fairchild (ed.), 'On location heritage cities and sites', in Barrett, R. James, *The Heritage of Social Class and Class Conflict on Chicago's South Side*, Springer, 2012, p.29.
62. Rowley, *Richard Wright*, John Macrae/Owl Books, p.102.
63. *Chicago Defender*, Big Weekend edition, 5 August 1916, p.9.
64. Ibid., 10 February 1917, p.3.
65. Goldfield, *Black, White and Southern*, pp.8–9.
66. Gordon, *Can't Be Satisfied*, p.217.
67. Merrill, *Blues Route*, p.91.
68. Speckled Red (Rufus Perryman) had worked on a medicine show in the South, and then moved to Memphis from Detroit to play in the logging and levee camps; he recorded 'The Dirty Dozen' in 1929 – see Oliver, *Story of the Blues*, pp.64, 88.
69. Big Joe Williams arrived in Chicago in the mid 1930s and recorded with Lester Melrose's Bluebird label; he plays guitar on Sonny Boy Williamson's 1937 recording of 'Good Morning Little Schoolgirl'. See Rowe, *Chicago Blues*, p.20.
70. Davis, *History of the Blues*, p.141.
71. Iglauer, Bruce, personal interview at Alligator Records, 23 September 2012.
72. Ibid.
73. Ibid.
74. Ibid.
75. Ibid.
76. Oliver, *Story of the Blues*, p.142.
77. Rowe, *Chicago Blues*, pp.20–1.
78. Glover et al., *Blues with a Feeling*, p.28.
79. Oliver, *Story of the Blues*, p.181.
80. Glover et al., *Blues with a Feeling*, p.35.
81. Oliver, *Story of the Blues*, p.181.
82. Palmer, *Deep Blues*, p.251.
83. Oliver, *Story of the Blues*, p.187.
84. Rowe, *Chicago Blues*, p.160.
85. Ibid.
86. George, Nelson, *The Death of Rhythm & Blues*, Omnibus Press, p.107.
87. Ibid.

2 Lord, Sixty-One Highway:
JOLIET TO ROCK ISLAND

The itinerary Richard and I had planned would take us 160 miles west of Chicago, where we would join Highway 61 and meet the Mississippi River just after Galena. This route would allow us to take in the spectacular scenery of the Mississippi bluffs below Dubuque. Nevertheless, we couldn't resist departing Chicago along a few miles of Route 66. Driving south from the centre of Chicago along Route 66 takes you to Joliet Correctional Center, the penitentiary from which Jake gets paroled at the beginning of *The Blues Brothers*. It's also where Sal Paradise, Kerouac's autobiographical character from *On the Road*, hitches his first lift westward in search of freedom:

To get out of the impossible complexities of Chicago traffic I took the bus to Joliet, Illinois, went by the Joliet pen, stationed myself just outside the town after a walk through its leafy rickety streets behind, and pointed the way. All the way to Joliet by bus, and I had spent more than half my money.

My first ride was a dynamite truck with a red flag, about thirty miles into the great green Illinois, the truck driver pointing out the place where Route 6, which we were on, intersects Route 66 before they both shoot west for incredible distances.[1]

What makes both *The Blues Brothers* and *On the Road* fascinating for blues pilgrims is that their characters offer clues regarding the construction of the blues narrative from a white perspective.

Jake and Elwood personify a view of the travelling musician on the fringes of society, freed from the constraints of women and family, yet seeking redemption on the road. However, as Francis Davis reminds readers in his *The History of the Blues*, Jake and Elwood were developed originally as comic characters, caricaturing 'a breed of white blues enthusiast who had come to *think* of himself as black' (adding that, as with Spinal Tap, their audience 'failed to get the joke but laughed anyway').[2] Jake and Elwood share many of the country bluesmen attributes that were emphasised in books published in the late 1950s and early '60s.

Fredric Ramsey undertook five trips to the Southern countryside between 1951 and 1957 and outlines the image of the itinerant musician in *Been Here and Gone*, published in 1960:

The men who carried the devil on their backs, the box pickers and songsters who were the vagrants, easy riders and drifters of a period just past, are hardly ever to be encountered along the southern highways today. Yet the paths they traced are known, and it is still possible, in traveling, to discover something of their world by following their routes.[3]

Other writers have recognised the deliberate romanticism of a particular lifestyle within such accounts of the blues. Samuel Charters, whose book *The Country Blues* inspired a generation of young white males to go on pilgrimage to find surviving blues artists, acknowledged that if his 'books from this time seem romantic it's because I tried to make them romantic' for the very reason of 'trying to describe black music and black culture in a way that would immediately involve a certain kind of younger, middle-class white American'.[4]

Kerouac, whose existential character Sal Paradise and Sal's hero, Dean Moriarty, exhibit the white notion of the uninhibited and unrestrained black man, laid down a blueprint for the beat generation. In *On the Road* Sal Paradise articulates this white notion: 'I wished I were Joe. I was only myself, Sal Paradise, sad, strolling in this violet dark, this unbearably sweet night, wishing I could exchange worlds with the happy, true hearted, ecstatic Negroes of America.'[5]

In the same year as *On the Road*'s publication, Norman Mailer's *The White Negro*, originally published in *Dissent*, attempted to articulate the hipster's characterisation of the Negro:

Knowing in his cells of his existence that life was war, nothing but war, the Negro (all exceptions admitted) could rarely afford the sophisticated inhibitions of civilisation, and so he kept for his survival the art of the primitive, he lived in the enormous present, he subsisted for his Saturday night kicks, relinquishing the pleasures of the mind for the more obligatory pleasures of the body, and in his music he gave voice to the character and quality of his existence … it was indeed a communication by art because it said 'I feel like this, and now you do too.'[6]

Commentators such as Marybeth Hamilton have suggested that the romance of the 1950s and '60s blues revivalists was kinder and gentler than the 'sexual existential outlaw' portrayed by the beat movement. Both the beats and the revivalists were 'enthralled by the primitive' and Hamilton, like Adelt (see below), recognises these similarities:

What united both movements was their almost exclusively male constituency and their romance with outsider manhood, with defiant black men who seemed to scorn the suburban breadwinner's stifling, soul destroying routine. For revivalists, that model was the country bluesmen, at heart a 'beggar, outcast, near criminal'; for Beats, it was the black urban jazzman, 'a frontiersman in the Wild West of American nightlife' as Norman Mailer described him, who had taken the only route possible if one was to find authenticity in a conformist world: 'to divorce oneself from society, to exit without roots, to set out on that uncharted journey into the rebellious imperatives of the self.'[7]

Undoubtedly, most of the histories written by white authors in the 1960s were genuine attempts to document blues both as an important part of African American culture as well as expression of black suffering. However, in so doing these accounts often excluded women from the story of the blues and projected the deeper desires and anxieties of white males in the 1960s. As Marybeth Hamilton suggests:

In their celebration of blues poetry's profoundly personal character, its expression of intense inner feeling, enthusiasts infused their romance with the unfettered self with a highly charged sense of the supreme realness of rural black men. A defiant drifter, scorning convention, breaking free from domestic ties, the bluesman embodied the tensions of modern masculinity that from its earliest stirrings in the 1950's simmered beneath the surface of the blues revival.[8]

She also suggests that it is therefore not surprising that many of the early blues revivalists did not find authenticity in the voices of the women blues artists (such as Bessie Smith, Ida Cox and Ethel Waters, or guitarists like Memphis Minnie or Rosetta Tharpe), but instead locate authenticity in the voice of the male bluesman.

Ulrich Adelt argues in *Blues Music in the 1960s* that one must take account of the masculinisation of the blues, in terms of the inclusion of white men and the exclusion of black women, and that in the 1960s there was a 'valorisation of an older and rurally based lower-class black culture by mostly young, urban, middle-class white people'.[9] Elijah Wald reminds his readers that for most of us the blues is the image presented by Keith Richards and Mick Jagger, which he summarises as one of 'sex and drugs, and raw, dirty, violent, wild, passionate, angry, grungy, greasy, frightening outlaw music' and adds:

Check any popular image of an old-time blues singer. He is male and black, of course. He plays guitar. He is a loner and a rambler, without money or a pleasant home. He is a figure from another world, not like the people next door, or anyone in your family, or anyone you know well. And his music is haunting, searing, and cuts you to the bone.[10]

To a large extent this view arises from the inescapable fact that in the 1960s blues moves from being played by black musicians for primarily black audiences to being played primarily by white musicians for a young white audience; or, as Ulrich Adelt argues, 'in the larger context of the burgeoning counterculture, audiences for blues music became increasingly white and European. Yet, while blues was becoming white, blackness, in particular black masculinity, remained a marker of authenticity.'[11] And it is the equation of blackness and uninhibited male sexuality that Adelt argues became a central component of Eric Clapton's construction of blues authenticity. Comparing Clapton's notion of blackness with Kerouac's, Adelt suggests, 'like Sal Paradise in Kerouac's narrative, Clapton felt it legitimate to identify as a White Negro and take everything but the burden from black culture'.[12]

Maybe we need to look further than the hipsters, beatniks or comic reflections like *The Blues Brothers*. In 1928, one year before Charley Patton recorded 'Down the Dirt Road', the white pioneering American sociologist Howard W. Odum published *Rainbow Round My Shoulder*. The novel's hero, Left Wing Gordon, is referred to throughout the novel as Black Ulysses. From the opening chapter, 'A Twelve String Laura in the Rough', the narrator spits out lines of blues; hardly a page passes without a verse included to support the narrative. Black Ulysses describes his itinerant lifestyle from the outset: 'Sometimes I works an' sometimes I don't. 'Long with work or travelin' I plays my box an' sings my blues an' gits to help me out when I need 'em, mo' specially good-looking womens.'[13]

For me, making this journey, these arguments about race and gender were as important as the places we would visit; building my own story of the blues would be greatly dependent upon an awareness of how others had built theirs.

It took us four days to reach Mississippi, Lomax's land, where the blues began. Where the name of every other town jumps out from a blues lyric. Where miles of cotton fields, decaying shotgun shacks, run-down juke joints, freight trains fifty carriages long and endless dusty highways can still be found from a time when drifters wandered the landscape creating music that captured the tension between the reality of black suffering and unfettered freedom.

Muddy Waters's gravestone, Restvale cemetery.

Upon leaving Chicago our intention was to pay our respects at the graves of some of the principal musicians of Chicago blues. The first cemetery on our itinerary was the Restvale cemetery in Alsip, about 15 miles south of Chicago. Restvale, like other cemeteries we planned to visit, was situated well outside of the city, which seemed odd, as most of the musicians had lived in the South Side or West Side of Chicago. However, an article in the *Chicago Defender* from 1963 shed some light on burial practices and we started to understand why we'd had to drive out to Cook County: 'The Chicago racists are not satisfied with segregating the living on the indefensible basis of race, they have pursued their prejudice to the burial grounds with the same unconscionable determination.'[14]

A system of lot sale discrimination had been practised, and 'blacks responded to discriminatory policies by creating their own segregated spaces, beginning with Mount Greenwood in 1908, and followed by Lincoln, Burr Oak and Restvale, all located on the south side of the city.'[15]

The list of the musicians buried at Restvale read like a roll call of Chicago blues artists from the 1930s through to the '60s: guitarist and mandolin player Charles 'Papa Charlie' McCoy (1909–50), guitarist and singer John Henry Barbee (1905–64), harmonica player Jazz Gillum (1904–66), guitarist Earl Hooker (MW, 1929–70), harmonica player Big Walter 'Shakey' Horton (MW, 1918–81), guitarist Samuel 'Magic Sam' Gene Maghett (1937–69), guitarist Kansas Joe McCoy (1905–50), blues musician and composer James Burke 'St Louis Jimmy' Oden (1903–77), guitarist and songwriter Eddie Taylor (1923–85), guitarist and singer Theodore Roosevelt 'Hound Dog' Taylor (1915–75), and guitarist and singer Luther Tucker, (MW, 1936–93). The most well-known blues artist buried at Restvale is the king of Chicago blues, McKinley Morganfield, known from childhood as Muddy Waters (1915–83).[16]

On the day of Muddy's funeral a cavalcade drove through Chicago's South Side. According to reports, the streets were lined with people who wanted to pay their last respects. Over the course of three days thousands of mourners visited the body at the Metropolitan Funeral Parlours on the South Side. In attendance at Muddy's funeral service were Willie Dixon, Buddy Guy, Junior Wells, Memphis Slim, Johnny Winter and Pops Staples.[17] A report in the *Observer-Reporter* stated, 'The Rolling Stones, who studied under Waters and took their name from a song he made popular in the 1950s, sent flowers, with a note saying "We shall never forget you, Muddy". It was signed by Mick Jagger, Keith Richards, Bill Wyman, Charlie Watts and Ron Wood.'[18]

Another one of Chicago's legendary harmonica players, Big Walter Horton, is to be found in Restvale cemetery. Born in Mississippi, Horton came up to Chicago via Memphis and replaced Junior Wells in Muddy Waters's band in 1952.

It was a 2-mile drive from Restvale across to Burr Oak, the next Cook County cemetery. There we hoped to find the grave of Willie Dixon, who'd been a hugely influential part of the Chicago blues scene. Dixon, whose grandson Keith had been our guide on the tour of Chess Studios, had by the 1950s become part the Chess establishment, gaining a position within the company that enabled him to wield a high degree of influence over its artists and the material the label recorded. It's been said that before Leonard Chess put out any record, he would send it to four people in the company, one of whom was Dixon, the only one with a musical background.

Willie Dixon was also a prolific composer of blues material and his compositions are still covered by bands today. Elijah Wald described Dixon as one of the young Turks who, along with Waters, Wolf, Sonny Boy Williamson II, Big Walter Horton, Elmore James, John Lee Hooker and B.B. King, would 'electrify their music and turn it into the toughest roots sound on the urban landscape'.[19] In 1954 Waters had Dixon to thank for writing 'Hoochie Coochie Man', which became Waters's biggest hit. Waters followed this success with two more Dixon compositions, 'Just Make Love to You', which reached number four in the Billboard R&B charts three months later, and then 'I'm Ready', which peaked at number four in October of the same year.[20]

Dixon's success was to a great extent due to the fact that he found a formula that straddled the old and the new. One foot in the past and the other firmly set in Chicago's urban future. Benjamin Filene argues that 'Dixon's songs could appeal to newcomers from the South, but his language and imagery suggest that he was primarily speaking for and to migrants who had been settled in the North longer.'[21] It's the understanding that Dixon had of the appeal of Waters's music, with which he'd been familiar since the 1930s, that facilitated Waters's and Chess Records' transition from a product of down-home Delta blues to one that successfully combined the emotion of the Delta with what Dixon described as a peppier form.[22]

In 1954 Chicago blues reached its peak just as non-white unemployment doubled and rose to 10.1 per cent the following year. As Muddy pepped up with a more aggressive style, other blues artists released songs that captured the spirit of troubled times. As Mike Rowe remarks, 'the blues responded immediately' to these harder times, reflected in the material artists recorded. John Brim recorded 'Tough Times'; J.B. Lenoir recorded 'Eisenhower Blues' and, the next year, recorded 'Laid Off Blues', which went out as 'Everybody Wants to Know' and included the lyric 'If we poor people get so hungry we gonna take some food to eat'. Bobo Jenkins recorded 'Democrat Blues' and J.B. Hutto recorded 'Things are so Slow', which included the lines 'I had a dream last night, I was standing in a great long line – a line like they had boys in 1929', making reference to unemployment queues during the Depression.[23]

Willie Dixon's gravestone, Burr Oak cemetery.

The same year that Chess released Waters's 'I'm Ready', the US Supreme Court reached its historic decision in Brown v. Board of Education. This decreed that segregated schooling was unconstitutional. Yet despite the success of this landmark case for the lawyers of the National Association for the Advancement of Colored People (NAACP), it was just one step in the decades of struggle for civil rights.

As the four of us gathered round Dixon's grave a young woman approached us. She was with the only other group of white people in the Burr Oak cemetery. 'I'm looking for Emmett Till's grave – have you found it?' she asked hopefully.

In the distance her parents and a brother or boyfriend were methodically inspecting graves in other sections of the cemetery. I explained we'd found Willie Dixon's grave, but as soon as the words left my mouth they seemed to underplay the significance of the young woman's search.

Emmett Till's name struck a chord with me from my first blues pilgrimage. On that occasion I'd taken a wrong turn a few miles outside of Tutwiler, Mississippi, the town famous as the place where the black band leader W.C. Handy first heard the blues.

It was late in the afternoon and a storm was brewing. A calm came over the flat landscape and the sky resembled a dark curtain that came down till it joined the horizon. There were no clouds, nor wind, just a stillness, and then we saw the sign by the side of the highway informing us we were on the Emmett Till Memorial Highway. I stopped and swung the car round in the gravel entrance to an old wooden farmstead and headed back west along the highway to Tutwiler, passing the memorial sign a second time. My companion commented that he was sure Emmett Till had met an appalling death at the hands of whites, although at the time neither of us could recall quite how or why.

A few months later I came across Till's story. When he was 14 he was sent south by his mother from their home in Chicago to his relatives in Money, Mississippi, for the summer vacation. His 'mistake', a result of teenage bravado, was to ignore the unwritten code of behaviour expected of blacks in the South.

The Chicago Defender reported that, according to one of Till's friends, he had gone into Bryant's store in Money to buy some bubble gum and had been urged by his friends to 'look at the pretty lady behind the counter'.[24] Reports vary as to what happened next. Some suggest that he said goodbye to Mrs Bryant, the pretty storekeeper, and then whistled when she followed him from the shop. Other reports suggest his mistake was to say, 'Bye, honey.' Either way, Till had transgressed the boundaries of acceptable behaviour imposed by whites on blacks in the South.

Three days later, on a Saturday night, Roy Bryant and his half-brother came looking for Till. The brothers took him at gunpoint from his bed at his uncle's house, whereupon he was tortured, mutilated and eventually shot in the face before being tied with barbed wire to a cotton gin fan and thrown in the Tallahatchie River. Bryant used the fact that Till had wolf-whistled at his wife in his defence. The all-white male jury took an hour to find Bryant and Milam not guilty of Till's murder.

Till's broken body was brought back by his mother to be buried in Chicago, causing an outcry across the country. His mother insisted that her son be displayed in a glass-topped casket for the world to see.

The musicians whose graves we'd come to find at Burr Oak and Restvale – Dixon and Waters – had grown up in the South and would have experienced fears of similar treatment in their everyday lives. They would certainly have been aware of Till's murder and may have even been among the tens of thousands of black Chicagoan's who attended Till's funeral. They would doubtless have shared many of the same disappointments upon arriving in the North; disappointments captured by black writers such as Langston Hughes and Richard Wright.

There were eight of us spread out across Burr Oak looking for Emmett Till's grave. The young woman had downloaded a photograph from the internet that showed the grave had a bronze vase. For thirty minutes we searched, each working independently, each of us with our own thoughts as we walked the lines of graves, each for a moment forgetting the excitement of the Chicago blues.

Richard questioned the inclusion of Galena on our itinerary because it added a few hundred miles to the trip. I'd got most of Pat Middleton's five-volume guide, America's Great River Road, prior to the trip and had been thinking about how best to build a sense of the Mississippi, which is such an intrinsic part of the blues story, into our journey. Whilst Middleton does not come across as a big blues fan, she provides a useful guide of the landscape's natural geographic features and towns' economic backgrounds. Middleton also recognises that, without planning, a traveller can drive south and the Mississippi can remain conspicuous by its absence:

> Only the Great River we found was missing. Like Tom Sawyer, who shows up at his own funeral, it seems a ghost. This gateway to a wilderness, a natural highway for the westward expansion, moulder of land and culture, the Great River today has either been veiled in levees that separate it from its villages or it has wandered away on its own. We speak of it, we protect ourselves from its careless meanders, we test ourselves against it, but we seldom see it.[25]

In the preface to Volume IV, which covers the states of Arkansas, Mississippi and Louisiana, Middleton alludes to the fact that one will see 'both poverty and great wealth in extremes that are seldom seen in the United States'.[26] I knew that within a couple of days we'd be visiting some fairly poor areas, whereas in Galena poverty isn't much in evidence. As well as that, the route between Chicago and Galena cuts across beautiful rural landscape, which is by no means just tedious Corn Belt.

The old railroad depot, Bouthillier Street, Galena, Illinois.

Galena feels like an indulgence for the blues pilgrim. This restored Victorian gem, with its quaint streets subtly illuminated by the glow of fake gas lamps, its old shopfronts full of arts and crafts interspersed between little restaurants and taverns, had nothing, as far as we were aware, to do with the blues. Lamp-lit flights of steps ascend the bluff that dominates the town leading to neat residential avenues of timbered detached houses overlooking Main Street and the river below. People come here at weekends on vacations from the city and for some Chicagoans it's the place where they have a second home.

We drove down Main Street and made for the DeSoto House Hotel, the best in town; it opened in 1855 and was once known as the largest in the West. A grand curved staircase led up from the lobby, which still has an original ornately decorated tin ceiling. From the hotel one can see the levee built to protect the town following severe flooding that brought water to a height of 4 to 5ft along Main Street in 1937. Unlike so many of the towns in the United States, Galena still has a feel that invites you to explore on foot, walk its levee or meander from bar to bar – something that the blues pilgrim is told is inadvisable in some parts of the larger towns and cities further south.

In a first-floor atrium of the DeSoto we found William Christopher Handy in a display case, staring out from a framed photograph alongside five other prominent African Americans who had visited Galena. The sign read: 'W.C. Handy, musician, "Father of the Blues", composer of "St Louis Blues".'

One night, returning from an engagement in the Delta, Handy had to wait at Tutwiler for a train that had been delayed by nine hours. It was there that he heard a ragged black guitarist who pressed a knife across the strings and sang 'Goin' where the Southern cross the Dog' – a reference to the Southern and Yazoo Delta railroads. Handy had heard the blues for the first time, an event that the blues historian Paul Oliver suggested 'quite literally altered the life of William Christopher Handy and also, to a considerable degree, the course of the blues …'[27]

We adjusted our schedule in order to visit the town's museum and library and try to find out what Handy had been up to in Galena. The likelihood is that Handy and his orchestra had an engagement here; however, despite making enquiries and consulting a number of sources we never found out what had brought Handy to Galena.

The plan was to cross the Mississippi into Iowa and stop at the port town of Dubuque. An ice harbour was built at Dubuque between 1882 and 1885 and it was here that the river's great steam boats would shelter during severe winters. The Woodward Riverboat Museum, situated by the ice harbour, is a good reason to make a stop in Dubuque, as it's one of the best museums on the river and offers an excellent overview of its history.

After crossing the Mississippi, we at last joined Highway 61 and got our first sight of those classic black-and-white 'US Highway 61' signs.

Three hundred and fifty miles to the north, Highway 61 leads to Thunder Bay and the Canadian border, and the last big American town, Duluth, Minnesota. It was here, on 24 May 1941, that one Robert Allen Zimmerman, aka Bob Dylan, was born – a man who for a brief moment represented the hopes of all who looked for a future built on America's folk traditions. And 1,000 miles to the south it ends at New Orleans, the city that many claim to be the birthplace of jazz, and blues.

Our journey followed the route that had brought young Englishmen to Chicago in the early 1960s. Young men whose roots were steeped in rock 'n' roll, jazz and skiffle and who thought they recognised something both exciting and akin to their own music in the sounds of the Chicago blues.

We took Highway 61 South out of Dubuque, then turned south along Highway 52 and drove across a causeway out into the Mississippi to the island city of Sabula, a marooned agricultural town, which today has the feel of a small fishing village. This nineteenth-century town is defended by a levee and a series of lakes that hold back the mighty waters of the Mississippi. The main highway winds past small dusty roads that lead down to the waterfront before crossing the Mississippi on a box-frame iron bridge into Illinois and the town of Savanna. On the Illinois side signs directed us onto Highway 84 North and towards the Mississippi Palisades Park. Dusk was starting to draw in as we ascended to the parking areas, near the top of the bluffs. Boardwalks enticed us from the cover of the forest's foliage and out onto precarious wooden jetties which jut out from the palisades. An immense expanse of water and forest filled the entire view across the horizon, a view that captured both the magnitude and magnificence of the Mississippi. Just then the sun set, and the Great River and Buffalo Lake stretched out before us, illuminated in a golden glow. A whistle blew as a freight train slowly came into view, crawling along an arching bend between the edge of the bluff and the shore. I started counting the freight wagons, each one as long as a passenger carriage. After the fiftieth, I gave up.

The following morning's journey brought us to Le Claire, a small riverside town which claims Buffalo Bill as a native son. It would be hard to drive through Le Claire without making a stop, as it's the closest we would come to a cowboy frontier town on the whole trip. We found Sneaky Pete's tavern, a three-storey wooden and brick building, conspicuous by the large Union flag painted on the wall, in the main street, aptly named Cody Street after Buffalo Bill. Our eyes slowly adjusted as we made our way through the front bar, with its darkened wood interior which sported bullet holes in the ceiling. Sneaky Pete's served a good breakfast and the restaurant at the back overlooked the railway sidings and the comings and goings of barges of the Mississippi beyond.

Pointing out the bullet holes in the ceiling, one Le Claire resident informed us that the building had been a hotel and cow herders' saloon. Le Claire was situated on an old cattle drover's route, at the head of rapids that ran from here down to Davenport until the river lock and dam had been built in the last century. This was plausible as we'd already discovered that Bellevue, a town situated some 60 miles further upriver, had been infamous as a shelter for

William M. Black steamboat, Dubuque Harbor, Iowa.

Views across the Mississippi River from the bluff, Mississippi Palisades State Park, Illinois.

Julien Dubuque Bridge across the Mississippi River, Dubuque.

cattle thieves and outlaws. It was also the scene of the so-called Bellevue war, the largest western shoot-out, which arose when the town's people took on and rid themselves of the Brown Gang in 1840.[28]

We'd included Rock Island on our itinerary because of the 'Chicago, Rock Island and Pacific Railroad', which in 1854 established the first service to link Chicago to the Mississippi. The railroad is referred to in 'Rock Island Line', the song made popular by Lonnie Donegan. He recorded it for Decca in 1955, with Chris Barber on bass and Beryl Brydon on washboard. As blues historian Robert Palmer states:

> The skiffle craze began early in 1956 when Lonnie Donegan, formerly the banjoist with Chris Barber's trad band, became an overnight star with a hit record called 'Rock Island Line'. It was a songster ballad that Donegan had learned from a Leadbelly recording, and Donegan had performed it in a kind of jug band style, with acoustic guitar and bass, washboard percussion, and kazoo leads. These were the basic ingredients of skiffle.[29]

The importance of the song 'Rock Island Line' is not only as part of Donegan and skiffle's contribution to the evolution of British blues-orientated rock music. It's the song's connection with Leadbelly that also takes us to the Lomaxes. It was Alan Lomax's father, John Lomax, who first recorded Leadbelly in 1933, during a trip to record black folk music for the book *American Folk Songs and Ballads*, which he undertook with the then 18-year-old Alan. In the summer of 1933 the pair visited Angola Penitentiary, southern Louisiana, close to the Mississippi border and Highway 61. On the fourth day of recording the songs of prison inmates, the Lomaxes were introduced to guitarist and singer Huddie Ledbetter, who sang seven songs for them. John Lomax recorded in his notes that 'we found a Negro convict that was so skilful with his guitar and his strong, baritone voice that he had been made a "trusty" and kept around Camp A headquarters as a laundryman, so as to be near at hand to sing and play for visitors.'[30]

By the following year Huddie Ledbetter had been released from Angola for 'good time'. Contrary to the myth that developed around Ledbetter's release, he was not pardoned following John Lomax's intervention to Governor Allen. As well as becoming accepted fact, this popular myth also became Ledbetter's understanding of events leading to his release. By the end of September 1934 the ever-grateful Ledbetter was employed by John Lomax as his driver and together they embarked on a tour of the South, undertaking further field recordings for the Library of Congress of 'Negro' folk songs. By October they arrived at Cummins Prison Farm in Arkansas, 30 miles west of the Mississippi River. It was while at Cummins Farm they recorded a prisoner named Kelly Pace leading a group of prisoners in work songs while they cut logs with axes. The song was 'Rock Island Line'.

Notes

1. Kerouac, Jack, *On the Road*, Penguin, 1991, pp.14–15.
2. Davis, Francis, *The History of the Blues: The Roots Music and the People*, Da Capo, 2003, p.242.
3. Ramsey, Fredrick, *Been Here and Gone*, Cassell and Company Ltd, 1960, p.95.
4. Chartres, Samuel B., *The Country Blues*, Da Capo, 1975, p.x.
5. Kerouac, *On the Road*, p.180.
6. Mailer, Norman, *The White Negro*, City Light Books, 1957, p.4.
7. Hamilton, Marybeth, *In Search of the Blues: Black Voices White Visions*, Jonathan Cape, 2007, p.193.
8. Ibid., pp.192–3.
9. Adelt, Ulrich, *Blues Music in the 1960s*, Rutgers, 2011, p.6.
10. Wald, Elijah, *Escaping the Delta: Robert Johnson and the Invention of the Blues*, Amistad, 2005, p.221.
11. Adelt, *Blues Music in the 1960s*, p.1.
12. Ibid., p.59.
13. Odum, W. Howard, *Rainbow Round My Shoulder*, Bobbs-Merrill Company, 1928, p.9.
14. *Chicago Defender*, daily edition, 5 March 1963, p.12. *ProQuest Historical Newspapers: The Chicago Defender (1910–75)*.
15. Yalom, Marilyn, *The American Resting Place*, Houghton Mifflin, 2008, p.171.
16. MW denotes artists that were members of Muddy Waters's band at one point in their career. Robert Gordon states that Waters was born in 1913 – Gordon, Robert, *Can't Be Satisfied: The Life and Times of Muddy Waters*, Pimlico, 2003, p.4.
17. Gordon, Robert, *Can't Be Satisfied* pp.272–3.
18. *Observer-Reporter*, 6 May 1983, p.19.
19. Wald, *Escaping the Delta*, p. 90.
20. Gordon, *Can't Be Satisfied*, Appendix C, p.292.
21. Filene, Benjamin, *Romancing the Folk: Public Memory and American Roots Music*, University of North Carolina Press, 2000, p.106.
22. Palmer, Robert, *Deep Blues*, Penguin, 1992, interview with Willie Dixon, p.166.
23. Rowe, Mike, *Chicago Blues: The City and The Music*, Da Capo, 1975, pp.122–3. Originally published in 1973 as *Chicago Breakdown*.
24. Collin, Mattie S. and Elliott, Robert, 'Grieving Mother Meets Body of Lynched Son', *Chicago Defender* national edition, 10 September 1955, p.5.
25. Middleton, Pat, *Discover! America's Great River Road Volume 3*, Heritage Press, 1998, p.x.
26. Middleton, Pat, *Discover! America's Great River Road Volume 4*, Heritage Press, 2005, p.x.
27. Oliver, Paul, *The Story of the Blues – The Making of Black Music*, Pimlico, 1997, p.28.
28. Middleton, Pat, *Discover America's Great River Road, Volume 2*, Heritage Press, 1992, p.61.
29. Palmer, *Deep Blues*, p.257.
30. Wolfe, Charles K. and Lornell, Kip, *The Life and Legend of Leadbelly*, Da Capo, 1999, p.113.

3

Down to St Louis:

ST LOUIS

For every rock 'n' roller who claims to have been inspired by skiffle you can find a hundred more who will acknowledge Chuck Berry, the man from St Louis, Missouri, as their most important musical influence. That's why on my first blues pilgrimage I'd included a stopover at Berry's home town. Yet on that occasion I'd left St Louis disappointed and discovered little to connect me with Berry and his music. I remember still struggling to place the city in the broader context of the overall journey. Maybe it was partly to do with the fact that St Louis sees itself as a jazz city, celebrating its connections with Miles Davies and Scott Joplin. Even W.C. Handy's 'St Louis Blues' has become a staple for numerous rearrangements by jazz musicians over the years. For much of its history the city's African American middle class had viewed the neighbourhoods from which blues emanated disparagingly. This time I would give the city another shot. Perhaps if I looked for Chuck he'd help me find the spirit of the blues rolling in with the mist from the Mississippi.

The city of St Louis is a little less than 300 miles south from Davenport and Rock Island, or about a five-hour drive along Highway 61. About 50 miles out of Davenport we passed a diner that caught our eye; I drove back and parked up in the forecourt. Turning a big automatic with soft suspension round in a single arc onto the opposite lane never fails to give me a little shot of adrenalin, which I guess is wrapped up in that 1950s imagery that Chuck Berry conveys in songs such as 'Maybellene'.

The diner was at Muscatine and it made sense to grab a bite to eat before settling into the journey. At the beginning of the nineteenth century this riverside location had been home to the Mascoutin Indians; it was later developed by German immigrants towards the latter half of the century. Wood was the town's most profitable commodity until a German named John F. Boepple established the Boepple Button Factory; within a matter of years the town had become the centre of the Mississippi River freshwater pearl button industry and Muscatine gained a reputation as the pearl button capital of the world.

Mark Twain was familiar with Muscatine, as his brother had part ownership in the *Muscatine Journal*. Twain honed his literary skills contributing travel articles to his brother's paper while training as a printer. He also referred to Muscatine in his autobiographical *Life on the Mississippi*, in which he describes the town from his vantage point aboard a riverboat passing the town. Twain was working as a steamboat pilot in the 1850s, just at the time that the town started to develop.

The year following the publication of *Life on the Mississippi* saw the publication of *The Adventures of Huckleberry Finn*; probably Twain's most important novel and one that would prove to be a source of controversy from its publication through to the present day. The very existence of *Huckleberry Finn* continues to form part of the discourse on race in modern America and as such retains relevance irrespective of whether one views its themes as abolitionist and antislavery or steeped in racist language and minstrelsy. Only a few months prior to our visit to Dubuque, the town where we had first joined Highway 61, a teacher was reported to have been sacked from a local school for allegedly telling a classroom of students that *Huckleberry Finn* was a racist novel.[1] The American Library Association's Office for Intellectual Freedom reported that *Huckleberry Finn* appeared in the top ten most challenged books for 2007, based upon the number of written complaints made for a book's removal from public access in schools and libraries.[2]

The diner was empty; it was between meal times and the staff sat around a table on the far side. It was fitted out in 1950s retro style, complete with red-and-white leather seats and Formica tables. The waitress explained that the original diner had been situated a couple of miles up the road on the banks of the Mississippi before being relocated to Highway 61. The model juke boxes on each table were stocked with a selection of classic rock 'n' roll from the 1950s and '60s but even though we'd be in Chuck Berry's home town by nightfall, it seemed a little too corny to choose one of Chuck's songs so early in the day.

As I sat and surveyed the scene, I contemplated my feeling of unease about why the celebration of the ordinary seemed so comfortable, even an essential part of our American road trip. The diner was typical of the short-term immersion in Americana that Europeans crave yet don't ever fully understand why they seek it. They turn the American dream on its head. The antithesis

Le Claire riverboat, Mississippi.

to individualism succeeding over the ordinary, the diner is where ordinariness has itself succeeded. Roadside temples not to modernity but to the mundane, where those who dine are no longer objects but are instead the participating subjects of mass society.

The Mississippi didn't reappear for another 100 miles or so, until we passed the bend in the river at Fort Madison. When it did, the Great River was about a mile wide, which is what's so impressive about the Mississippi, even though it's still nearly 1,000 miles from the Gulf of Mexico. It just keeps collecting water as it makes the journey south. You have to seek the river out and each time you find it it's bigger and bigger. When you can't see it you know it's still constantly with you, just behind the tree line or beyond the bank of a levee, because it's too big to disappear. I thought of Huck and Jim being carried downriver on their raft, heading for the mouth of the Ohio River, seeking a route to safety and away from the Southern slave states. But the current of the mighty Mississippi swept them past the lights of St Louis, in the distance on the other side of the river, and on past the mouth of the Ohio River, which was lost in the fog, taking them ever deeper into the South.

Highway 61 drifts away from the river, and then returns once again to offer glimpses of the water just before Canton is reached. After Canton the

Sneaky Pete's Bar and Grill, Le Claire, Iowa.

wide road allows a little time to be made up. Time was pressing, because we needed to negotiate our way through to downtown St Louis and a hotel we'd pre-booked, close to the Gateway Arch. A hundred miles from St Louis, Highway 61 dipped back towards the river and a sign invited us to Hannibal, Mark Twain's home town. Hannibal, or St Petersburg, as Twain names the town in *The Adventures of Tom Sawyer* and *Huckleberry Finn*, is considered to be one of the most attractive towns on this part of the river. Our two guidebooks, now creased backwards and sitting with broken spines on the dashboard, made Hannibal sound inviting. It was described as 'still picturesque' and 'a town which has given itself over to Twain'; passing Hannibal was a difficult call.

However, St Louis and the evening beckoned and unfortunately even our three-week schedule didn't allow enough time for us to join the pilgrims who had come to pay homage at the childhood home of Samuel Langhorne Clemens, aka Mark Twain. Irrespective of what Twain might have to tell us about life in the South, Chuck Berry was the key reason for making a stopover in St Louis.

It was clear in my own mind that our trip to St Louis was to pay homage to a man who had made my life immeasurably happier. An artist of whom Nelson George said, when comparing him to Presley in the *Death of Rhythm and Blues*, 'Chuck Berry, the real genius of what we call rock & roll, whose guitar licks, humour, and storytelling skills produced a catalogue of intense, personal music'.[3] But, Eric Clapton suggests that Berry was not fully aware of the enormity of his own position: 'I'd heard stories he was very bitter and thought people had ripped him off and in order to think that you must be aware of how far your influence has spread. I don't really know if he's completely aware of how much people really love his music.'[4]

Sunset over the Mississippi River, Highway 52, Savannah, Illinois.

I'd found an article by Peter Egan published in a collection of automotive writing, in which he recounts his adventures driving down Highway 61 in a 'royal maroon 1963 Model Sixty-Two Cadillac'. A car that he informs his readers is 'perfect for a blues pilgrimage. Chuck Berry would approve.' After leaving Hannibal, Egan cruises up Cardiff Hill to where Huck and Tom would watch the river. He then takes Highway 61 and stops off at Wentzville, a town a few miles west. This is where Berry Park is situated, Chuck's family ranch house, which featured in the Taylor Hackford film *Hail! Hail! Rock 'n' Roll*.

Highway 61 works its way through the outer suburbs of St Louis until 40 miles from the city's centre it merges with Interstate 64. Except one is never really sure of where the city's centre really is, because half of the city is on the other side of the Mississippi River and falls under the jurisdiction of the State of Illinois. At Midtown we ran into the tail of the St Louis rush hour. From there on in we were in Chuck's city, bumper to bumper but hardly rolling from side to side as the traffic around us settled down to a steady crawl.

Dusk fell and the skyscrapers of downtown St Louis lit up before us. Beyond them peeked Eero Saarinen's 630ft-high stainless steel monument commemorating Jefferson's Louisiana Purchase and America's great expansion westward. St Louis's Gateway Arch is not only the largest man-made monument in the United States, but is also the tallest accessible building in the State of Missouri. We kept catching glimpses of the arch between the downtown skyscrapers, its towering silver form illuminated by the search lamps that surround the base of the arch, until their beams became lost in the cool mist rolling in off the Mississippi River.

I recalled driving into St Louis for the first time, Berry's 'Route 66' playing in the car, and passing the signs for the Cahokia Indian Mounds. These were the mounds of the Mississippians, a Native American culture that inhabited large areas around the Mississippi between 800 CE and 1500 CE.

In the narrative of the blues, St Louis, like Memphis, represents a gateway to the Northern cities – away from Jim Crow. A gateway through which some of the key exponents of urban blues passed. Yet St Louis also represented a gateway to freedom through which Dred Scott, in 1857, found he couldn't pass when the US Supreme Court considered him to be private property rather than a man. A decision that meant even free blacks could not be citizens of the United States.[5] Dred Scott challenged the limits of the Missouri Compromise, which had banned slavery in any new state north of Missouri's southern boundary, arguing that having lived in Illinois, a free state, he had the right not to be sold as a slave in Missouri.[6]

I was determined that on this trip we'd find the St Louis that had a story to tell about the blues. But first we had to find the Hilton, dump our bags, and find where the music was. On my last trip to the city I had been greeted on arrival by a 100ft cut out of Chuck Berry standing by the side of the interstate, announcing his return to the city for a homecoming concert.

Now, five years later, Berry was 86 years old and still gigging. He puts on a regular show each month at the Blueberry Hill in Delmar, situated only a couple of miles from the Greater Ville neighbourhood of St Louis, where he grew up.

We planned that the following day we would visit some of the sites connected with Berry's early life, but on this first evening in the city we'd make for the jazz and blues clubs located on South Broadway. The receptionist at the Hilton recommended that although the clubs were only a mile or so away it would be best to take a taxi. So we got into a yellow cab and headed downtown. Many of the venues are in buildings dating back to the nineteenth century and now survive in an area bordered between the pillars supporting the interstate and the rail tracks that cross the Mississippi.

Our taxi dropped us outside BB's Jazz, Blues & Soups club. This is situated in a three-storey building that has served numerous purposes over the last century and a half, including a period as a brothel. We paid BB's $5 cover charge, ordered a rib basket and a couple of Blue Moons, and joined the other punters, all white and middle-aged, for the Monday night session of blues, courtesy of the Hadden Sayers' band.

Sayers' band played original soulful blues material, with an undercurrent of rock running through most numbers, taken from Sayers' *Hard Dollar* album, released the previous year. They were all consummate musicians and 'Back to the Blues' had been nominated for song of the year at the Blues Blast Music Awards. Sayers had also been working with Ruthie Foster, who had received the accolade of Contemporary Blues Artist of the Year a couple of years back. The band broke between sets, so I took the opportunity to ask Sayers about the session work he'd been doing and get him to sign a copy of the album.

We left the band to their break and made our way under the railway bridges that crossed Broadway to stroll the 100 yards or so down to the Broadway Oyster Bar, which had a four-piece band playing some live blues in its garden bar. The sound of rail freight clanked continuously between songs as wagons rolled over the MacArthur Bridge and across the river to East St Louis. The evening air still held the city's warmth and the waitress brought us a couple more beers. People wandered out from the bars onto the streets to talk and smoke, and the rhythmic beat of the bands merged with the sound of people mingling on the street outside the Broadway bars.

Hadden Sayers' band got into its second set, but the sound of Latin music mixed with the excited chatter of the younger customers in the open-air bar opposite dominated the street beneath the railway tracks. Revellers were illuminated by a series of coloured lanterns strung from a canvas awning. Taxis came and went and a group of young women with short dresses and carefully groomed hair rummaged in shoulder bags to find fares and cigarette lighters, while others came out to see if taxis had arrived to take them on to bars at Soulard.

We returned to BB's to catch the end of the second set. I still wanted to visit the Soulard neighbourhood, the city's Latin Quarter, renowned for its bars and live music, including a good offering of jazz and blues. After hailing a cab outside

BB's Jazz, Blues & Soups Club, Downtown St Louis.

Hadden Sayers Band, BB's Jazz, Blues & Soups Club, South Broadway, St Louis.

Election posters on the site of the Cosmopolitan Club, East St Louis.

the Broadway Oyster Bar, we took the short ride along Broadway over to Soulard Market, and strolled along Geyer Avenue between Seventh and Thirteenth Street. Here, amongst quaint nineteenth-century residential brick properties on lamp-lit avenues, Soulard's famous bars and restaurants are to be found.

At the weekends Soulard is filled with revellers moving from bar to bar, and in February Soulard hosts its own Mardi Gras festival, which attracts thousands of visitors to its charming streets. But as Soulard closed down that night, and the last few drinkers sat in the bars that were still serving, there was a calmness about this historic French enclave. A guitarist sang in a corner bar to a group of students as he wound up his set.

We rose early next morning, as our plan was to drive across the river into East St Louis and find the site where the Cosmopolitan Club had been. I'd come across accounts of the club in Chuck Berry's autobiography and seen Taylor Hackford's film *Hail! Hail! Rock 'n' Roll*. Made in 1986, the film, in which Chuck Berry and Keith Richards starred, revisits scenes from Berry's early career. The Cosmopolitan, which had been a supermarket prior to being refurbished as a club, stood at the crossroads of Seventeenth Street and Bond Avenue.

Our search for the site of the Cosmopolitan club took us onto the Poplar Street Bridge over the Mississippi and into Illinois. This eight-lane bridge takes vehicles in and out of St Louis on an elevated stretch of the freeway, detached from the lives of those in East St Louis below. I'd read reports that suggested the area's high homicide rate, which ran at seventeen times the average for the United States, was linked to East St Louis' endemic poverty and lack of economic opportunity, combined with extensive crack cocaine use. Our early start was partly due to a naive notion on my part that crack users weren't early risers. We didn't see anything to reassure us that times had changed since Jonathan Kozol – the educationalist and writer, who has been described as 'today's most eloquent spokesman for America's disenfranchised' – painted a frighteningly vivid and disturbing picture of life for many East St Louis inhabitants:

The decimation of the men within the population is quite nearly total. Four of five births in East St Louis are to single mothers. Where do the men go? Some to prison. Some to the military. Many to an early death. Dozens of men are living in the streets or sleeping in small isolated camps behind burnt-out buildings.[7]

Despite our reservations about East St Louis (and the fact that the hotel receptionist, after asking us where we planned to go that day, asked if we were really sure we wanted to do that) it only took a couple of minutes from the exit of the interstate to reach the junction of Seventeenth and Bond, the site of the Cosmopolitan Club. For me this was the second symbolic crossroads of our trip. The Cosmopolitan Club represented the crossroads of Chicago blues and rock 'n' roll. It was here that Chuck Berry and Johnnie Johnson had first come to prominence in the city, combining a myriad of musical influences into something that would become known as rock 'n' roll. Within eighteen months of the first gig at the Cosmopolitan, Berry had been offered a contract and recorded his first session with Chess in Chicago, which included 'Maybellene', 'Wee Wee Hours', 'Thirty Days' and 'You Can't Catch Me', with Willie Dixon on stand-up bass. 'Maybellene' was chosen for release in July 1955; the song, which Berry had based on the white country song 'Ida Red', quickly made its way to number one in the Billboard R&B chart.

Berry had idolised Muddy Waters, to the extent that when Waters came to East St Louis and visited the Cosmopolitan Club Berry describes himself as being 'enthralled to be so near one of his idols' and delegated himself 'to chaperone him around the spots of entertainment in East St Louis'.[8]

With the influences of St Louis's piano tradition ever present it seems hardly surprising that the rock 'n' roll of Chuck Berry and Johnnie Johnson incorporated piano riffs from swing and rag-time, combined with the guitar licks of Carl Hogan, Lonnie Johnson, T-Bone Walker and Charlie Christian to establish a distinctive space within the newly emerging rock 'n' roll genre. When I listen to Peetie Wheatstraw's 'Peetie Wheatstraw Stomp', recorded in Chicago in 1937 with Kokomo Arnold accompanying on guitar, it's more 'Maybellene' than 'Ida Red'.

Pianist Johnnie Johnson asked Chuck Berry to join him and drummer Ebby Hardy for a New Year's Eve gig with Johnnie's band, the Sir John's Trio, at the Cosmopolitan in 1953. The performance went down so well that the owner of the club rebooked the Johnnie Johnson trio with the proviso that Berry fronted it. It was at the Cosmopolitan that the band built its reputation, playing to a mixed audience that responded enthusiastically to a varied repertoire of Nat 'King' Cole and Muddy Waters covers interspersed with hillbilly and country and western songs. The act soon started to attract packed houses with an audience that might be 40 per cent white on some nights.

Because East St Louis was in the State of Illinois it was a little more liberally inclined towards races mixing than was the case in St Louis, Missouri, across the river. Berry's story betrays the dissonance felt by an artist whose creativity produced a musical form that so successfully captured the experience of white youth, yet whose own experience was informed by the stifling constraints of life as an African American growing up in 1940s and '50s Missouri. He tells how the custom of the police in St Louis upon stopping a mixed-race couple would be to take them to the police station for a mandatory shot for venereal disease.[9]

Memories of racism continually come to the fore in Berry's accounts of his early life. Such as the time he was picked up by the police because he had been reported by a jealous ex-boyfriend for having sex with a white Canadian woman, a tenant in a house Berry was renovating. He describes one officer tilting his head as the sergeant swung a baseball bat menacingly whilst trying to establish if he'd had sex with a white woman.[10]

In the Taylor Hackford film Berry recounts how at the age of 11 he was taken by his father to the Fox Theater in St Louis. With a touch of irony he recalls that it could have been to see *The Tale of Two Cities*, and remembered the woman in the box office telling his father 'you know your people can't come in here – go away', adding that his family had to wait two years for the production to come to the black theatre. In the film Berry crosses the threshold to the foyer of the Fox Theater, where he is due to play that night with Keith Richards, and poignantly observes that 'this is a far cry from years back when my forefathers were sold a few blocks away on the steps of the Civil Court House.'[11]

Berry's response, rather than capitulation, is to allude to his experience as a black man within lyrics framed specifically for his white audience in songs such as 'Brown Eyed Handsome Man', 'Johnny B Goode' and 'Promised Land'.[12]

In *Blues and the Poetic Spirit* Garon argues that many white practitioners of blues miss the fact that blues was not only entertainment but also a means of expressing 'an eloquent and coded protest against white rule and oppression'.[13] Garon cites the example of Chuck Berry's 'Promised Land', in which the 'poor boy' in question takes a Greyhound bus to reach the 'promised land', the West Coast of America. However, when the hound breaks down and strands its passengers in Birmingham, Alabama, he buys a ticket 'across Mississippi, clean', which means without making a stop in the state. As Garon points out: 'For a black man to be stranded somewhere in the Deep South was bad enough, but in Mississippi? Stranded? Never!'[14]

East St Louis, although once the heart of the St Louis blues scene, is today exactly as Richard Knight describes it, 'a run-down and semi-deserted suburb with nothing like the music it once enjoyed'.[15] In Jonathan Franzen's novel *The Twenty-Seventh City* East St Louis is portrayed as a location of fear; a place where those living over the river don't go; erased from the minds of the St Louis populace across the bridge. In the novel, Barbara is lost in a wet, empty street in East St Louis and looks towards the river. She recognises the names on the green interstate signs on the elevated highway that passes above her but she can't climb up to the shoulder to flag a car down. She can see the skyline of downtown St Louis and the Gateway Arch. At the end of the street she sees her city but can't reach it; she can't find an escape from what she describes as 'a Hiroshima neighbourhood in the spring of '46, so flat and lifeless that it almost promised to offer safe passage'.[16]

The East St Louis Franzen describes is:

A small-scale version of the South Bronx, of Watts, of North Philly. These cratered streets three miles east of the Arch would have been a menace or a social issue for people in St Louis if they weren't protected by a wide river and a state line. … The town was a black hole in the local cosmos, a place so poor and vicious that even organised crime stayed away.[17]

My first encounter with East St Louis five years previously was due to a miscalculation. I'd inadvertently left the elevated interstate too early, having just crossed the Martin Luther King Bridge into Illinois. I remember the sense of abandonment about the place and thinking that the width of the streets seemed at odds with a town largely deserted. In my diary for that day I'd noted that the streets were 'noticeably shabbier than the downtown area we'd just come from on the other side of the river'.

Through misreading the interstate signs I'd dropped down into what was once known as the Valley, an area which Paul Garon describes as having been a notorious district that 'provided steady work for a number of blues singers, as well as for pimps, prostitutes, gamblers, bootleggers, crooked politicians and assorted hustlers'.[18] The Valley was situated north of Railroad Avenue, across Broadway and along Third and Fourth Street as far as St Clair Avenue.[19]

It was here in July 1917, after white mobs burned black homes, that the worst race riot of the twentieth century in the United States occurred, leaving thirty-nine people dead. The headlines in the *Chicago Defender* claimed that police and soldiers failed to defend local people and left children and men to be killed while refugees flocked into St Louis.[20] The roots of the disturbance had been brewing for some time due to rumours that employers were encouraging black labour to replace white strikers. A report in the *Chicago Defender* published the month prior to the riot suggests this was the case and that employers were publicly talking about importing Chinese labour.[21]

The blues historian Paul Oliver suggests that 'outside of Chicago and Detroit, St Louis was undoubtedly the richest (city) musically'. He also captures the important role of music within the squalid conditions of East St Louis when he states:

Across the Mississippi River from St Louis lies the crude, unlovely town called East St Louis, which had been the scene in 1917 of an appalling race riot when black labour was brought in to replace white workers. The scars remained, but for those who worked and lived in the squalor of its factories and disintegrating wood houses, there was some outlet in the joints and bars of Market and Main, and Main and Broadway, where at Katy Red's honky-tonk for instance, Henry Brown, Roosevelt Sykes, Alice Moore and Peetie Wheatstraw might be heard.[22]

Piano featured prominently in the East St Louis blues scene of the 1930s and '40s. As East St Louis pianist Henry Townsend recalled in an interview with Paul Garon in the early 1970s, 'in St Louis there were so many piano players. It was really a piano town. There were lots of good piano players like Roosevelt Sykes and Henry Brown. And Lee Green, he was much older than all of us – he was a good rag timer too.'[23]

One of East St Louis's most prolific recording blues pianists was Peetie Wheatstraw. Having first worked with Vocalion in 1930, Wheatstraw went on to record 160 songs on eighty records. He worked up until his violent death in December 1941, when the car he was travelling in left the road and hit a stationary freight wagon in the sidings on Third Street. The accident occurred in the Valley, only a few yards away from where I'd inadvertently turned off the interstate on my first trip to St Louis. Garon describes the Valley as being an extremely tough area at the time Wheatstraw lived there and a neighbourhood that 'many of the bourgeois black citizenry of East St Louis looked down upon'. Today, you won't find much of the Valley, and the expressway has taken the place of North Third Street where Wheatstraw's home had been.[24]

To add to Wheatstraw's mythology, Big Joe Williams, who was in the back of the car with him just prior to the crash, but was drunk and decided to catch a streetcar back across the river to Missouri, told Paul Garon that Wheatstraw had been playing '61 Highway' on the guitar.[25] According to a report in the East St Louis Metro Journal, the three men were thrown from the car and the impact of the crash moved ten freight cars in the siding. Wheatstraw's wife had witnessed the crash from their home 'but was unaware her husband was involved until she ran to the scene'.[26]

The Martin Luther King Bridge took us back over the Mississippi to St Louis and we made our way west along Dr Martin Luther King Drive for a few miles, passing through North St Louis towards the Ville neighbourhood, where Chuck Berry grew up. As we drove further through North St Louis and away from the downtown area the deterioration of the brick-built properties that lined the avenues either side of Dr Martin Luther King Drive became starker. Yet it was clear that most of these avenues had once been impressive and sought-after residential areas.

The shops on the opposite side of Dr Martin Luther King Drive had been boarded up, as had a good many other properties, and as we turned we were met once again by a series of vacant lots with patches of grass where buildings had once stood. A little way along the street we reached a number of the brick villas, which were characteristic of the architecture to be found in North St Louis. Some of the buildings were in good repair but others had missing windows, roofs partially stripped of their tiles, and shuttering nailed over any opening that would allow access.

Berry was born in a three-room brick cottage at 2520 Goode Avenue. Situated in a nicely kept area in the best of the three black sections of the city, it is from Goode Avenue that the country boy and protagonist in his song 'Johnny B Goode' takes his name. Ironically the hero of the song was originally penned as 'a coloured boy', but was subsequently changed by Berry to 'country boy' when he recorded the song, so as not to alienate a white audience.[27] Partly autobiographical, Johnny's life is also a metaphor for the development of blues music (or at least one view of it); rather than being born in St Louis, Johnny is born in a log cabin near New Orleans. Berry places Johnny's log cabin at the beginning of the African American experience, a place that Berry interestingly describes in his autobiography as the 'gateway from freedom' that he 'was led to understand, was somewhere close to New Orleans, where most Africans were sorted through and sold'.[28]

A few properties had trees growing through the roof. Then within the distance of a few metres the buildings changed yet again and the streets were lined with well-maintained new and refurbished properties. I was becoming aware of just how quickly areas could alter within a very short distance, as though an investement tap had been turned on and off. It appeared that Chuck's first family home had been demolished but one could easily imagine this as having been a smart, middle-class black neighbourhood. The Antioch Baptist Church still stands at the corner of Goode Avenue and North Market Street, where Chuck's parents sang in the church choir. Berry suggests that the choir practices at the family home, the constant singing and harmonising by family members, were how his musical roots were laid down.

We returned to Martin Luther King Drive and made our way a couple of miles west to Delmar Boulevard and the Delmar Loop area in search of the statue of Chuck Berry that had been unveiled opposite the Blueberry Hill restaurant and music club. The square is known by locals as simply Chuck Berry Plaza. Joe Edwards, the restaurant's owner, together with Charlie Brennan from KNOW-AM, raised $100,000 to fund the Harry Weber commission, an 8ft bronze statue of Chuck Berry. The statue was unveiled in 2011. Joe Edwards explained to me that the steel walls that define the plaza have musical notes depicted in them and at night they illuminate in blue to visually 'play' 'Johnny B. Goode'.

It was not yet midday so unfortunately we couldn't enjoy the full illuminated glory of Chuck's plaza, but the Blueberry Hill restaurant had already opened and a glance at the menu told me I would not be able to resist the pulled pork. For the sake of research I'd been sampling this mouth-watering Southern favourite of shredded slow-cooked pig shoulder and barbeque sauce at every opportunity. Strolling along the Delmar Boulevard Walk of Fame seemed the sensibly healthy precursor to tasting another plate of pulled pork.

The Walk of Fame, like the statue honouring Berry, is another initiative of Joe Edwards. More than 100 brass stars embedded in the pavement along Delmar Boulevard honour past inhabitants of St Louis who've contributed to the cultural heritage of the United States. Walking west from the restaurant we found stars honouring ragtime pianist Scott Joplin and Ike Turner, who was closely connected with East St Louis – Ike's band were Berry and Johnnie Johnson's main rivals back in their Cosmopolitan Club days – and then we finally found the star honouring Chuck's pianist, Johnnie Johnson.

Henry Townsend's bronze plaque describes him as the patriarch of St Louis blues, who played with Robert Johnson. Born in Shelby, Mississippi, Townsend grew up in Cairo, Illinois, before travelling and settling in St Louis, where he

Goode Avenue, The Ville historic neighbourhood, North St Louis.

Chuck Berry statue, Harry Weber, Chuck Berry Plaza, Delmar Boulevard, opposite the Blueberry Hill restaurant.

was influenced by the East St Louis pianist Roosevelt Sykes.[29] He was one of the only artists to have recorded in every decade between the beginnings of recorded blues in the 1920s through to his death in 2006.

I wandered back down Delmar Boulevard looking for more brass stars. Amongst the notable inclusions were stars commemorating Miles Davis, born across the river in East St Louis; Tina Turner, whose name was Anna Mae Bullock, and who met Ike Turner when he was playing in the clubs in East St Louis; Maya Angelou; and Josephine Baker. Then, just outside the Pin-Up Bowl, we found a star we didn't expect: one commemorating the poet T.S. Eliot. It is a little ironic that the author of *The Waste Land* was born so close to the urban prairie of East St Louis and the urban decay now in evidence in parts of North St Louis:

> Out of this stony rubbish? Son of man,
> You cannot say, or guess, for you know only
> A heap of broken images, where the sun beats,
> And the dead tree gives no shelter, the cricket no relief,
> And the dry stone no sound of water.[30]

(from *The Waste Land*, T.S. Eliot, 1922)

Notes

1. Flood, Alison, 'Teacher's aide sacked over claim that Huckleberry Finn is "racist"', *Guardian* (website), 18 July 2012, http://www.theguardian.com/books/2012/jul/18/teacher-sacked-huckleberry-finn-racist.
2. 'Book banning alive and well in the U.S.', ALA-PIO Media Relations press release, 9 September 2008.
3. George, Nelson, *The Death of Rhythm and Blues*, Omnibus Press, 1988, p.63.
4. Interview with Eric Clapton, *Hail! Hail! Rock 'n' Roll*, Taylor Hackford (producer), Universal, 1986.
5. Cooper, William J. Jr and Terrill, E. Thomas, *The American South, Vol. 1*, McGraw-Hill, 1991, pp.321–2.
6. Wilkinson, Brenda, *The Civil Rights Movement*, Crescent Books, 1997, p.25.
7. Ahmed, Safir, *St Louis Post-Dispatch*, quoted in Kozol, Jonathan, *Savage Inequalities*, Crown, 1991, p.15.
8. Berry, Chuck, *Chuck Berry: The Autobiography*, Faber and Faber, 1988, p.101.
9. Ibid., pp.89–90.
10. Ibid., pp.82–5.
11. *Hail! Hail! Rock 'n' Roll*, Hackford.
12. Berry, Chuck, *The Autobiography*, pp.141–62 for explanations of lyrics. See also Garon, Paul, *Blues and the Poetic Spirit*, City Lights, 1996, p.198.
13. Garon, *Blues and the Poetic Spirit*, p.198.
14. Ibid., p.198.
15. Knight, Richard, *The Blues Highway*, Trailblazer Publications, 2001, p.198.
16. Franzen, Jonathan, *The Twenty-Seventh City*, Fourth Estate, 2010, pp.490–8.
17. Ibid., pp.387–8.
18. Garon, Paul, *The Devil's Son-in-Law*, Charles H. Kerr, 2003, p.9.
19. Rudwick, Elliot, *Race Riot at East St Louis*, Illini Books, 1982, p.277.
20. *Chicago Defender*, Big Weekend edition, 7 July 1917, p.1. *ProQuest Historical Newspapers: The Chicago Defender (1910–1975)*.
21. *Chicago Defender*, 16 June 1917.
22. Oliver, Paul, *The Story of the Blues: The Making of Black Music*, Pimlico, 1997, pp.99–100.
23. Garon, *The Devil's Son-in-Law*, p.5.
24. Ibid., pp.80, 106.
25. Ibid., p.109.
26. *East St Louis Metro Journal*, 22 December 1942, reproduced in Garon, *The Devil's Son-in-Law*, p.107.
27. Berry, Chuck, *The Autobiography*, pp.xxii, 1, 156, 335.
28. Ibid., p.156.
29. Davis, Francis, *The History of the Blues: The Roots Music and the People*, Da Capo, 2003, pp.149–50.
30. Eliot, T.S., *The Waste Land and Other Poems*, Signet Classic, 1998, p.32.

Interstate 55 took us out of St Louis and past the city's stainless steel homage to America's great westward expansion. The cluster of skyscrapers around it soon became distant images in the rear-view mirror. The interstate carved its way through the edge of Soulard and within twenty minutes the suburbs were behind us. I was leaving with a good feeling. Finding a little of Chuck's history had helped me connect the city with him. This time around, I'd reconfigured the narrative I carried with me to one in which the Chuck Berry I'd seen perform comes home. This was a man who was finishing his career playing in his home town, in a club on Delmar Boulevard, where sixty-five years earlier he'd rented a single bedroom and kitchenette with his new wife, Themetta, just a stone's throw from Goode Avenue and his birthplace.

With our schedule only allowing two days in Memphis, the largest city on the Mississippi River, we decided to stay on Interstate 55, which runs parallel with Highway 61, for most of the 285-mile journey. However, we decided to drop onto Highway 61 for 50 miles of two-lane highway between Perryville and Cape Girardeau, to take in the scenery and break the monotony of the interstate. What we found was an undulating rural landscape punctuated by small farmsteads, timber-framed barns and a highway bordered by neat little country communities of well-maintained timber-clad properties.

I'd made sense of St Louis by seeing it first and foremost as the piano town described by Henry Townsend. The city had laid down a marker on our journey that symbolised the merging of ragtime, jump blues, boogie woogie and hillbilly into a form of pop music that became known as rock 'n' roll, whose notable exponents included Johnnie Johnson, Chuck Berry and Ike Turner. Memphis represented transformation in a different order of magnitude. If Chicago and St Louis were spaces where historical trajectories were stirred, sometimes shaken and set on their way again, then Memphis was a space where historical trajectories got sucked in and then spun out in new directions. Memphis was where country blues came to town and left as rhythm and blues; where black music crossed over and became white; where Southern sharecroppers escaped from what Lewis Jones described as something akin to feudal fiefdoms and

became conscious of an urban future. And it's where African Americans lost a leader while glimpsing a promised land.[1]

We crossed the Hernando de Soto Bridge from Arkansas into Tennessee, and our first sight of Memphis must have been from a similar vantage point to the one Twain had aboard the *Gold Dust* as it rounded the broad sweeping bend in the Mississippi and crossed the mouth of Wolf River. However, Steve Cheseborough reminds blues travellers that this is not Chuck Berry's bridge, where Marie lived 'high upon the ridge, just a half mile from the Mississippi Bridge'. Cheseborough places Marie's house somewhere close to McLemore Avenue.[2] Looking south as we crossed the Mississippi River we could see the E.H. Crump Bridge, built in 1949. This traditional steel truss bridge is the one Berry would have been referring to in his song 'Memphis Tennessee'.

E.H. Crump, whom the old bridge is named after, also has a connection with the history of the blues. Crump commissioned band leader W.C. Handy to write a song for his 1909 mayoral campaign; Handy wrote 'Mr Crump', based on a blues tune he had heard played by local black musicians. Myth has it that the song was so popular that it helped Crump become mayor of Memphis, and it was eventually published in sheet music form as an instrumental under the title 'Memphis Blues', subtitled 'Mr Crump'.

The proposition that this was the first published blues song is keenly disputed because Hart Ward, a white musician from Oklahoma, had published 'Dallas Blues', an instrumental, months earlier. Arthur Seals, a black vaudeville comedian, had had 'Baby Seal's Blues' published that summer.

Halfway across the Hernando de Soto Bridge we were greeted by our first view of Memphis's tallest buildings, perched compactly on the high point of the Chickasaw Bluffs, overlooking the river. There is something about this first sight of Memphis when driving across the bridge from Arkansas that creates a sense of excited expectation. As the city's skyline unfolded, my consciousness flooded with innumerable lyrics that reinforced the centrality of the city's position within the story of the blues. Like Jim Jarmusch's blues pilgrims, I gazed at the silhouette of downtown Memphis knowing that therein lay Union Street and

Lauderdale Courts: Elvis Presley's home when the family moved to Memphis in 1949.

Sam Phillips's Sun Studios. Less than a mile along Union Street from Sun Studios is WDIA, the home of the first radio station to target black listeners.

Between Sun Studios and WDIA stands the palatial Peabody Hotel, where labels like Vocalion and Paramount recorded artists such as Furry Lewis, Frank Stokes, Willie Brown and Tommy Johnson, before the emergence of recording studios. Today the Peabody lobby is the location of Lansky Brothers outfitters – Elvis Presley and B.B. King bought their suits from Lansky's former shop on Beale Street. The Southern writer David L. Cohn wrote in 1935 that 'the Mississippi Delta begins at the lobby of the Peabody Hotel and ends on Catfish Row in Vicksburg.'[3]

On the Tennessee side of the river, the tallest buildings of downtown Memphis overshadowed the road at the foot of the bluff. Only three blocks away is Lauderdale Courts, where Elvis Presley's family took possession of a two-bedroom Housing Association apartment on 20 September 1949, following the family's move the previous winter from Tupelo, Mississippi, where they had lived in one of three houses designated for white families on North Green Street, an African American neighbourhood.[4] A few miles south, Third Street runs into Highway 61 and on towards Graceland.

Undoubtedly, Memphis is a music city. Tom Downs described it as one that was 'steeped in blues and was at the epicentre of rock and roll'.[5] But the problem that confronts the blues pilgrim is the temptation to read the city through a narrative that's embedded in our consciousness through the lyrics of countless songs. It's all too easy to become beguiled by the innumerable myths of music industry folklore because, more than anything, we want to believe. Just the enormity of what Memphis represents in terms of the transition of rhythm and blues into rock 'n' roll is so seductive and waiting to be found within a Jim Jarmusch film set. During the course of the next two days we would see how those preconceptions played out.

When you reach Memphis you feel you've truly reached the South, particularly in the summer months, when the heat and the clinging humidity envelop you as soon as you get out of a car. As the cotton capital of the Delta, Memphis has served as the cotton trading town for the Lower Mississippi Valley and many consider it the capital of the Delta, despite the fact that the city is situated in Tennessee and not Mississippi. In the nineteenth century, cotton was America's biggest export, and the huge demand was met by the plantation system. Cotton was shipped up the Mississippi to Memphis with vast quantities being exported to Britain and Europe. It was in Memphis in the months leading up to the Civil War that the slogan amongst those supporting succession was 'cotton is king', and after the war the city re-emerged as a cotton centre, with the Memphis Cotton Exchange established in 1874.

Cotton of course is central to the blues narrative because the production of cotton under the plantation system was inextricably linked to forms of labour organisation dependent upon slavery. In broad terms, slavery only flourished in states where agricultural production adopted the plantation system.[6] Following emancipation, cotton production was organised through a quasi-feudal organisation of labour, taking the form of sharecropping until the development of mechanised picking in the 1940s. Increased cotton production necessitated a fourfold growth in the numbers of the South's captive African American population, commensurate with the rapid expansion of cotton manufacture. This appetite for cotton was largely driven by the phenomenal growth of the British and European cotton industry, which lay at the heart of the industrial revolution and European capitalism. Output of cotton increased from 73,000 bales per annum in 1800 to 4,500,000 bales per annum by 1860.[7] Over the same period the number of black slaves living in the South increased from 1 million in 1800 to 4 million.[8] Industrial cotton manufacture, which had turned English children into wage slaves, had in America's Southern states transformed an earlier form of 'more or less patriarchal slavery into a system of commercial exploitation'.[9]

In April 1882 the *Gold Dust*, a double-decked Vicksburg steam packet, berthed overnight at Memphis. On board was Mark Twain, researching what has been described as his most quintessential book, *Life on the Mississippi*, which was published two years after his journey. During its voyage down the Mississippi it would make stops at Helena, Natchez, Baton Rouge and Vicksburg – all towns we would visit in the following days.

Twain had time to pen a description of late-nineteenth-century Memphis. His observations describe the town's renaissance following yellow fever epidemics of the previous decade that had reduced the city's population by three-quarters. Twain informed his readers of the horror the yellow fever's visitation had bestowed on Memphis through an eyewitness account of a German tourist. The German described how 'the city was become a mighty graveyard, two thirds of the population had deserted the place, and only the poor, the aged and the sick, remained behind, a sure prey for the insidious enemy'.[10] What Twain observed was a town that was taking off economically for the second time:

A thriving place is the Good Samaritan City of the Mississippi; has a great wholesale jobbing trade; foundries, machine shops; and manufactories of wagons, carriages, and cotton-seed oil; and is shortly to have cotton mills and elevators.

Her cotton receipts reached five thousand bales last year – an increase of sixty thousand over the year before. Out from her healthy commercial heart issue five trunk lines of railway; and a sixth is being added.[11]

However, Twain also observed other important changes in society. His trip down the Mississippi River came only seventeen years after the Southern slave population had been freed by the Emancipation Act of 1865, and a mere five years after the collapse of the Reconstruction, which failed following the Compromise of 1877 (whereupon Southern Democrats gave their support to the Republican candidate, Rutherford B. Hayes, in the electoral college in

A cotton bale at the Abbay & Leatherman office. This was a traditional method of wrapping for shipment.

exchange for the removal of federal troops from the South).[12] The withdrawal of troops from the South effectively put an end to the Reconstruction and enabled the post-Civil War gains made by African Americans in the Southern states to be reversed. As well as the beginning of the South's post-war recovery, Twain notes the upheaval of the Southern black population in the post-Reconstruction period:

> We were getting down now into the migrating negro region. These poor people could never travel when they were slaves; so they make up for the privation now. They stay on a plantation till the desire to travel seizes them; then they pack up, hail a steamboat, and clear out. Not to any particular place; no, nearly any place will answer; they only want to be moving.[13]

Yet, in Tennessee the first of the 'Jim Crow' laws was passed in 1875, segregating public transportation. Further legislation was passed which prohibited a labourer to break a work contract, in addition to vagrancy laws making it unlawful not to have any visible means of support. Furthermore, by 1890 the Southern states had started to pass a series of laws which would once again disenfranchise African Americans.[14] In effect, within twenty-five years of the Emancipation Act abolishing slavery, a series of laws had supplanted slavery with a system of peonage or forced labour in the South.[15]

For thousands of African Americans, Memphis was a halfway house between Jim Crow and the hope of moving to, as an article in the *Chicago Defender* in 1925 described it, a part of the country that would recognise them as human beings:

> Memphis, the assembling point for those who have turned their faces northward, is fast becoming crowded with persons from farther south who are patiently awaiting the opportunity to cross the line into a free country. … (P)eople are tired of working all summer for nothing, starving in winter, refused proper educational facilities and civic protection, and tired of seeing their homes at the constant mercy of bigoted whites.[16]

Today, to the south of Downtown, one will find parts of Memphis that are still very poor. The city has more than its share of problems arising from poverty. I was shocked the first time I drove into the city, approaching it as I did from Highway 61 to the south and driving through what Tom Downs refers as 'some gritty South Memphis Neighbourhoods'.[17] Considering that a report published in 2012 by the University of Memphis shows that the number of the city's inhabitants living below the poverty level is 27.2 per cent, which rises to 33.7 per cent for African Americans, it's hardly surprising that beyond the security-conscious Beale Street tourist area between Second and Fourth Street, the number of panhandlers can seem a little unnerving. One blues historian described 'the panhandlers on Union Street as the most aggressive I've encountered anywhere – or maybe just the most desperate'.[18]

Chicago was now 500 miles behind us and we had another 400 miles to go before we reached New Orleans. Memphis for us was also the halfway house and it seemed appropriate that somewhere in the midst of the city's towering buildings was Beale Street. It runs up from the riverfront through downtown Memphis, and probably no other street in the world boasts such a mythical association with the blues. Rufus Thomas called it a heaven for a black man. It is here that R.A. Lawson suggests that 'among fellow share-croppers, stevedores, domestics, loggers, and roustabouts, the blues musicians took the realities of white-controlled places and then talked about them with relative freedom'.[19]

Nowadays the clubs lining Beale Street cover little more than two blocks, somewhat less than when Beale was a thriving centre of black entertainment and in the heart of the African American commercial centre of the city. As we walked away from the river towards Handy Park, sounds of contemporary renditions of blues songs drifted through the open doors of the clubs and out into the Memphis night air, along with the smell of alcohol and fast food. It was tempting to conjure up the ghosts of the acoustic blues guitarists from whom so many of the songs were derived – travelling guitarists of the like of Sam Chatmon, Tommy Johnson and Robert Johnson. Yet the reality, as Cheseborough suggests, is that on Beale Street during the 1920s and '30s it was the pianists and the jazz combos that got to play in the clubs, whereas the guitarists found a role as street entertainers.[20]

Delta guitarist Honeyboy Edwards, an associate of Robert Johnson and an artist I'd been lucky enough to see perform in Clarksdale, recalled in an interview with Robert Palmer that in 'Memphis, you could play in front of the big hotels, sometimes in the lobbies. And in the evening, you could always go down to Handy Park, there off Beale Street.'[21] Similarly in Margaret McKee's description of music on Beale Street it is guitarists such as Furry Lewis, Booker White and Sleepy John Estes who were relegated to street corner performances. Furry Lewis, who originally hailed from Greenwood, Mississippi, was a musician whose own story closely parallels the development and changes of Memphis blues music. In interviews undertaken by Margaret McKee and Fred Chisenhall, recorded between 1972 and 1976, Furry Lewis recalled recording with Vocalion as early as 1927 and how he lost a leg falling under a freight train while hoboing in 1916. He also recalled how he occasionally worked with and filled in for musicians in W.C. Handy's band, although he acknowledged that 'Handy preferred trained musicians who could read music and follow his elaborate orchestrations.'[22]

Working as a street cleaner for the Memphis Sanitation Department from the 1920s, Furry Lewis remained a city employee for forty-four years, which supported his music career; he was described as 'one of the street's most familiar figures, playing in Honky-tonks, in Beale Street Park and on Amateur Nights at the Beale Street Palace Theater'.[23]

Furry Lewis's death in Memphis on 14 September 1981 brought to an end a life story that was entwined with the history of the city's relationship with the blues. He had been given his first good guitar by W.C. Handy and had travelled the South as a musician with medicine shows, prior to recording with the first wave of blues guitarists in the late 1920s for Vocalion and RCA Victor, including the Vocalion session in September 1929 at the Peabody Hotel.[24] Following Furry Lewis's rediscovery in the blues revival of the early 1960s, his career experienced a resurgence. He went on to record on a number of occasions during the following two decades and appeared at numerous festivals, including Madison Square Garden.

As late as the early 1950s, Howlin' Wolf talked about busking on Beale Street in the days when he was playing the small clubs in South Memphis, and it was only after his recording success in 1952 that he was booked to play the Hippodrome, a large club at 500 Beale Street.[25] Memphis-born pianist Memphis Slim recalled that he and Roosevelt Sykes, who hailed from

Riverfront landing, Memphis, near the end of Beale Street.

across the Mississippi in Helena, Arkansas, both played blues at the Midway on Beale Street but said that the blues guitarists could only play in the park or the street.[26] Even Muddy Waters recalled playing in Handy Park and how other musicians 'in that park was running rings around us'.[27] Today the music emanating from the bars consists of contemporary interpretations of country blues guitarists played through the filter of the 1960s and '70s and the predominance of amplified Chicago blues.

Even if the acoustic blues guitarists were for the most part confined to the street, the ghost of Robert Johnson still haunts at least one building on Beale Street. In 1935, on the first floor of the Kings Palace Café at 162 Beale Street, in a photographic studio belonging to two black photographers named the Hook brothers, one of the only two known photographs of the 'King of the Delta Blues' was taken. The photograph of Johnson in a pinstriped suit would later feature on the front of his million-selling album, released by Columbia sixty years after his death. The image, Elijah Wald suggests, portrays a smiling, confident Johnson, which is at odds with our need to see him as part of the 'James Dean/Marlon Brando dreams of pained, sensitive, brilliant, masculine rebellion'.[28]

Today, enjoying blues in the bars along Beale Street is a generally safer pastime than when Beale was at its height and lined with barrelhouses, dance halls, brothels, gambling dens, music halls and the sounds of the jug bands and the blues guitarists playing in the park and streets. It's certainly a lot safer than in 1916, when the Prudential Insurance Company reported the murder rate in Memphis was the highest of all cities in the South, at 89.9 per 100,000 people.[29] It's believed it was in a Memphis gambling den that the infamous folk hero Stackolee killed Billy Lyons one Friday night.[30] As the lyrics of W.C. Handy's composition 'Beale Street Blues' morbidly forewarns:

You'll meet the honest men and pickpockets skilled,
You'll find that business never closes 'til somebody gets killed.[31]

It was in 1925, the same year that the *Chicago Defender* had reported that the great north trek was on again, that a young Richard Wright arrived on Beale Street on a cold Sunday morning looking for a room. Wright had been warned to expect a Beale Street 'filled with danger: pickpockets, prostitutes, cut-throats and black confidence men'.[32]

The percussive back beat of a snare found space between the thump of a bass drum emanating from one of the Beale Street bars. The road block set up at the entrance to the Tourist District of Beale Street was reinforced by the usual line of Memphis Police Department cars parked across the street. MPD officers gathered around their cars, enjoying the cooler air of the evening, chatting with one another and the few passers-by who stopped to talk to them on their way to the bars and restaurants. Beyond the road block a myriad of illuminated signs transformed Beale with an electric neon glow that held the

promise of a night of alcoholic revelry. The Beale Street flippers hand-sprung and back-flipped at a terrifying velocity down the centre of the street, which was lined with younger members of the team shaking buckets and inviting tourists to make donations.

The first time that I really tried to evaluate what had survived on Beale was on a late June morning. By ten o'clock the temperature had reached 106°F and the awnings outside the Beale Street businesses offered little respite from the heat. I crossed the street to A. Schwab's General Store (established by Abraham Schwab, an immigrant from Alsace, in 1876) and purchased a tourist's sun hat. The store has moved to three different premises on the same block, where it has sold a rather bizarre mix of hardware, clothing and voodoo powders. It moved to its present location in 1911 and at some time started selling 78rpm records. I rummaged through Schwab's oak-coloured wooden trays and shelves, the like of which I hadn't seen since preschool days when my mother would take me to town on shopping day. The store's distinctive name runs the length of its red-brick facade in 2ft-high letters. It made an appearance in Jarmusch's *Mystery Train* as the destination on Beale where Nicoletta Braschi is dropped by a taxi.

Although Beale Street is nearly 2 miles long, today the area that has live music runs for less than a quarter of a mile, in what is known now as the Beale Street Historic District. Today all the music is to be found between B.B. King's club at the junction of Beale Street and Second Street down to the junction of Fourth Street and Beale, where, standing a little way back from the road, W.C. Handy's home can be found. He lived in the house following his move to Memphis from Clarksdale in 1905, but it was then situated ten blocks south of Beale Street in Janette Street.

Standing in front of the shotgun house, I wondered to what extent Handy's home was representative of the Memphis tourist experience, where things are not quite as they appear. Or perhaps even worse, as Francis Davis quips, 'blues fans go to Memphis for the same reason they go to Mississippi, to stare at things that aren't there anymore'.[33]

It's easy to dismiss Beale Street as a mere tourist attraction of little historic value and even easier to find worthy critics who bestow upon it derision similar to that aimed at the blues clubs in downtown Chicago. However, unlike many of the Chicago blues clubs that have moved to locations where a receptive audience is to be found, in Memphis the action still takes place on the street that claims long-standing historic connections with the blues, going back a century or more. It's a fact that as far back as when blues was first heard on Beale Street in the clubs and theatres or played by the jug bands and guitarists who worked in the park or on street corners, people have bemoaned the death of Beale Street, fearing it no longer to be the place that figured in their recollections. Even W.C. Handy, who at the time had only just begun the process of popularising blues to a wider public (and within three years of the success of the publication of his 'St Louis Blues'), chose to incorporate

W.C. Handy statue, Handy Park, Memphis.

B.B. King's Company Store, Beale Street, Memphis.

the demise of the old Beale Street into the lyrics of a new song, 'Beale Street Blues'; he described the song as a 'hail and farewell to the old Beale, the street that was'.[34] The street's losing 'something essential to its former character' had arisen, as Handy saw it, from the passage of a local option law allowing for the prohibition of alcohol – a move that he suggested owed much to lobbying by excursion boat operators, whose aim had been to increase their share of the liquor trade.[35]

Beale Street today is different from the one Hugh Merrill described in 1986. On his drive across America in search of the country's purest music, he stopped over in Memphis to take a walk down Beale Street but didn't find much happening in the way of music. But Merrill had arrived at a time when the city was just starting to get on its feet again two decades after the assassination of Dr Martin Luther King Jr – an event of seismic proportions that reflected the fault lines that ran through America.

A photograph taken just after the area around Beale had been flattened in a 1970s urban renewal programme shows the hotchpotch of flat-roofed brick buildings that made up the surviving two blocks. Yet in spite of the mass demolition that took place all around Beale, only fifteen of the fifty-seven properties that existed prior to the urban renewal period were demolished.[36] Therefore there is still plenty of architecture that dates back to Beale in its heyday as an area of African American commerce and entertainment.

Many of the historic Beale Street buildings east of Rufus Thomas Boulevard have been lost under the tracks of the bulldozer. Such landmarks include the Palace Theater at 326 Beale Street, the Midway Café at 357 and the Panama Club at the corner of Beale and Fourth.[37] The Palace Theater had hosted the great female blues singers of the 1920s including Bessie Smith, Ma Rainey and Ida Cox, who performed on the Theater Owners Booking Association (TOBA) circuit until it folded in the Depression of the 1930s. The Palace Theater was

W.C. Handy's shotgun house and Memphis Police Department cars in background.

also the venue where, in the 1940s, the Mississippi-born African American promoter Robert Henry brought acts such as Count Basie, Cab Calloway, Duke Ellington and Fats Waller. Henry continued to run a pool hall on Beale until 1974, and was one of the last tenants to leave the street.[38]

Rigid segregation was maintained in Memphis and the only time whites came to Beale Street was for the Midnight Rambles, a show put on for the city's white citizens at midnight.[39] Preston Lauterbach suggests that 'White Memphians crossed Beale on their Main Street errands, catching scents of cornbread, fish frying, and pork shoulder sweetly barbecuing, though most dared not explore further.'[40] For the few whites that did venture down Beale Street, by the early 1940s they could find themselves unwelcome, as did Alan Lomax when he returned to the street he loved in 1942 and walked into the Monarch Club, put a blues record on the jukebox and called the bartender for a beer. The bartender refused to serve him and pointed to a card pinned to the wall and informed Lomax that no whites would be served. He apparently grinned as he told Lomax that Mister Crump had pronounced 'if we gonna segredate one way, we gonna segredate the other'.[41]

The Midway Café at 357 Beale Street was where the barrelhouse pianists of the likes of Roosevelt Sykes and Memphis Slim played and Sykes also recalled playing the Palace Theater with his touring band in the early 1940s.[42]

In the short term the city's plans for urban renewal left Beale as a series of vacant lots, which Nat D. Williams described as leaving it looking 'like a coffin'.[43] Nevertheless, even if what the blues pilgrim sees today is a mere fraction of the area that stood prior to renewal, there is as much that is truly of historic interest to the blues pilgrim as there is fabricated, if one takes the trouble to find it.

It wasn't until the 1980s that clubs started to reappear on Beale, and Steve Cheseborough suggests that it was when B.B. King's club opened in 1991 that Beale Street began to become a tourist destination (although King's club was preceded by the Rum Boogie Café, which opened in 1985). B.B. King's restaurant at the corner of Beale and Second Street, despite being a consolidation of four buildings, retains much of its pre-urban renewal appearance. In any case the original building that stood here had been demolished in 1924, long before the urban renewal programme.

The demolition of the surrounding area, linked to the urban renewal programme, had effectively cut off what remained of the old Beale Street from the remaining African American neighbourhoods. Nevertheless, many buildings in the streets to the south of Beale Street, around the vicinity of the National Civil Rights Museum, the Lorraine Motel and the Arcade restaurant, still possess plenty of historic character, with many dating back to a time prior to the arrival of blues in the city.

Arriving in Memphis in late September, Richard and I didn't experience the searing heat of my visit in June. The morning was still warm as we wandered down Beale Street and across Third Street, passing the entrance to Handy Park.

My gaze caught Handy's bronze statue and I paused momentarily to watch the handful of visitors assembled round the smaller of two stages, listening to a lunchtime session. The band worked its way through a few well-tried standards, which I knew I'd no doubt hear again before the day was out. In a break between numbers, the singer requested that a panhandler working the park desist from bothering the audience. I remembered reading one blues writer who'd interpreted the words of H.C. Speir, the talent scout from Jackson, to suggest that blues was an idiom that 'was essentially a panhandling device on the part of alcoholics'.[44]

We zig-zagged back across the street to Wet Willies Bar, one of five businesses in the block opposite Handy Park. Wet Willies dominates the corner of Beale and Rufus Thomas, the peeling whitewash on its walls giving way to red brick underneath. Built in 1884, the building has acquired a place in the story of the blues as the base of operations for the entertainment business of Sunbeam Mitchell and his wife Ernestine McKinney in the 1940s. The pair rented two floors above the Pantaze Drug Store from Abe Plough, a Jew originally from Tupelo, Mississippi, who through his cosmetics and pharmaceuticals business, offering products such as skin bleaches and hair straighteners to the black community, became one of the wealthiest businessmen in the city.

Stopping halfway across the street, I looked up at the rows of Victorian windows above Wet Willies. Sunbeam and Ernestine had opened a rooming house on the third floor; it became the Mitchell Hotel, where it's been said some rooms could be paid for by the hour – it's also said that this was Ernestine's side of the business. On the second floor they established a club called the Domino Lounge, with a small bandstand and a bar. It would later become known as Mitchell's Club Handy. Bobby 'Blue' Bland recalled how in the 1950s he and other musicians like B.B. King would play for five dollars a night and the hot chilli. And it was B.B. King and actor and comedian Stepin' Fetchit that the Mitchells asked as guest stars to the opening night of Club Handy in 1958.[45] The aftershow jam sessions were legendary and the Mitchells' establishment became a key networking venue for musicians in the South. While the Mitchells cultivated an image of blues patrons lending a supportive arm to the up-and-coming local and itinerant musicians coming through Memphis, the reality was that they were shrewd operators who could be dangerous if crossed. Preston Lauterbach suggests that Sunbeam soon developed an 'interstate vice distribution system that looked like an old medicine show, albeit with sex, gambling, bottled-in-bond booze, and entertainment by the rising stars of black music'.[46]

By the end of the 1940s Sunbeam Mitchell was acting as the area's informal employment agency for musicians and the hotel had become a regional hub of what became known as the 'chitlin' circuit'. Mitchell's network consisted of other club operators, such as Harold 'Hardface' Clanton, based across the state border in Mississippi. The prohibition laws Mississippi retained until 1966 helped consolidate the position of the many clubs whose management

Early evening on Beale Street, Memphis.

Building that housed the Mitchell's Hotel and Club Handy, Beale
Street, Memphis.

were inextricably linked with the bootleg liquor industry. It was through the Mitchells' network of contacts that artists could secure bookings. For the up-and-coming B.B. King this meant gigs in juke joints along Highway 51, south down Highway 61 and across the river in Helena, all within a range that could be advertised by B.B. King over the airwaves of WDIA.[47]

The Palace Theater was renowned for its Tuesday show, known as amateur night, which up until 1940 had been hosted by Professor Nat D. Williams, who had taught history at the Booker T. Washington High School.[48] One of Williams's pupils was Rufus Thomas, who had worked a number of years on the travelling tent shows with the Rabbit Foot Minstrels before returning to Memphis and forming a close relationship with his former teacher; a relationship that would impact upon the black Memphis music scene for the next three decades. Thomas took over the MC's job for the Palace's amateur night from Williams. One of the many hopefuls who would appear for the $1 appearance fee was Riley B. King, later known as B.B. King. As Thomas recalled to Peter Guralnick, 'B.B. used to come with holes in his shoes, his guitar all patched up, just to get that dollar.'[49] Other hopefuls at the Palace's amateur night included Bobby 'Blue' Bland, Johnny Ace, Roscoe Gordon and Isaac Hayes, who would all go on to make substantial contributions towards Memphis's reputation as the city at the centre of rhythm and blues.

After leaving the site of the Palace Theater, we continued past the New Daisy Theater, which today hosts live bands and boxing. The next building on the block is the building that housed the original Monarch Club, a plush gambling house owned by the Memphis politician Jim Kinnane, who was also known as the czar of the Memphis underworld. It has been said that W.C. Handy enjoyed listening to the club's piano players, so perhaps it is fitting that Handy's shotgun house has been relocated next door.[50]

By 1949 Nat D. Williams was DJing for WDIA, which was the first American radio station aimed at black listeners, known as 'Mother station of the Negroes'. A Tennessee historical plaque marks the spot where the station started in 1949, and the building has a restored Memphis historic building plaque outside. In addition to promoting black music across the airwaves, Williams used his 'Tan Town Jamboree' programme to include a regular slot about black history.[51]

The following year, B.B. King joined Williams as a DJ at WDIA, and in the aftermath of King's success with '3 O'Clock Blues', recorded in 1951, Rufus Thomas was brought in to host the station's 'Sepia Swing Club' and later the 'Hoot 'n' Holler' show, which went out each evening. In terms of crossover, WDIA played a crucial role indirectly, because it had made rhythm and blues accessible to a new audience of white teenagers in Memphis and the Mid-South. It also featured a young Elvis Presley and introduced him to a black audience. Thomas was, as Harrison notes, the only black DJ to play early Stones and Beatles records on a black show. It was Williams who commented upon the wider impact Presley was having amongst young African American Memphians, when he wrote in the *Pittsburgh Courier* on 22 December 1956 that:

A thousand black, brown and beige teen-age girls in the audience blended their alto and soprano voices in one wild crescendo of sound that that rent the rafters … and took off like scalded cats in the direction of Elvis … But further, Beale Streeters are wondering if these teen-age girls' demonstration over Presley doesn't reflect a basic integration in attitude and aspiration which has been festering in the minds of most of your folks' women folk all along. Huhhh?[52]

Within two years of Presley's initial success the *Chicago Defender*, whilst far more supportive of Presley than many white newspapers, argued that bias had prevented black artists from reaching the emerging youth market on a similar scale to that of Presley:

He's playing the type of music and in the style introduced by the late Lonnie Johnson and T-Bone Walker that the latter pair have been unable to take before the nation's jitterbugs on a mass scale. Neither T-Bone nor Lonnie could have appeared in this hall, before same jam (sic), because of bias.[53]

This sense of black dispossession of rhythm and blues comes across in an interview the Memphis artist Rufus Thomas, who started with Sun Records around 1951, gave to Hugh Merrill. In the interview he recalled how the Sun Records stable had been all black, saying that it was all over for black artists after Sam Phillips had hired Elvis and those people – referring to Jerry Lee Lewis, Carl Perkins and Johnny Cash. Thomas argues that 'he dropped everybody black like a hot potato … And we were developing a Memphis blues sound. They say that once he got white people, it was the beginning of rock and roll. But we were already doing it.'[54] Thomas points to Joe Turner, Chuck Berry and Little Richard as the pioneers of rock 'n' roll.

By the time that Beale Street effectively closed down and nailed up the shuttering boards – in the aftermath of the riots that followed Martin Luther King Jr's assassination in 1968 – many of Memphis's blues artists had already been rediscovered in the folk blues revival of the early 1960s. Sam Charters wrote about Furry Lewis, Gus Cannon and the Memphis jug bands in his seminal book *The Country Blues*, published in 1959.

On Tuesday 12 February 1968, two sanitation workers were tragically crushed to death while sheltering from the rain in the rear of their compressor garbage truck – the only shelter permitted for black workers by the city's sanitation department rules. Within two months their deaths would lead

The New Daisy Theater, Beale Street, Memphis.

to a pivotal shift in African Americans' struggle for civil rights. Immediately following the deaths of the two city employees, Memphis sanitation workers went on strike, not for any material gain but simply for the right of trade union recognition. The sanitation workers adopted the slogan 'I am a man', which reflected their demand to be treated with human dignity.

By early March seven of the sanitation workers had received ten-day prison sentences and fines for contempt of court. Two weeks later, on 20 March, 17,000 people attended a rally to hear Dr Martin Luther King Jr speak in support of the strikers, and the following week King led a march through the city, which ended in the shooting of 16-year-old Larry Payne by police. On 3 April King returned to Memphis and delivered his 'I've seen the Promised Land, I may not get there with you' speech, which was primarily in support of the sanitation workers. The following day King was shot dead, by sniper James Earl Ray, as he stood on the balcony of the Lorraine Motel.[55]

Bill Patton, a Memphian who has written a useful history of the city and its buildings, and who also runs Backbeat Tours, a company offering guided tours of the city, suggests that following the assassination, the label of 'the city that killed King' stuck. This was despite the fact that, as Patton states, 'James Earl Ray had no previous connection with the city.' Patton's book portrays a dramatic image of capital flight from downtown Memphis that took the city years to recover from and suggests that:

the city deteriorated into desolate, abandoned storefronts on desolate, abandoned streets as citizens fled the violence, the uncertainty, the confusion. Building after building – the Peabody Hotel, the Orpheum, Goldsmiths and Lowenstein's department stores, even Beale Street itself – all were boarded up and left to die.[56]

Similarly, McKee and Chisenhall describe the aftermath of the riots that began around Beale Street and the surrounding area following the sanitation workers' strike and King's assassination as leaving the area bereft of stores and dying. The area's economic malaise presented the Memphis Housing Authority with the opportunity to buy up land and tear down many of the buildings that it had been hankering to demolish for a number of years. The original renewal proposals, which would have displaced 1,400 families from their homes, were met with enthusiasm by the majority of Memphis's white citizens, but did not receive the same jubilation amongst the city's black population. Perhaps it was somewhat ironic that the initial plan for the demolition of much of Beale Street had been proposed in the very same year that W.C. Handy died. Commenting on the dilapidated state of Beale in 1974, the Chicago Defender paraphrased the lyrics that Handy had penned in Pee Wee's Café on Beale Street: the 'evening sun had gone down on Beale Street'.[57]

I crossed the junction of Beale and Rufus Thomas Boulevard and passed the Hard Rock café. It was at this junction that police lines had been drawn during the riots, just days before King's murder. Three days prior to the first riots, an article in the Chicago Defender reported a new kind of militancy amongst Memphis citizens in their support for the sanitation workers' strike.[58] The day after the riot the Chicago Defender lay the blame for it on the mayor and the city council, arguing that tension had been high for two months and 'all that was needed was an appropriate occasion for the full release of smothered anger and resentment'. The article added that the city authorities had to make what amounted to a fatal choice between 'settling the strike and clubbing the marchers into submission, they chose the latter'.[59] Within a week of King's assassination, US insurance companies estimated that the cost arising from the riots amounted to over $30 million in property damage compensation.[60]

We caught a trolley bus from Beale to take us south down Main Street for five blocks. The Memphis trolleys that run down Main Street were first introduced in 1891 by the Memphis Street Railway Company. It ran seventy-five cars over a network of 100 miles of track. In 1947 the service was replaced by transit buses, but in 1993 a trolley service aimed at serving the historic tourist district was reintroduced. We left the trolley at the Huling Avenue stop and stood by a vacant lot next to the red-brick building that had once been Canipe's amusement store and rooming house on the upper floors. It was from this rooming house, on 4 April 1968, that James Earl Ray is said to have fired the fateful shot that killed Martin Luther King Jr. In 1998 a Memphis jury found in favour of the King family's wrongful death lawsuit against a local café owner, Loyd Jowers, and declared that King's murder had been part of a larger murder plot and had not been committed by a lone assassin.

Given both the enormity of the tragedy and its timing, in the minds of many Americans the assassination also marked a crossroads in race relations in the US. The Johnson administration's Civil Rights Act of 1968, the aim of which was to end housing segregation, was enacted within days of the assassination and amidst the aftermath of the riots that followed.

I stood by what had once been the flank wall of Canipe's amusement store, which was acquired by the National Civil Rights Museum in 1999. Today it serves as an annex to the main museum and houses items of evidence used in the trial of James Earl Ray. Following the line of sight that Ray would have had from the rooming house towards the Lorraine Motel on 480 Mulberry Street, one is drawn to a scene of retro Americana that is both tantalising and disturbing. The museum's owners have restored the motel's forecourt to how it was on the day of King's assassination, grimly complete with a 1959 Dodge Royal and a 1968 Cadillac parked under the balcony of room 306.

The façade of the Lorraine Motel that appeared on television newsreels around the world following King's murder has cleverly been incorporated into the frontage of the National Civil Rights Museum. An audio guide takes visitors through an emotional rollercoaster of a tour, outlining the history of African Americans' struggle for civil rights from slavery to the present day. Life-size reconstructions of key moments represent some of the campaigns adopted by

The Lorraine Motel, site of Dr Martin Luther King Jr's assassination, Memphis.

organisations such as the National Association for the Advancement of Colored People (NAACP), the Student Non-Violent Co-ordinating Committee (SNCC), the Southern Christian Leadership Conference (SCLC) and the Campaign of Racial Equality (CORE), and are reinforced by newsreel footage, enabling visitors to walk through a series of desperately poignant tableaux.

This is a story that leaves one overwhelmed by the tenacity of ordinary people who in exceptional circumstances confronted a Southern white hegemony sustained through the perpetuation of state violence and racism. The exhibits, such as the burnt-out Freedom Rider's bus fire-bombed in

The Lorraine Motel, site of Dr Martin Luther King Jr's assassination, now the National Civil Rights Museum.

Alabama, honour these courageous acts of defiance. Others testify to the bravery of the black and white youngsters whose conviction gave them the strength to face mob violence and humiliation in lunch counter sit-ins, and the lone action of Rosa Parks's defiance, which led to collective resistance in the form of the Montgomery bus boycott in 1963 and brought Martin Luther King Jr to prominence.

The tour culminates on the motel balcony with visitors viewing a recreation of room 306, which King shared with Ralph Abernathy on the night of his murder. In the late 1950s and 1960s the Lorraine Motel was one of the few establishments where black visitors to Memphis could find overnight accommodation. Therefore, many notable African Americans took rooms at the Lorraine when business brought them to the city, and the motel was often used by artists visiting the Stax studios a few blocks to the south. So, in addition to political, religious and business guests, the motel hosted many black musicians, including Ray Charles, Lionel Hampton, Aretha Franklin, Ethel Waters, Otis Redding, the Staple Singers and Wilson Pickett.[61]

King's last words from the balcony outside room 306 were to Ben Branch, the one-time Plantation Inn band leader and an official of the Musicians Union. King asked him to play Thomas Dorsey's 'Precious Lord Take My Hand' at the meeting for the sanitation workers, whom King was due to address that evening.[62]

Walking down the stairs from the balcony – the same stairs that Jesse Jackson ran up to reach King immediately following the shooting – one can't fail to sense a shared feeling amongst other visitors of the injustice and gravity of what occurred here.

Nevertheless, there is also something disturbing about the scene outside the Lorraine Motel because there is also a celebration of iconic post-war modernity: the symmetry of motel utilitarianism and the perfect chromed gas guzzlers with their rocket tail fins. This scene, complete with the restored electric tubed signage of the Lorraine Motel is disconcertingly rock 'n' roll. Perhaps this is part of the museum's strength, which makes it all the more challenging because everything about the scene reminds us that what we see on the outside is the aspirational future of 1960s America. Conversely, what confronts the visitor inside the National Civil Rights Museum and beyond the façade of the Lorraine Motel are the tensions inherent within American society: a country grappling with the legacy of a population whose ancestors arrived either to pursue a dream by way of Ellis Island or were imported as slaves and traded in the markets of Charleston, Savannah, Mobile, Natchez and New Orleans.

It has been estimated that up until 1820, for every European that crossed the Atlantic there were five Africans who made the crossing.[63] The New World was a land of involuntary pioneers. For this, the National Civil Rights Museum is an outstanding international achievement. The Blues Highway advises visitors to Memphis that 'if you see just one thing in Memphis, see this'.[64]

We left the Lorraine Motel and walked one block to the Arcade Restaurant on South Main Street, another Mystery Train location. It is also reputed to have been a favoured diner of Elvis Presley, who was attracted by the delights of fried peanut butter and banana sandwiches. Richard and I found a table but I passed on the sandwich and resisted the all-day Southern breakfast with bacon and grits. Ordering just a coffee, I scanned the faces of the largely white customers sitting along the line of Formica tables. Many, like me, had just come out of the National Civil Rights Museum. We discussed an account I'd read of Elie Wiesel, a Holocaust survivor and Nobel laureate, who'd visited the museum and left saying it was the first time in his life that he felt ashamed to be white, and the story of an elderly former Ku Klux Klan member from Tennessee who wept before the museum's education director before confessing that he had done terrible things when he was younger and, having visited the museum, he felt that it was the right place to apologise.[65]

We took a trolley along Main Street towards Beale and picked up the car to drive the 2 miles or so to the Stax Museum on East McLemore Street. We'd been advised that it would be sensible to drive rather than walk, as some of the neighbourhoods between Beale and the museum could be a problem for tourists. Memphis Slim's house, which stands across the street from the museum, languishes amongst creeping vegetation, an uninhabited wreck. Its roof is stripped, windows are missing and much of its rotting clapboard frontage has fallen away. Only the notice in the front garden stating 'The Historic Home of Memphis Slim on Soulsville USA' was in reasonable repair.

That the outward appearance of neighbourhoods could change so rapidly intrigued me. We drove past blocks of proudly maintained homes, whose drives were lined with faux Victorian lamps and box hedge borders around manicured lawns, and then within a block or so house after house would be boarded up and we'd look down side streets that bore closer resemblance to overgrown country lanes than city streets.

A red neon sign spelling out STAX across the top of the restored cinema marquee makes the Stax Museum difficult to miss. The perfectly restored studio and Satellite Records store stand apart from many of the single-storey brick buildings at the nearby crossroads. A restaurant was boarded up, another business had a 'For Lease' sign above its shutter-boarded windows and the burger bar looked as though it hadn't sold burgers for some time. The congregation of buildings around the crossroads all had the feel of a little country town that had died, rather than a neighbourhood in the middle of the largest city on the Mississippi.

Maybe it's just a feeling that's all too easy to read into Memphis, based on the gravity of events that occurred in the city. The Stax Museum, like the National Civil Rights Museum, screams out for us not to read Memphis as the city that closed down in 1968, yet when we find the ossified America of our dreams, untouched since the 1960s, the temptation is to blame an event. As I pulled up outside Stax, those were the feelings I carried with me. Not only

The Arcade Restaurant, South Main Street,
Memphis.

The Stax Museum, McLemore Avenue,
Memphis.

had we come straight from the Lorraine Motel but I'd also just read Peter Guralnick's *Sweet Soul Music* prior to coming to Memphis.

Soul music is, according to Guralnick, 'ultimately derived from the Southern dream of freedom', and while he found that the motivation of the independent labels (who had found a space within what was essentially rhythm and blues and one free from the major labels) was to make money, he places this in a historical context that aligns soul's rise with the success of the 1960s Civil Rights Movement and its fragmentation following the assassination of Martin Luther King Jr.[66] The sign on the footway outside the studio lists Booker T and the MGs, the interracial house band, as well as many of the black artists who brought Stax its phenomenal success throughout the 1960s, such as Isaac Hayes, Otis Redding, Sam and Dave, the Staple Singers, Johnnie Taylor, Albert King and Carla and Rufus Thomas.

Stax took over the old Capital Theater, a rundown movie house in a rundown white neighbourhood that was becoming black. Jim Stewart and Estelle Axton, the founders of Stax, managed to rent it for $150 a month. It had not been used as a picture house for some time and had occasionally hosted country and western bands. Peter Guralnick argues that one of the keys to Stax's success was its location:

> Where else could Packy Axton have gotten the benefit of Gilbert Caples's long-time experience? Where else would an ambitious young guitar player like Steve Cropper have had the chance to play with a bass player like Lewis Steinberg (of the musically prominent black Steinberg family) or drummer Curtis Green from the PI (Plantation Inn)? Where else would a wet-behind-the-ears Booker T. Jones ever have gotten the chance to escape both the ghetto *and* the black bourgeoisie, to interact with such a lively and different musical intelligence as Chips Moman's? Where else could a partnership like the Memphis Horns, uniting a white West

Memphis dirt farmers son like Wayne Jackson with black counterparts like Andrew Love and Floyd Newman (Newman was studying to be a teacher when they met), ever have come about?[67]

Today, what visitors see at the Stax studio owes much to the Soulsville Foundation, which funds and operates the museum. The foundation also funds and operates the Soulsville Charter School and the Stax Music Academy, which both work closely with young people from the local area.

I crossed the road to the recently built business premises opposite the museum, whose modern smoked glass windows and neat lines contrasted with the boarded-up shops at the crossroads. A hopeful sign announcing 'Town Center Soulsville USA' had been planted in the newly laid grass verge. Looking across McLemore Avenue towards the studio, I smiled at the thought that somewhere down at the other end of the avenue, not far from the river, Marie's house had stood. Then I imagined the picture that Guralnick describes of the day in the studio when Martin Luther King Jr was shot and the anger on McLemore Avenue soon after.

Isaac Hayes and David Porter heard the news and jumped in a car to make the same journey we'd made that afternoon, round to the Lorraine Motel, but they couldn't get near to the building because thousands of people had come out onto the streets in a moment of collective anger and grief. Steve Cropper and Duck Dunn had to be escorted to their cars by black musicians working at the studio because of the intensity of feeling on the streets and the next day the police pulled their guns on Hayes when he came out of Stax to talk to Dunn, who'd come to the studio to retrieve his bass. The very act of talking to someone of another colour could now be misconstrued as threatening if undertaken in the wrong part of town. The day of King's murder, June Dunn said, everything at Stax changed.[68]

Notes

1. Lomax, Alan, *The Land Where the Blues Began*, The New Press, 1993, p.94. See also 'South called No. 1 problem by President', *Chicago Defender*, 16 July 1938, p.5. Lomax quoted the African American scholar Lewis Wade Jones, from Fisk University, who joined him on the 1941 and 1942 research trips to Coahoma County, Mississippi, as saying: 'The big white house over there is really a castle, you see, and we are riding through a fief, right out of olden times. We can't do that without permission from the lord of the manor.' The *Chicago Defender* reported that on 15 July 1938 President Roosevelt attacked 'the South's hangover feudal system and unsound business structure as the nation's No.1 Economic Problem'.

2. Cheseborough, Steve, *Blues Traveling: The Holy Sites of Delta Blues*, University Press of Mississippi, 2009, pp.37–8.

3. Cohn, David L., 'Where I was born and raised' in Abbott, Dorothy (ed.), *Mississippi Writers: Reflections of Childhood and Youth Non-Fiction* University of Mississippi Press, 1985, p.125.

4. Guralnick, Peter, *Last Train to Memphis: The Rise of Elvis Presley*, Abacus, 1995, pp.25–33.

5. Downs, Tom, *Blues and BBQ*, Lonely Planet, 2005, p.8.

6. Cooper, William J., Jr and Terrill, Thomas E., *The American South: A History Volume 1*, McGraw-Hill, 1991, pp.204–5.

7. Ibid., p.194.

8. Ibid., p.222.

9. Marx, Karl, *Capital Volume One*, Lawrence and Wishart, 1954, p.711.

10. Twain, Mark, *Life on the Mississippi*, Wordsworth Classics, 2012, p.201.

11. Ibid., p.202.

12. Wilkinson, Brenda, *The Civil Rights Movement*, Crescent Books, 1997, p.48.

13. Twain, *Life on the Mississippi*, p.204.

14. Wilkinson, *Civil Rights Movement*, p.51.

15. See Carper, N. Gordon, 'Slavery Revisited: Peonage in the South', *Pylon* 37:1, 1976, pp.85–99.

16. *Chicago Defender*, 21 February 1925, p.9.

17. Downs, Tom, *Blues and BBQ*, Lonely Planet, 2005, p.18.

18. Davis, Francis, *The History of the Blues: The Roots Music and the People*, Da Capo, 2003, p.45.

19. Lawson, R.A., *Jim Crow's Counterculture: The Blues and Black Southerners*, Louisiana State University Press, 2010, p.58.

20. Cheseborough, *Blues Traveling*, p.24.

21. Palmer, Robert, *Deep Blues*, Viking Penguin, 1992, p.120.

22. McKee and Chisenhall, *Beale, Black and Blue*, p.105.

23. Ibid., p.107.

24. Charters, Samuel B., *The Country Blues*, Da Capo, 1959, pp.103–6.

25. Segrest, James and Hoffman, Mark, *Moanin' at Midnight: The Life and Times of Howlin' Wolf*, Avalon, 2004, p.93.

26. Cheseborough, *Blues Traveling*, p.33.

27. Gordon, Robert, *Can't Be Satisfied: The Life and Times of Muddy Waters*, Pimlico, 2003, p.307 for notes of interview with McKee and Chisenhall.

28. Wald, Elijah, *Escaping the Delta: Robert Johnson and the Invention of the Blues*, Amistad, 2005, p.248.

29. Palmer, *Deep Blues*, p.152.

30. Oliver, Paul, *The Story of the Blues: The Making of Black Music*, Pimlico, 1997, p.24.

31. Handy, W.C., 'Beale Street: Another Memphis "Blues"', Pace and Handy Music Co., Memphis, Tennessee, 1917 (audio recording).

32. Wright, Richard, *Black Boy*, Longman, 1984, p.182.

33. Davis, *History of the Blues*, p.42.

34. Handy, W.C., *Father of the Blues: An Autobiography*, Da Capo, 1991, p.124.

35. Handy, *Father of the Blues*, p.124.

36. Gulyas, Sandor, 'Creating A Blues Playground: A Comparison of Beale Street in Memphis, Tennessee, and Farish Street in Jackson, Mississippi', 2008, p.37. Thesis Submitted to Louisiana State University and Agricultural & Mechanical College, MA in Department of Geography and Anthropology, August 2008. Can be found at Deltablues.org.

37. *National Register of Historic Places Registration Form*, United States Department of the Interior, National Park Service, Section 8, p.2.

38. Lauterbach, Preston, *The Chitlin' Circuit and the Road to Rock 'n' Roll*, W.W. Norton, 2011, p.296.

39. Merrill, Hugh, *The Blues Route*, Morrow, 1990, p.62. Interview with Rufus Thomas.

40. Lauterbach, *The Chitlin' Circuit*, p.275.

41. Lomax, *The Land Where the Blues Began*, p.4.

42. McKee, Margaret and Chisenhall, Fred, *Beale, Black and Blue*, Louisiana State University Press, p.176.

43. McKee and Chisenhall, *Beale, Black and Blue*, pp.96–7.

44. Calt, Stephen, *I'd Rather be the Devil – Skip James and the Blues*, Chicago Review Press, 2008, p.138.

45. *Chicago Defender*, 31 May 1958, p.18.

46. Lauterbach, *The Chitlin' Circuit*, p.187.

47. Ibid., p.199.

48. George, Nelson, *The Death of Rhythm and Blues*, Omnibus Press, 1988, p.49.
49. Guralnick, Peter, *Lost Highway*, Penguin, 1992, p.60.
50. See Cheseborough, *Blues Traveling*, p.31 and Patton, William, *A Guide to Historic Downtown Memphis*, The History Press, 2010, p.25.
51. Harrison, Jennifer, *Elvis As We Knew Him: Our Shared Life in a Small Town in South Memphis*, Universe, Inc., 2003, p.47.
52. Williams, Nat D., *Pittsburgh Courier*, 22 December 1956, quoted in Guralnick, Peter, *Last Train to Memphis*, p.370.
53. *Chicago Defender*, daily edition, 6 August 1956, p.19.
54. Merrill, Hugh, *The Blues Route*, Morrow, 1990, p.65.
55. '1968 AFSCME Memphis Sanitation Workers' Strike Chronology', AFSCME, www.afscme.org/union/history/mlk/1968-afscme-memphis-sanitation-workers-strike-chronology.
56. Patton, William, *A Guide to Historic Downtown Memphis*, p.30.
57. 'The Rise and Fall of Beale Street', *Chicago Defender*, Big Weekend edition, 25 May 1974, p.84.
58. *Chicago Daily Defender*, 25 March 1968, p.5.
59. *Chicago Daily Defender*, 1 April 1968, p.13.
60. *Chicago Daily Defender*, 11 April 1968, p.18.
61. 'Mission and facts', The National Civil Rights Museum, www.civilrightsmuseum.org/Mission-Facts.aspx?pid=9&spid=20#sthash.SizHbgOU.dpbs.
62. Reider, Jonathan, *The Word of the Lord Is Upon Me*, Harvard University Press, 2008, p.231.
63. Johnson, Walter, *Soul by Soul: Life Inside the Antebellum Slave Market*, Harvard University Press, 1999, p.4.
64. Knight, Richard, *The Blues Highway*, Trailblazer Publications, 2001, p.151.
65. Kamin, Ben, *Room 306: The National Story of the Lorraine Motel*, Michigan State University Press, 2012.
66. Guralnick, Peter, *Sweet Soul Music: Rhythm and Blues and the Southern Dream of Freedom*, Back Bay Books, 1999, pp.2–3.
67. Ibid., p.111.
68. Ibid., p.355.

WALLS TO ROBINSONVILLE

As if to beckon us further into the Delta region, the now familiar black-and-white Highway 61 signs appeared with increasing frequency. Sounds of Memphis Minnie's 'Me and My Chauffeur Blues' rang out from the car's sound system – hauntingly in tune with the flat landscape all around as we crossed the state line into DeSoto County, Mississippi. For the last four days our journey had run parallel with the great river, since first meeting it at Galena; it had taken a week to cover the 800 miles from Chicago to the Delta. The road trip had taken us through Illinois, Iowa, Missouri, Arkansas and Tennessee, and we were just about to cross into the state of Mississippi and the Delta region, which, in the words of Alan Lomax, is 'the land where the blues began'. For blues pilgrims it's a mythical landscape where it's all too easy to imagine that one feels the spirit of lone, itinerant bluesmen who once captured the essence of the South.

Yet the South isn't just about the ghosts of rootless male guitarists. This stretch of the blues highway between Memphis and the little town of Walls, situated just across the Mississippi state line, could perhaps more fittingly have been named after one of the region's best female blues guitarists from the 1930s and '40s. In the space of an hour the highway had taken us from the bars where Memphis Minnie had worked on Beale Street, past her final residence just 5 miles before the state line, and now we were on our way to find her grave at the New Hope Baptist Church, just outside Walls on old Highway 61.

Memphis Minnie, aka Lizzie Douglas, was born on a summer's day in 1897 in Algiers, Louisiana. The town today has been swallowed up into the New Orleans conurbation and was annexed by Orleans Parish in 1870. Douglas moved the 400 miles north to Walls with her family when she was 7 years old. She was a woman who would set her sights further than the cotton fields of the Mississippi and went on to play a formative role in the creation of the new style of urban blues. By the late 1940s she was playing places like the 708 Club in Chicago's South Side, where we'd started our own journey. She started recording for Lester Melrose's Bluebird Label in the late 1920s, which is when she adopted the name Memphis Minnie, and is considered an important influence on the development of the Chicago blues sound. Blues historian Paul Oliver argues that there were few other women singers in Chicago that could compare with Memphis Minnie and suggests that she was 'in the opinion of many the finest female blues singer outside of the classic idiom'.[1]

The Memphis Minnie story could have been invented by a rock 'n' roll publicist – except most of it is probably true. Despite being an impoverished farmer, her father managed to buy her a guitar when she was 11 years old. Within two years she had left the farm and tried to scrape a living as a street musician on Beale Street, using the name 'Kid Douglas'. It's said that she would resort to prostitution to support her musical career and attracted the relatively high fee of $12 for her services.[2] She sang about the subject in 'Hustlin' Woman Blues', which deals with the problems women on the street faced from violence and pimps.

Johnny Shines, who had travelled widely with Robert Johnson, recalled Memphis Minnie as something of a tough cookie, recalling how she'd go for any man that would fool with her, using anything at hand whether it be a guitar, pocket-knife or a pistol.[3] Minnie's relationships reflected the centrality of music in her life and her best-known partners were other notable street blues musicians, including Casey Bill Weldon of the Memphis Jug Band, who was nine years younger than her. In her early 30s she married Joe McCoy, and the pair worked together in Jed Davenport's Beale Street Jug Band playing the streets, parks and barbershops of Memphis until being spotted by Lester Melrose, a talent scout for Columbia Records. Following her success with 'Bumble Bee' she went on to record numerous sides during the course of her career up until the late 1950s, before succumbing to a series of health problems in her 60s.

In Elijah Wald's analysis of blues artists who had had more than 100 sides recorded between 1920 and 1942, Memphis Minnie ranks eighth with 158 sides, just two places below Bessie Smith.[4] Undoubtedly she lived a fast and hard lifestyle and as Denis Mercier noted, writing in *Notable Black American Women*, 'the blues life, with its drinking and late hours, caught up with her in the late 1950s'. Her last recording was made for JOB in 1954, two years after she rerecorded 'Me and My Chauffeur' for Checker, which had not secured her place amongst the newer Chicago blues artists of the likes of Waters and Wolf as she had hoped it would.[5]

Langston Hughes, an African American poet and intellectual, captured the extent to which Minnie on the one hand pushed the boundaries of blues whilst on the other retaining within it the essence of a rural South. Reviewing her performance at Chicago's 230 Club in 1942, aptly entitled 'Here to Yonder', Hughes wrote:

> through the smoke and racket of the noisy Chicago bar float Louisiana bayous, muddy old swamps, Mississippi dust and sun, cotton fields, lonesome roads, train whistles in the night, mosquitoes at dawn, and the Rural Free Delivery that never brings the right letter. All these things cry through the strings on Memphis Minnie's electric guitar, amplified to machine proportions – a musical version of electric welders plus a rolling mill.[6]

Memphis Minnie was a trendsetter and it would be another couple of years before Muddy Waters's uncle, Joe Grant, would buy him an unbranded electric guitar.[7] Hughes's review recognised a dual direction that was emerging in 1940s urban blues, similar to the theories of the urbanisation of country blues that follow more than a decade later. As Charters stated in 1959, referring to the 1940s, 'there was a restless and aggressiveness in the new young coloured audience that was much more excited by the fierce shouting of newer singers – Lightnin' Hopkins, B.B. King, John Lee Hooker, Muddy Waters, Smokey Hogg and Bo Diddley – than it was in the more sophisticated styles of Big Bill or Brownie McGhee.'[8] Willie Dixon told *Living Blues* in 1988 that his lyrics described the South from the viewpoint of nostalgic migrants who had adopted an urban way of life, 'by using some of the past it fitted a lot of the people and fits also our hopes for the future.'[9] Paul Oliver goes further suggesting that:

> (By) 1954 the nation's African American population had a median age of 25.1 and in the northern cities more than half the black masses were under this age; they did not want to hear the blues of the South that their parents liked – the South meant nothing to them. Muddy Waters, Howlin' Wolf and Elmore James were already seeming 'old' but their dynamism, their fierce shouting and collective power of their bands expressed the swelling anger of the younger Blacks.[10]

For blues pilgrims, paying homage to Memphis Minnie at her final resting place has an added advantage because it's an excuse to leave Highway 61 and explore old Highway 61. This has the benefit, for those that have the time, of going into the backwaters of a rural Mississippi, not easily found by staying on the newer road. It's old Highway 61 that, as Cheseborough points out, 'is really the road they're singing about in all those songs'.[11]

Our car bumped over the single-track railroad crossing at Walls as we passed a few timbered shotgun shacks. After a couple of miles we pulled into the New Hope Baptist Church car park and walked a little way from the church to find Minnie's grave. A few large trees provided much of the cemetery with a little welcome shade and within minutes we'd located a new granite gravestone decorated with a small oval photograph of Minnie, with the silver earrings, necklace and the gold tooth that the tobacco-chewing guitarist was renowned for.

Memphis Minnie returned to Memphis in the mid 1950s, her health failing following a series of strokes. Her care had to be funded through a combination of welfare and the local church up until her death in 1973, whereupon she was buried in an unmarked grave in the cemetery at Walls.[12] Prior to 1996 there would have been little to signify Minnie's final resting place, but the Mount Zion Memorial Fund started its work of establishing memorials for blues artists who had been buried in unmarked or poorly marked graves.[13] Her new gravestone was funded by donations from John Fogerty and Bonnie Raitt and would not have happened without the perseverance of the fund founded by Skip Henderson.[14] An inscription on the stone reads 'Lizzie "Kid" Douglas Lawlers, AKA, Memphis Minnie, June 3, 1897, Aug. 6, 1973'.

The little Baptist church seemed isolated, surrounded as it was by acres of perfectly flat cotton and soybean fields. A landscape that felt as if it held the unwritten history of those that had lived and worked here. The wail from a freight train's whistle drifted like a lone harmonica across the flat landscape as we read the memorial text on the stone.

Leaving the shade of the cemetery, I drove back along dusty roads as far as the collection of houses that formed DeSoto County's little town of Walls, once again bumping over the single-track level crossing, and then turned south back onto old Highway 61. After a few miles our route cut away from the levee and hot deserted countryside and found the newer highway. The occasional truck would gradually gain on us, its chromium hubs, gas tank and exhaust stack slowly gliding past in the outside lane. In the South one doesn't meet the frenetic pace of driving found in the cities. Overtaking appeared to be determined by minor variations in vehicle cruise control settings rather than engine performance. Ships pass one another with greater disparities of speed than American drivers do down South. The relaxed style of driving means people cover vast distances without arriving stressed and having to unpeel white knuckles from the steering wheel. In Mississippi there seems to be more danger from sleeping drivers than from speeding drivers, and in case one becomes too relaxed and allows the speed to slowly creep over the state limit there is always the randomly parked highway patrol officer's car, inconspicuous amongst the long grass of the central reservation, to remind one that in the state of Mississippi speed limits will be strictly enforced.

Gateway to the Blues Visitors Center, Tutwiler, in an old Illinois Central Railroad depot, Mississippi.

Highway 61 brought us through DeSoto County and down into Tunica County, which until recently was considered one of the poorest counties in the United States, with an estimated half of the population dependent upon Federal Assistance.[15] In 1985 Reverend Jesse Jackson called Tunica 'America's Ethiopia' and on national television drew the nation's attention to Sugar Ditch Alley, where people had to inhabit a collection of shacks lining an open sewer. Then Tunica took a gamble, which according to the County Administrator was more out of desperation than genius. Following the passage of legislation allowing for dockside gambling on the Mississippi Sound and the Mississippi River, the small town of Robinsonville, where Robert Johnson grew up, became home to gaming casinos. Ten had opened by 1997 attracting 17.4 million visitors, making the town the third largest gaming resort in America.[16]

A red-and-blue neon sign informing drivers that they were passing the Gateway to the Blues Visitors Center caught my attention. The sign was mounted on the roof of a weathered wooden rail freight depot, which stood alone at the edge of a far-reaching expanse of cotton that lay between the highway and the levee. The building could have stood there since the railway came to Tunica, but I knew it hadn't as I had no recollection of the building from the last time I'd driven this section of the highway, five years previously. I swung round at the first convenient turning point and drove back and parked outside the freight depot.

Piped Delta blues started playing as we closed the car doors and crossed the car park. I felt as if someone in the centre had popped a CD on especially for our arrival; however, the truth was perhaps that a device had been installed that could detect a blues pilgrim crossing the car park from 50m. Maybe this was to limit the visitor centre's staff from having to listen to a never-ending loop of Delta blues unless visitors were in attendance. As if to emphasise that we'd arrived at an old freight depot, a short section of rusting railroad track had been laid next to the small loading platform. Built in 1895, the depot had served as a transportation hub at Dundee, a small town on the Illinois Central Railroad (ICR), situated about 30 miles south along old Highway 61. It had been donated to Tunica County by the owners, Edgar and Janet Hood.

Inside the depot, staff warmly greeted us and enquired as to how far we'd travelled as we perused the collection of blue artefacts on display. The centre sells a wide selection of CDs, books and T-shirts and holds a good stock of literature informing visitors about where to find historic blues sites in the Mississippi. It also had free maps and guides informing visitors about the Mississippi Blues Trail markers – which serve as the perfect excuse to go and find out-of-the-way, lazy and often dying Delta towns.

Nevertheless, perhaps the old ICR depot is in itself the most fitting welcome to the Delta region, for the simple reason that the railroad represents an important historical link between the Delta and many of the towns and cities we'd stopped at on our journey. It was the coming of the railroad that had opened up numerous Delta towns, linking them with Memphis and New Orleans and the Midwest cities further north, such as St Louis and Chicago, alleviating the region's total dependency on river transport. Furthermore, the ICR provided new avenues for commerce between manufacturing bases and the rural South.

The railway also provided a conduit for consumer goods into the Delta, such as the low-priced Stella guitars from the Sears Roebuck catalogue, as well as the arrival of 78 records and the Victrolas advertised in papers such as the *Chicago Defender*. Muddy Waters recalled that his first introduction to the blues was listening to music played on a phonograph owned by a woman who lived across the field from his house on the Stovall plantation, Clarksdale.[17]

In the 1920s mail order businesses advertising in papers opened up the race record market in the Southern rural states, just as record shops had in the cities of the North and Midwest.[18] Professor John Wesley Work III, one of the African American scholars who worked with Alan Lomax during the 1941–42 joint Fisk University/Library of Congress study of black musical habits and history in Coahoma County, noted that among 'the plantation folk … phonographs and records were fairly well distributed'; one family had eighty-five records, sixty-nine of which were dance records, mostly commercial blues. Another had forty-five records, of which thirty-six were dance records.[19]

Despite country blues guitarists seldom receiving royalties beyond the initial payment for their recordings, records served as useful marketing tools that often enabled country blues musicians to gig further afield. A record would often bring regional kudos and help an artist access a wider audience, thereby attracting larger audiences and increasing a musician's geographic reach to juke joints, dances and gambling houses in towns up and down the railroad lines.[20] The railroads increased labour mobility for workers in the rural states, thereby facilitating an increased movement of musicians with country blues influences to urban centres.

We left the visitor centre and took a right turn off of Highway 61 onto one of the new roads that cut through the cotton fields, past the casino resorts, and headed towards the levee and old Highway 61. Under a blazing midday sun one morning in August 1942, Alan Lomax drove down this stretch of old Highway 61 en route to Tunica, having departed Memphis an hour or so earlier. According to Lomax, his objective was to find the home of 'Little Robert', or Robert Johnson.[21] More importantly, he knew he was returning to continue the work he had commenced with John Work the previous summer – surveying the music found in Coahoma County for the Library of Congress/ Fisk University Study.

Lomax had been made aware of Johnson's small body of recorded work by John Hammond, a record producer from New York City. Not only did Hammond work for Columbia Records, he also had a particular interest in African American artists and was a keen civil rights activist. In 1938 he organised the programme for the *From Spirituals to Swing* concert, held at Carnegie Hall on 23 December, which showcased a selection of African American music to a mainly white audience. Included on the bill was Robert Johnson, Hammond's choice of what he considered a truly outstanding blues singer. Unknown to both Hammond and Lomax at the time, Johnson had been murdered, probably poisoned by a jealous lover's husband, four months earlier. Instead. Hammond brought in Big Blue Broonzy as Johnson's replacement, and the Carnegie Hall audience were played records of Johnson's 'Walkin' Blues' and 'Preachin' Blues'.[22]

It was through his connection with Hammond that Lomax had been able to listen to Columbia's original recordings of Johnson, recorded in Texas in 1936 and 1937. Lomax referred to Johnson's recordings in his recollections of the Coahoma Study and, obviously making reference to white music aficionados, remarked that 'in 1939 only a handful of us appreciated him'.[23] Lomax and Hammond were both part of a larger reappraisal that had got under way in the mid 1930s of what constituted folk music. Such a reappraisal included another father and son team, namely Charles and Pete Seeger. William G. Roy, professor and Chair of the Sociology Department at the University of California, argues that Charles Seeger's influence was immense. Not only was Seeger seen as a founding father of ethnomusicology, but he also convinced the American left of the idea that folk music should be racially inclusive. Seeger had developed the view that working people 'through their structural position

Casinos amongst the cotton fields, in Tunica, Mississippi.

in society could better appreciate the music for its content, not just the idle fixation on technique' and was instrumental in providing 'the Communist Party with the justification for adopting folk music as the music of the people'.[24] Charles Edward Smith, writing in the *Daily Worker*, encapsulated this view when he suggested that spirituals, the blues and hot jazz were the authentic voice of the black working class, unlike other forms of commercialised music.[25]

In his account of the Coahoma Study, which Lomax wrote over fifty years after the study, he described how Highway 61 'ran straight for mile after mile of flat, treeless plantations, where the houses of black sharecroppers rose like grey stones in the green sea of cotton'.[26]

On the day Richard and I arrived, the flatlands surrounding Robinsonville exhibited an abundance of cotton. It was the last week in September; the green pods had ripened and the cotton had burst from the bolls, turning the fields into a sea of white. The sharecropper's shacks Lomax recollected from his visit had been replaced by huge temples to Tunica County's leisure and entertainment industry. Today it is Tunica's casinos that stand like huge ocean liners in the sea of white cotton, served by a flotilla of accommodation complexes – the flagships of the big hotel chains – which dwarf the few remaining abandoned sharecropper's shacks, roadside chapels and dilapidated commissaries.

We continued a little distance along the highway looking for another crossroads in the history of the blues: the junction of Clack Road and Old Highway 61. A solitary Blues Trail marker stood on the verge at the side of the highway, close to the office of the Tunica Convention and Visitors Bureau, so I pulled the car over to take a closer look at the plaque. It stands on the site of Clack's grocery, where on 3 September 1941 Alan Lomax and musicologist John Work III recorded a performance by Eddie James House, better known as Son House. Along with him were Willie Brown, fiddle and mandolin player Fiddlin' Joe Martin and harmonica player Leroy Williams. This session was later transcribed by Work from the discs that were recorded.

Interestingly, Lomax's recording of Son House took place eleven years after House had recorded for Paramount at Grafton, Wisconsin, with Willie Brown and Charley Patton.[27] John Work refers to House as being part of a generation of guitarists who 'created a mild vogue for guitar records in the twenties'.[28] In terms of how this translated into record sales, this is almost an overstatement in House's case: the four Son House records released by Paramount failed to sell. Their rarity is testament to their limited sales. According to record collector and blues writer Gayle Dean Wardlow, there are no known copies of 'Clarksdale Moan', only one copy of 'Preaching the Blues' and only a very few copies of 'My Black Mama' and 'Dry Spell Blues'.[29]

What Lomax and Work were engaged in at the Clack crossroads was a new approach to folklore collection. As Marybeth Hamilton suggests:

the aim … was 'to explore objectively and exhaustively the musical habits of a single Negro community in the Delta, to find out and describe the function of the music in the community, to ascertain the history of music in the community, and to document adequately the cultural and social backgrounds of music in the community.[30]

The Coahoma Study broke new ground. Not only were the majority of its researchers African Americans, but unlike previous folk studies it adopted the approach that folk music wasn't a constant expression that held within it an underlying purity. It moved away from a view that authenticity was dependent upon a lack of contamination from external influences. Instead it looked at the music of Delta people as something dynamic rather than static, examining it in the context of a society in change.

The unpublished manuscripts of the Fisk University scholars were uncovered by blues historian Robert Gordon and finally published in *Lost Delta Found* in 2005. Together with Alan Lomax's account of the study, in his book *The Land Where the Blues Began*, it gives an insight into the music played in the juke joints, churches and homes in and around the Delta town of Clarksdale, together with documentation of the lives of the people who consumed, as well as produced, the music.

On that hot September day when Lomax and Work met Son House, he informed the two researchers that he was near to quitting music, considering himself an old man, although he was only 39. House suggested that they seek out another local guitarist, who played in a similar style to Robert Johnson and himself, and who he described as 'an old boy called Muddy Waters round Clarksdale, he learnt from me and Little Robert and they say he gettin' to be a pretty fair player'.[31]

Lomax's foray into the Delta in 1941 doesn't just document events; it also serves as a good example of how research seldom has a neutral effect. The Coahoma Study captures the music of Son House, a local artist who had experienced very limited success with record sales a decade previously and who was close to retiring. The intervention of the Coahoma Study and the Library of Congress recordings begs the question as to whether House would have been rediscovered in the 1960s blues revival if it had not been for the existence of the Lomax recordings, which were released on a Folkways album, *Son House and J.D. Short – Blues from the Mississippi Delta*, in 1963. The second side contained the Son House tracks recorded in the 1942 session.

In the summer after the album's release three youngsters, Nick Perls, Dick Waterman and Phil Spiro, who were that 'certain kind of middle-class white American' Sam Charters had hoped to inspire with his 1959 book *The Country Blues*, arrived in Robinsonville in search of Son House.[32] After receiving a tip-off, the three eventually located him in Rochester, New York; he had left Robinsonville just a year after the 1942 Lomax recording.[33] What they found was a man suffering from the long-term effects of alcoholism, surviving on welfare payments and who hadn't picked up a guitar for years. With the help of Al Wilson, the guitarist with Canned Heat, who tutored House on how to play his own songs again, he was relaunched to the public at the 1964 Newport Folk Festival. In 1965 he went on to record *Father of the Folk Blues* for Columbia, produced by John Hammond.

However, the three blues hunters weren't the only young people from the North to arrive in Mississippi that summer. Nine hundred young volunteers went down to Mississippi as part of Freedom Summer to help with black voter registration. Sam Charters described one area of Mississippi in the liner notes of the Folkway's album issued the previous year as 'one of the most vicious areas of human intolerance and brutality on the face of the earth'.[34] Andrew Goodman, aged 20; James Earl Chaney, aged 21; and Michael Henry Schwerner, aged 24, discovered just how vicious Mississippi could be. Arrested on 21 June in Philadelphia, Mississippi, for an alleged speeding offence, the three civil rights activists would not make it out of Mississippi alive. On 4 August their bodies were found buried at a dam in Philadelphia. It has been said that the police conspired in the crime. Chaney was so badly beaten that the pathologist stated that he had 'never witnessed bones so severely shattered'.[35]

I stood next to the Mississippi Blues Trail marker that honoured Son House and surveyed the flat landscape that spread out every which way. It was almost impossible not to contrast the parts of the landscape that would have been familiar to House and his fellow musicians, with the newness of the casinos rising out of the cotton fields. The resorts were separated by a mile or so of rural landscape that appeared to have remained unchanged for centuries: the winding levee a few hundred yards across the cotton fields, a few surviving remnants of sharecroppers shacks and dusty plantation tracks that led off from the highway to cut through the fields of blossoming white bolls. Except, of course, the reality was somewhat different. The Delta we see isn't a landscape frozen in time; yet it's the sense of being remote from change and external influences that makes the region so appealing to the blues pilgrim. The longer one spends in the Delta the greater the temptation is to conjure a narrative of how the land had impacted upon the lives of its inhabitants, shaped their future and, along with it, the music. Of course, this is the very reason why the Delta is so appealing to blues pilgrims. However, in our eagerness to read from the landscape a narrative that suits our preconceptions there is a danger that we construct a version that does not always fit comfortably with the facts.

For the likes of Son House and his fellow musicians at Clack's store the reality was that they inhabited a relatively new landscape. Less than a century prior to House meeting Alan Lomax here in 1941, much of the Delta and Yazoo flood plain had been a fetid land of forest and swamp. During the 1850s Tunica County experienced nearly a five-fold increase of land that had been cleared, drained and brought into cultivation.[36] Marybeth Hamilton journeyed to the Delta in 1999, aware of the many inconsistencies that exist between reality and the narratives that blues travellers bring to the region, all too easily reinforced by the landscape. Hamilton describes how it took months before the spell of the landscape was broken and she could see a photograph she had taken of a ruined wooden railroad bridge submerged in a swamp somewhere off of Old Highway 61 for what it truly represented:

> At some level I knew that these photos were hackneyed, that they had been taken by every blues pilgrim before me. But the power of the tale was too strong to resist … Over time, once I'd retuned to a frenetically urban, post-industrial London, that railway bridge began to tell a new tale and I came to see the hand of modernity in my photograph.[37]

Yet looking around, it also occurred to me that the most recent changes in Delta society – the casinos among the cotton fields – were actually less incongruous with the past than might at first be imagined. There is in fact a long-standing and close connection between gambling and the blues in Mississippi.

Blues guitarist Albert King is said to have told Detroit Junior a story about how he once walked into a juke joint to see Howlin' Wolf play. A man lay on the floor and people were resting their feet on him whilst gambling. When King enquired as to why they had their feet on the man, he was informed that they'd just killed him. King rounded the story off by saying that not only did the men carry on gambling, but that the Wolf carried on howlin'.[38] As if to confirm that gambling is nothing new to the area, the Tunica Museum, which also reminds visitors that the Chickasaw Indians were the first people to own slaves in the area, has an exhibit from one of Harold 'Hardface' Clanton's establishments, established in conjunction with Sunbeam Mitchell, who had his club on Beale Street. Preston Lauterbach refers to the black entrepreneur Clanton as someone who proved exceptional to the rules of the sharecropper system that dominated Tunica society and states:

> Sunbeam forged another long-standing alliance not fifty miles south of Memphis in the Mississippi Delta, where he and Tunica County kingpin Harold 'Hardface' Clanton partnered in a dice and entertainment venture. Segregation and Prohibition: The Laws and customs implemented to keep men like Sunbeam, Milt Barnes, and Hardface in line instead made them wealthy playboys.[39]

Maybe echoes of Johnson's *The Last Fair Deal Gone Down* still reverberate where old Highway 61 crosses Casino Strip Boulevard. The links between gambling and the blues are neither new nor unusual; Webster Franklin, the CEO of the Tunica Convention and Visitors Bureau said that he hoped the centre would 'draw the blues enthusiasts to the state and give them an authentic experience while they're here, and at the same time they'll stay in our hotels and hopefully play a few slot machines'.[40]

After Alan Lomax made the 1942 recordings he didn't see Muddy Waters again for ten years, and when he did Waters was driving a big Cadillac.

Cypress swamp outside Clarksdale, Mississippi.

Clarksdale and the Stovall plantation, where Waters had lived with his mother from the age of 3, was just 50 miles down Highway 61 from the little town of Robinsonville. Here we'd find one if not more of Robert Johnson's mythical crossroads. Because Clarksdale's already good communication links continuously improved, with the coming of the railroad in 1884 and the construction of highways in the twentieth century the town found itself as one of the most important trade and cultural centres in the north-west of Mississippi.

Our schedule included a couple of days at one of the region's largest blues festivals, just over the Mississippi River at Helena, and so Clarksdale, the Delta's capital of blues and cotton, would have to be put on hold until mid-week. Accommodation being tight in Helena, with thousands of people visiting Arkansas for the King Biscuit Blues Festival, we'd taken advantage of the wealth of hotel accommodation around Robinsonville.

About a mile west of Robinsonville there was one more historic landmark that I wanted to find before we headed to the King Biscuit festival: the Abbay & Leatherman Plantation. This was where Robert Johnson grew up from the age of 7, having moved to Robinsonville from Memphis with his mother, Julia Major Dodds, and her then husband, Dusty Willis.

When Johnson first arrived in Robinsonville he was known as Robert Leroy Spencer, having taken the name of one of his stepfathers. Spencer Snr had had to change his surname from Dodds after being forced to leave his land and escape a lynch mob. This wasn't unusual for African Americans at the time, who had virtually no recourse to law if disputes arose with their white neighbours. In 1914 Robert joined his stepfather and lived with him for a while in Memphis. However, Dodds refused to reconcile with Johnson's mother, who had had an affair with Noah Johnson shortly after Dodds had been forced to flee. After Robert's mother married Dusty Willis, she was reunited with her son and brought him to live with her on the Abbay and Leatherman plantation near Robinsonville. Sometime in Robert's teens he started referring to himself as Johnson, having found out that his real father was Noah Johnson.[41]

The turning to the Abbay and Leatherman plantation was at the crossroads of Highway 61 and a single-track road running towards the river and Commerce. At the crossroads stood a brick building with a sign that promises the chance of a lunch stop and some Southern food. Swinging the car off the Old Commerce Road, we pulled onto the gravel forecourt of the Hollywood Café and parked adjacent to the raised wooden platform and balustrade at the front of the building. This appeared to be the heart of Robinsonville – just a handful of houses clustered round a crossroads surrounded by acres of cotton. A new road, Casino Strip Resort Boulevard, which could only have been named by committee, bypassed what remained of the town. Fortunately the new road's name belies the fact that the surrounding landscape has an overwhelming rustic, lazy Southern feel without a slot machine or craps table in sight.

The Hollywood Café is housed in an old commissary, built in the 1920s, that once belonged to the B.F. Harbert & Co. plantation. It was once the grocery store that served local plantation workers but it now served a menu of catfish, shrimps and frogs' legs to locals and the few tourists lucky enough to find it. Deep-fried dill pickle is one of the Hollywood's speciality dishes: a local delight that they've been frying for four decades. There's a saying with the locals that if something is edible then you can bet that someone south of the Mason-Dixon line has tried to cook it in oil.

We left the café and drove west, passing nothing but cotton fields on either side. Old Commerce Road eventually became subsumed into the new Casino Boulevard. The electricity poles, the tallest things visible for miles, lined the edge of the road, slanting from the ravages of the wind, each appearing a little shorter than the last until the line of wires and the road ahead narrowed to an infinitesimal point in the shimmering heat haze. Apart from cotton, all that stood between ourselves and the Mississippi was the uninterrupted form of the levee, and as usual it denied us sight of the great river itself.

'Commerce', announced a sign, although there appeared to be nothing more there than a couple of timbered houses and some old farm machinery on the parched earth beside the highway. I'd read somewhere that Robert Johnson may have attended school here, so I guessed the Abbay and Leatherman plantation was in the vicinity. Standing a little way back from the highway we noticed a building that stood out from the others because of its antiquity. This small brick building could easily have been an old schoolhouse or church hall. Its modest porch was supported by two white pillars and above the door was a metal sign screwed into the brickwork that simply read 'Abbay and Leatherman'. I pulled off the highway onto the verge at the edge of the cotton field. All around was a landscape that Robert Johnson would have been familiar with for the best part of his life. The Abbay and Leatherman office was nearly 100 years old when Johnson saw it for the first time and he would have looked across from these buildings to the levee and the river on the far side of the fields.

In the field next to the building stood a familiar blue enamelled sign, another Blues Trail marker, which by now we were pretty good at spotting. Just as I took the liberty of wheeling the dustbin round the side of the office and out of camera shot, a large truck pulled up and parked behind our car. The truck's occupants climbed out and the eldest of the two men offered a hand to shake, amused by my embarrassment at having been caught moving the bin. He introduced himself as Brad Cobb and explained that the other person was his son.

Brad said he farmed about 10,000 acres and this farm made up 2,500 acres of the total. Before he leased the land, the Leathermans had farmed it from 1828 right up until the last couple of decades. He is the first non-Leatherman to farm this land and he told us that, like his own son, very few children today

Abbay & Leatherman Plantation office, Commerce, near Robinsonville.

want to work the land their parents farmed. Brad invited us into the office and in pride of place was an old cotton bale wrapped as it would have been in preparation for shipment up the Mississippi River. Pointing to the fields around the office, Brad talked about how things had changed, explaining that most of the little tenement shacks and the mule barns had now gone and that the ones we see today are a mere fraction of what there had been prior to the mechanisation that took place in the 1950s. Brad's son added that the landscape was changing every year and what people romanticised about was definitely fading year on year.

The previous year they'd had floods here and the water had risen two-thirds of the way up the levee, Brad said, pointing across the top of the cotton field as his finger traced the run of the levee on the far side. The casinos took a battering that year and news reports showed the casinos, built on barges so as to comply with gambling legislation, floating. Many of the hotels flooded on the lower floors.

The height of the river last year had caused concern on the farm and there were concerns that the levee might break. It didn't, but the river had been predicted to rise to the highest since the 1937 flood. However, the worst flooding in the Delta was the Great Flood of 1927, immortalised in Charley Patton's 'Highwater Everywhere', recorded in 1929, in which he refers to the water at 'Greenville and Lula, Lord, it done rose everywhere'. It has been estimated that in the Delta Region alone over 200,000 people were displaced from their homes; levees failed in forty-two places. An official estimate puts the number of lives lost as a direct result of flooding at 500, before any account is taken of deaths through disease, exposure and malnutrition in the aftermath of the disaster.[42]

I asked Brad how many blues pilgrims pulled up here each week. He estimated he might see two or three and some would get out and take some photographs, adding that they've had rock and roll stars coming to see where Robert Johnson lived. About half the visitors to Brad Cobb's farm were from abroad and the others came from big cities like Chicago and New York. We thanked Brad and his son for their time and then just as we were about to leave Brad asked if we wanted to go and see where Johnson's home had been.

A dirt track led across the cotton fields past an old cotton gin. Another quarter of a mile and a track, rutted with tyre tracks in the soft dirt, abruptly turned and ran parallel with the levee on the other side of a strip of shrub land. By a bend in the shadow of the levee once stood the shack that had been home to the young Robert Johnson, his mother Julia Dodds and his stepfather Dusty Willis when they arrived from Memphis between 1918 and 1920.[43]

By the time Son House arrived in the area, sometime around 1930, Johnson was in his late teens. House had just been released from Parchman Farm, where he'd served time for shooting and killing Leroy Lee at a house party in 1928, which he claimed he'd done to defend his friend Sam Allen. After House had served less than two years, a judge released him and advised him to stay clear of Clarksdale. To comply with the judge's recommendation, House moved a few miles north to the Lula and Robinsonville area, where he found employment on a number of farms. However, there is no documented evidence beyond interviews that collaborates this story.

Among the farms where House found work was the Harbert plantation, back at the crossroads with Old Commerce Road, which we'd driven through that morning. House topped up his income playing blues at jukes and dances and somewhat surprisingly by preaching. But by the early 1930s the tension between House's religion and the blues, not eased by his problematic relationship with alcohol and womanising, was causing conflict not only for House but also amongst his congregations. The contradictions between his beliefs and lifestyle eventually brought his preaching to a close.[44]

Charley Patton had also moved into the area and was frequenting the musical haunts around Lula and Robinsonville. It was outside of Lula railway station that Patton first spotted House playing. House was invited to play outside Sara Knights Café in Lula and Patton was apparently impressed by the crowd House attracted, whereupon he approached him. Thereafter the pair established a friendship, which lasted until Patton's death from heart disease four years later. The friendship appears to have been based on common interests around the blues, women and a love of corn liquor.[45]

Johnson was 19, although House remembered him looking more like 15 or 16, when he started hanging around the juke joints of Lula and Robinsonville on a Saturday night, where he'd watch Charley Patton, Son House and their friend, the guitarist Willie Brown. By all accounts the young Johnson, whilst a fair harmonica player, was more of a nuisance when he took to playing the guitar – House described his playing as a racket.[46] Because of the violence that occurred at the Saturday night dances, Johnson's parents were opposed to him going, but like other youngsters bitten by a form of music that seems to make perfect sense of the world, Robert Johnson knew what he had to do.

I sat down in front of the levee and took in a scene that probably wasn't dissimilar to the one that Robert Johnson would have seen when he lived here. I picked up a handful of soil and let it slip through my fingers, and then noticed a small piece of brick. Picking it up, I cleaned it with some spittle and slipped it in my pocket – just maybe – it's nice to believe. We both picked a cotton boll. I guess this is what pilgrims do. I could've played one of the twenty-nine tracks on the Johnson CD I had in the car, which he recorded for Vocalion in the two years before his death.

The year after Son House's arrival in the Robinsonville area, Johnson left the Abbay & Leatherman Plantation – an act that after his death becomes elevated into the realms of musical folklore. It's believed he travelled the 240 miles to his birthplace at Hazlehurst, south of Jackson. Some months later, at the small town of Banks, 3 miles east of Robinsonville, Johnson walked into a juke joint where House and Willie Brown were playing. According to House, Johnson's guitar playing that night left them with their mouths wide open, whereupon House said, 'Well, ain't that fast! He's gone now!'[47]

Cotton gin, close to Robert Johnson's home at Commerce on the Abbay & Leatherman Plantation.

Johnson had left the Robinsonville area for between six months and two years. It is within that period that, according to myth, he went down to the crossroads and sold his soul to the devil in exchange for virtuoso guitar skills. The rest is history. But the problem with the crossroads myth is that early interviews with country blues guitarists fail to mention any pact that Robert Johnson made with the devil. It's not mentioned until Pete Welding's 'Hellhound On My Trail', an article published in 1966, which quotes Son House as saying that Johnson 'sold his soul to the devil in exchange for learning to play like that'.[48] The Welding article appeared the same year as Eric Clapton and the Powerhouse released Crossroads; two years before Cream released an amalgamation of Johnson's 'Crossroads Blues' and 'Traveling Riverside Blues' and three years before the Stones covered 'Love in Vain' on Let it Bleed. Wardlow states that the next mention of the crossroad myth is when Greil Marcus refers to the Son House interview in his book Mystery Train, published in 1975, and as such suggests the myth didn't reach its present form until the film Crossroads was released in 1986.

Given Wardlow's chronology above, if most blues pilgrims arrived at an awareness of Robert Johnson through listening to 1960s and '70s rock music, it is very unlikely that they would have incorporated the crossroads myth into their own narrative of Johnson until the late 1980s.

While the Melody Maker of July 1937 is often cited as one of the few references in the press to Johnson in his own lifetime, the weekly American Marxist magazine New Masses, firmly rooted in the material world, also carried coverage of Johnson's music on a number of occasions while he was still alive. In a column published on 2 March 1937, wedged between adverts for study tours to Soviet Russia, medical aid for the Spanish Civil War and an evening of analysis about the Moscow Treason Trials, Henry Johnson wrote:

We cannot but call your attention to the greatest Negro blues singer that has cropped up in recent years, Robert Johnson. Recording in the deepest Mississippi, Vocalion has certainly done right by us in the tunes 'Last Fair Deal Going Down' and 'Terraplane Blues', to mention only two of the sides already released, sung to his own guitar accompaniment.[49]

The following year New Masses funded the From Spirituals to Swing concert, staged at New York's Carnegie Hall with Johnson on the bill. The event has since been described as audacious for its time and one that 'proved to be the first major concert (and at such a prestigious venue) to feature black artists performing for an integrated audience'.[50] However, one week before the Carnegie Hall concert New Masses ran an article entitled 'Jim-Crow Blues', in which John Hammond broke the news to readers that Robert Johnson, planned as the big billing of the evening, was dead. Hammond finished the article by reminding readers of the difficulties black musicians had bringing certain musical forms to the public's attention. He was referring to the common practice of craft union segregation, which had the effect of isolating black musicians in Jim Crow unions, combined with the fact that 'hotel owners had definitely formulated a hostile policy towards Negro entertainment to go side-by-side with the exclusion of coloured patronage' and concluded that that 'Negro musicians still found themselves oppressed and ostracized'. Rather than pacts with the devil, the article offered a number of worldly changes such as 'the abolition of the colour line in the hiring of musicians rather than in the encouraging of more and better all colored bands'.[51]

Notes

1. Oliver, Paul, The Story of the Blues – The Making of Black Music, Pimlico, 1997, pp.122–3.
2. Aswell, Tom, Louisiana Rocks! The True Genesis of Rock and Roll, Pelican Publishing Company, Inc., 2010, p.199.
3. Rowe, Mike, Chicago Blues: The City and the Music, Da Capo, 1975, p.43. Originally published in 1973 as Chicago Breakdown.
4. Wald, Elijah, Escaping the Delta: Robert Johnson and the Invention of the Blues, Amistad, 2005, p.41.
5. Hardy, Phil and Laing, Dave, The Faber Companion to 20th Century Popular Music, Faber and Faber, 1992, p.539.
6. Chicago Defender, national edition, 9 January 1943, p.14. ProQuest Historical Newspapers: The Chicago Defender (1910–1975).
7. Gordon, Robert, Can't Be Satisfied: The Life and Times of Muddy Waters, Pimlico, 2003, p.79.
8. Charters, Samuel B., The Country Blues, Da Capo, 1959, p.233.
9. Corritore, Bob, Ferris, William, O'Neal, Jim, 'Willie Dixon, Part 1 (interview)', Living Blues, July/August 1988, pp.16–25. Quoted in Filene, Benjamin, Romancing the Folk: Public Memory and American Roots Music, University of North Carolina Press, 2000, p.107.
10. Oliver, Story of the Blues, p.184.

11. Cheseborough, Steve, *Blues Traveling: The Holy Sites of Delta Blues*, University Press of Mississippi, 2009, p.56.

12. Mercier, Denis, 'Memphis Minnie', in Smith, Jessie Carney (ed.), *Notable Black Americans; Book II*, Gale Research Inc., 1996, p.188.

13. Yellin, Emily, 'Homage at last for blues makers; Through a fan's crusade, unmarked graves get memorials', *New York Times*, 30 September 1997 at www.nytimes.com.

14. Ibid.

15. Snyder, Thomas James, 'The Effects of Casino Gaming on Tunica County', Mississippi, *Social Research Report Series 99-2*, University of Mississippi, September 1999, p.2.

16. Ibid.

17. Gordon, Robert, *Can't Be Satisfied: The Life and Times of Muddy Waters*, Pimlico, 2003, p.16.

18. Charters, *The Country Blues*, p.48.

19. Gordon, Robert and Nemerov, Bruce (eds), *Lost Delta Found: Rediscovering the Fisk University–Library of Congress Coahoma County Study, 1941–1942*, Vanderbilt University Press, 2005, p.86.

20. Wald, *Escaping the Delta*, p.122. Wald suggests that Robert Johnson's recordings 'would have increased his drawing power and hence his earnings at juke joints and house parties'.

21. Lomax, John, *The Land Where the Blues Began*, The New Press, 1993, pp.3–11. For discussion regarding when Lomax visited Johnson's home and the accuracy of his account see Beaumont, Daniel, *Preachin' the Blues*, Oxford University Press, 2011, p.104.

22. Wald, *Escaping the Delta*, pp.228–9.

23. Lomax, *The Land Where the Blues Began*, p.13.

24. Roy, William G., *Reds, Whites, and Blues*, Princeton University Press, 2010, p.117.

25. Smith, Charles Edward, 'Class Content and Jazz Music', *Daily Worker* (USA), 21 October 1933, referred to in Gennari, John, *Blowin' Hot and Cool: Jazz and its Critics*, University of Chicago Press, 2006, p.34.

26. Lomax, *The Land Where the Blues Began*, p.12.

27. Oliver, Paul, *The Story of the Blues: The Making of Black Music*, Pimlico, 1997, p.132. See also Davis, Francis, *The History of the Blues: The Roots Music and the People*, Da Capo, 2003, p.106.

28. Work III, John W., Coahoma Study – untitled manuscript, in Gordon and Nemerov, *Lost Delta Found*, p.88.

29. Wardlow, Gayle Dean, *Chasin' That Devil Music: Searching for the Blues*, Backbeat Books, 1998, p.139.

30. Hamilton, Marybeth, *In Search of the Blues: Black Voices White Visions*, Jonathan Cape, 2007, p.120.

31. Lomax, *The Land Where the Blues Began*, p.17.

32. Charters, *The Country Blues*, p.x.

33. Calt, Stephen, *I'd Rather Be the Devil*, Chicago Review Press, 2008, pp.241–2.

34. Charters, Samuel, (liner notes, p.1), *J.D. Short and Son House, The Blues of the Mississippi Delta*, Folkways Records FA 2467, 1963.

35. Wilkinson, Brenda, *The Civil Rights Movement*, Crescent Books, 1997, p.135.

36. Saikku, Mikko, *This Delta, This Land: An Environmental History of the Yazoo-Mississippi Floodplain*, University of Georgia Press, 2005, p.110.

37. Hamilton, *In Search of the Blues*, p.3.

38. Segrest, James and Hoffman, Mark, *Moanin' at Midnight: The Life and Times of Howlin' Wolf*, Thunder's Mouth Press, 2005, p.37; attributes the quote to Brisbin, John Anthony, Detroit Junior: 'You Got to Put Somethin' in it', *Living Blues*, September/October 1996.

39. Lauterbach, Preston, *The Chitlin' Circuit and the Road to Rock 'n' Roll*, Norton, 2012, p.223.

40. Klose, Roland, 'Tunica accustomed to tough times, takes trouble in stride', *The Commercial Appeal*, 20 September 2009, www.commercialappeal.com.

41. Guralnick, Peter, *Searching for Robert Johnson*, Dutton, 1992, pp.12–13.

42. Lawson, R.A., *Jim Crow's Counterculture: The Blues and Black Southerners*, Louisiana State University Press, 2010, pp.137, 140.

43. Guralnick, *Searching for Robert Johnson*, p.11.

44. Beaumont, *Preachin' the Blues*, pp.80, 85.

45. Ibid., pp.49–53.

46. Ibid., p.15.

47. Ibid., p.17. Beaumont, *Preachin' the Blues*, p.91, attributes the quote to Lester, Julius, 'I can make my own songs: An interview with Son House', *Sing Out!* 15:3, 1965.

48. Wardlow, *Chasin' That Devil Music*, p.203. Wardlow provides a chronological development of the crossroads myth from Welding's article in 1966 through to what he describes as its 'present form' in the film *Crossroads*, released in 1986.

49. Johnson, Henry, *New Masses*, 2 March 1937, p.29.

50. Wyman, Bill with Havers, Richard, *Bill Wyman's Blues Odyssey*, Dorling Kindersley, 2001, p.206.

51. Hammond, John, 'Jim-Crow blues', *New Masses*, 13 December 1938, p.27.

6

Pass the Biscuits – It's King Biscuit Time:

HELENA

The schedule Richard and I had worked up had been designed to take in a couple of the numerous blues festivals held throughout the Delta region. This in itself is not an easy choice, as many towns throughout the Delta that can boast a little blues history put on their own festival. Some towns, like Clarksdale, organise a number of festivals throughout the year, from smaller intimate festivals like the annual Juke Joint Festival in April to the annual Sunflower River Blues and Gospel Festival, which has both international and local artists and attracts thousands of visitors. Blues festivals in the state of Mississippi alone number more than sixty, starting as early as March and running through the year to November.[1]

Despite being spoilt for choice we settled on a solution that meant we would commence our road trip at the end of September so we could push on into the Delta by the beginning of October and catch the King Biscuit Blues Festival, one of the biggest of the annual Delta festivals. The King Biscuit Blues Festival is situated across the Mississippi River in historic downtown Helena, Arkansas, and attracts tens of thousands of blues fans from across America and around the world. The festival coincides within a week of the smaller Highway 61 Blues Festival, held at Leland, Mississippi, 100 miles south downriver from Helena. Not only is Leland close to Greenville, a town steeped in Delta blues history, but the festivals falling on adjacent weekends gave us time to branch out mid-week and explore Clarksdale, known as the blues capital of the Delta and the home town of Muddy Waters and numerous other Delta blues artists.[2]

The large neon sign with an enormous red arrow mounted on the roof of the Blue and White Diner makes it difficult to miss as one drives through Tunica. Inside, the diner was brimming with locals, although I had a feeling that the four men sporting ten gallon hats were maybe just passing through. The Blue and White became our pre-festival breakfast and coffee stop for the next three days as we commuted between Robinsonville and Helena for the King Biscuit Blues Festival. Despite having the appearance of a classic 1950s American diner, the Blue and White Diner dates back to just after the construction of the new highway, where it has stood since 1937. Originally it was located on Old Highway 61 in downtown Tunica, where it was established in 1924.

Fifteen miles beyond the Blue and White Diner we picked up Highway 49 to Helena. This dead-straight road, raised slightly above the surrounding farmland on a gravel bank, heads westward across the cotton fields towards the Lula and West Helena bridge over the Mississippi into Arkansas. A mile or so along the highway we passed an unmarked single track that led to Lula, the small farming town where both Charley Patton and Son House had spent a little time around 1930. A Blues Trail marker in the centre of Lula commemorates this small community's links with the two formative country blues guitarists.

Another 100 metres beyond the Lula turn-off we came to the Lula Fuel Center, a sprawling, yellow-painted single-storey block-built garage and store that overlooked a large gravel forecourt. In many respects the Lula Fuel Center had more 1950s retro about it than the Blue and White. Its size suggested that the truck stop had, in better days, grown to meet the demands of the highway connecting the once-thriving economies of north-west Mississippi and the port of Helena. Today the store offers a good selection of boxed beers and provisions for the passing motorist, so we put a few beers in the boot of the car for after the festival. Local people had warned us that during the festival Mississippi highway patrols would be out in force each evening on this section of Highway 49 looking for drivers who might have over-indulged at the King Biscuit Blues Festival, pulling them over as they crossed the state line.

Highway 49 maintains its approach towards the Mississippi River with a determination that doesn't deviate, as it starts a steady incline toward the crest of the levee. I eagerly expected a new panorama to greet us as the road passed over the highest point of the grass-covered sod mound that ran off on either side into the distance. This was man's attempt to redefine one of the world's great flood plains, and numerous guidebooks inform the reader that the Mississippi levee system is longer than the Great Wall of China. To either side, as we drove over the top of the levee, a sandy coloured track struck out tangentially on a course that hugged the levee's ridged spine. Yet, there was no river to be seen, not even a sleepy bayou or stretch of swampland. Instead there was 2 miles of continuous rich, black earth between us and the sandbanks lining the edge of the Mississippi. We were looking across one of the most fertile landscapes on earth, described as having the 'richest soil and the poorest people in the nation'.[3]

The stark iron grid work of the Helena Bridge loomed up ahead and a huge 'Welcome to Arkansas' sign hung above the westbound lane. On the Arkansas bank the highway ran directly over the levee. The scale of the levee reminded me of accounts of desperate attempts to defend the communities on both sides of the Mississippi as the waters rose during the Great Flood of 1927. In extreme circumstances the counties adjacent to the river would arm local workers to guard the levees, for fear that landowners from the opposite side of the river might send a dynamiting party across with the purpose of blowing a breach in the levee wall to release the pressure of flood water and safeguard their own land.[4] In Lomax's *The Land Where the Blues Began* he describes an interview with a one-time levee worker named Windy George, who recalled how one night when guarding the levee they captured four men in a skiff, who had rowed over from the Arkansas side when 'the river was so high it was about to bust'.[5] George told how following their capture, ploughs were tied round the necks of the two suspected saboteurs, and the two black workers who been forced to row them over from the Arkansas side were made to row the skiff out into midstream and throw the two suspected dynamiters into the river to drown. George Adam's account of the murder of the two levee saboteurs can also be found in Lewis W. Jones's introduction to John Work's Coahoma Study.[6]

Helena has been described as having been a little Chicago in the 1930s and '40s. The town even had a Chrysler plant at West Helena until the mid 1950s and a thriving port together with a cotton processing plant.[7] Mark Twain stopped over at Helena on his journey down the Mississippi on the *Gold Dust* and reported that it already had a population of 5,000, with 'plenty of coloured folk' and the 'commercial centre of a broad and prosperous region'.[8] Since then Helena's fortunes have peaked and during the last few decades its decline in population has reflected the absence of industry and far fewer opportunities for agricultural employment. The percentage of Helena's residents with an income less than the poverty level is just over 40 per cent – more than two and half times that for the whole of Arkansas. Moreover, more than one in six of Helena's residents have to survive on an income of less than half the poverty level.[9]

A large part of Helena's blues history is about the King Biscuit Time radio show and the town's most famous honorary son, harmonica player Sonny Boy Williamson II, with whom the show became synonymous. Broadcast from the city's radio station KFFA, the fifteen-minute King Biscuit show was the first to feature blues and was aimed at the station's black audience, estimated to comprise 70 per cent of its total number of listeners. With an initial 35-mile reach it influenced thousands of receptive listeners in Arkansas and the Mississippi Delta. Williamson, or Aleck Miller, aka Rice Miller, was actually born 60 miles further south down Highway 61 at Glendora, Mississippi, but, having found Helena in his 30s, he spent much of his life there. Despite finding success in Chicago and living in Europe for a short period, he chose to return to Helena when his health finally failed him.

King Biscuit's sponsors, the Interstate Grocery Company, aimed the show's advertising at African American cooks and housekeepers, because they were the people who purchased the flour for the larders of the white families that employed them. Sonny Boy Williamson and Robert Lockwood Jr, effectively sold the idea to KFFA boss Sam Anderson. It proved so successful that the show's allocated slot was increased to thirty minutes each day and by 1944 the station had increased its broadcasting coverage to a radius of 80 miles.

Lockwood told a story that one night he'd being doing a gig with Sonny Boy Williamson in the town of Tutwiler. Lockwood had bought a six-cylinder Pontiac so that he could get to gigs in the evening around the Delta and up towards Memphis, yet still get back to catch the last ferry over to Helena from Lula and catch a little sleep before getting to KFFA for the following morning's King Biscuit Time show, broadcast between 12 noon and 12.15 each day. One night as they were approaching Lula Lockwood caught sight of a highway patrol car parked up on the side of the road. Apparently, Lockwood cut his lights and he and Sonny Boy Williamson II turned onto the riverside road and made the 10-mile trip down to Friars Point, where they drove the car straight up onto the last ferry to leave that night.[10]

The town served as a funnel for black musicians from the Delta attracted to Helena, not only for the variety of work opportunities it presented but also as a centre of population – it was somewhere they could find receptive audiences in the bars and juke joints. For many musicians, such as Roosevelt Sykes, Little Walter and Jimmy Rogers, Helena served as a staging post for future forays up to West Memphis and onto the bigger cities like St Louis and Chicago. For Helena's most well-known musician, Sonny Boy Williamson II, the town was the base to which he would always return. According to Peter Guralnick, when Robert Johnson started travelling in the early 1930s he used Helena, Memphis, Greenwood and Robinsonville as bases to return to after gigs as far afield as St Louis, Chicago, Detroit and New York.[11]

The first time I drove into Helena was in 2007. I remember how overwhelmed I'd been by the feeling of decay, as though the town had shuttered up a couple of decades prior to my arrival. That day we'd driven down Missouri Street and parked under the levee. It was late morning sometime in the middle of April and already surprisingly warm. My diary entry for that day described 'how what had once been a thriving port side in the 1940s was now a partly desolate area with just the odd person wandering the deserted streets; where faded murals that had once advertised the products sold in the dock-side shops and bars could still be discerned on a few of the dilapidated buildings'.

Cherry Street, King Biscuit Blues Festival, Helena, Arkansas.

had a high school education and following a separation with his father took Robert to live in Helena so he could get a nine-month-a-year education rather than the seven months common in rural areas. When Robert was in his early teens his mother started a relationship with Robert Johnson, who was fifteen years younger than her. Johnson and Lockwood got along well and in an interview in 1979, Lockwood told Robert Palmer that:

> I had heard guitar players, but I wasn't interested in 'em. I didn't want to play an instrument if I had to have help … But then Robert came along and he was backing himself up without anybody helping him, and sounding good. He would go somewhere to play for people and tear the house up. So I got right on top of that. By him having a crush on my mother, I got a chance to be around him a little bit. I think I'm about the only one he ever taught.[12]

The guitar tuition served the young Lockwood well, for when he was about 20 years old he first saw Howlin' Wolf playing on the streets in the little town of Brickeys, situated about half an hour's drive north of Helena. Lockwood told Mark Hoffman in 2002 that he'd learned about Howlin' Wolf and Sonny Boy Williamson from Robert Johnson. The local whiskey store owner suggested to Lockwood that he play a few songs, whereupon, in the words of Lockwood, 'I started playing Robert Johnson's shit and drew all the people away from Wolf! It was funny. I looked out in the crowd and Howlin' Wolf had his guitar on his back.'[13]

It was about this time, around the mid 1930s, that the guitarist Johnny Shines met Johnson in Helena. As with Lockwood, Shines was knocked out by Johnson's playing and described him as 'the greatest guitar player I heard … Robert changed everything'.[14] In an interview with Guralnick, shortly following Shines' rediscovery in the 1960s blues revival, he recalled running into Johnson in Helena and began what he termed as 'journeying off'. Guralnick states Shines ran with Johnson for a period of about three years. Shines also described how exciting his time on the road with Johnson had been and connected the itinerant nature of the musician's life with the creative process:

> you leave here, you maybe go for five hundred miles, and you don't know anybody, everything is new to you. It's really, I mean if a person lives in an exploratory world, then this is the best thing that ever happened to them.[15]

Each day a handful of blues pilgrims trickle into downtown Helena, just as we had on that April morning, to catch the essence of a town that once attracted a coterie of musicians that would leave a great blues legacy, although many would only become aware of it very late in their lives, if at all.

The first stop that day was the Delta Cultural Center museum; no sooner had we arrived than Howard, the centre's manager, enquired if we liked blues and then whisked us over to the cultural center's studio on the opposite side of Cherry Street, where the legendary 'Sunshine' Sonny Payne was just about to start the daily lunchtime broadcast of King Biscuit Time.

We'd come to the town in the hope that we might see the original King Biscuit trailer, which was languishing in a field just on the edge of town, off of Highway 185. But instead Sonny Payne, who's been part of the King Biscuit team since the show's inception, called us over and invited us to 'come and join the show'. Visitors to the Delta Cultural Center are often invited onto the show and by chance, on that April lunchtime, we were the lucky ones. Just to make things complete, Sonny opened the show with the words that have made their way into blues folklore: 'Pass the biscuits, 'cause it's King Biscuit Time.'

Robert Lockwood Jr was a good musician by all accounts, even from a young age – he'd learnt to play the family's pump organ by the age of 12. His mother

Driving into Helena on the weekend of the festival was very different from that first visit. The shuttering had been taken down from the boarded-up shops and I dropped the car's speed down to a crawl to negotiate around groups of festival-goers congregating on Missouri Street. Vendors' stalls lined the footways along Missouri Street and Cherry Street. For a few days a small-time local economy flourishes, meeting the needs of the thousands of festival-goers who descend on Helena for three days of blues. We were waved onto a vacant lot by someone who asked for $10 and I was assured that in return the car's security would be down to him until we left in the evening.

Money comes into town, and for a brief few days at the beginning of October each year downtown Helena recaptures the spirit of its heyday. Indeed, in spite of a significant proportion of Helena's residents having little disposable income,

three of the festival's four stages are free and, as such, festival veterans say what they enjoy about King Biscuit is that much of it takes place on the streets and has an integrated feel about it. Buskers and street musicians line Cherry Street, running power from the local stores to compete with the sounds of the headlining bands from the festival's main stage. Crowds wander over rusting railroad tracks and down alleys that run between semi-derelict warehouses still standing in the streets running down to the levee.

King Biscuit Blues Festival, Helena, Arkansas, 2012.

It's on the smaller stages in the Cherry Street Historic District between Missouri Street and Perry Street where we found the hard-working street musicians that serve as the link between the big contemporary blues stars and the itinerant musicians who passed through countless towns just like Helena over half a century ago. On these stages could be found artists who are still knocking out the 200 gigs a year schedule, many of whom still remember criss-crossing the South in the days of the chitlin' circuit and whose careers have ebbed and flowed over the decades. Artists for whom a night hasn't finished until they've wiped the sweat from their face and sold a few CDs from the side of the stage. One of the highlights of the street stages included Vasti Jackson's rip-roaring lead, which he maintained throughout his ceaseless high-energy set. Jackson has been paying his dues for over four decades; he has been a session guitarist for Malaco Records and Alligator Records and was featured in the Scorsese documentary *The Blues* performing his own composition 'Train Rolling Blues'.

The evening brought with it a dark blue sky that accentuated the lighting on the main stage. A wind got up across the Mississippi and started to whip the large banners that hung at the back of the stage, advertising the bank and casino that supported the festival, as Roy Rogers approached the end of his set. The band toyed with a few bars of rhythmic boogie, and then Rogers ripped into Johnson's '32-20 Blues'. A warm glow came from electric lanterns strung across the stalls of street vendors and the aroma of alligator gumbo, hot tamales and pulled pork wafted across to the crowds sitting on the side of the levee. Halfway through the song Rogers teased the audience with an extended bridge before pulling the band back towards Johnson's song with a touch of Southern boogie. Eight bars of drum roll propelled the band back into Johnson's riff and as Rogers broke into the final verse, pockets of the crowd rose to their feet until everyone on the levee was standing. I welled up slightly, stirred by the artist capturing the moment and by the sudden awareness of the symbolism of a middle-aged, white guitarist rocking up a song that Robert Johnson may well have busked on the streets of downtown Helena or played in the rougher juke joints on Elm Street or the shotgun shacks to the north of the Walker Levee.[16] The juxtaposition of rock 'n' roll theatre and the backdrop of a decaying and dilapidated Southern town held my attention.

Walking into a juke joint a few days earlier, I had been greeted with a handshake from the owner, who'd asked me where I'd come from and enquired if I was going to play, before delivering an amusing yet thought-provoking quip: 'You've sure come a long way to hear your own kind of music.' Standing

by the Walker Levee, I thought back to what he'd said and became aware of how caught up I was with the image of Roy Rogers' triumphal delivery of Robert Johnson's '32-20 Blues' to an audience who had for the most part chosen Helena as the location to share the experience of that music with others. The moment represented for me all those white interpretations of blues that had brought me on this pilgrimage to the Delta. But the scene was being repeated at festivals throughout the Delta all summer. Only a few weeks earlier Robert Plant had played to an audience of thousands just a little further down Highway 61, at Clarksdale.

I'd been reading Paul Garon's *Blues and the Poetic Spirit*; we had visited him in Chicago on the first day of our pilgrimage. I wondered if I'd come all this way to celebrate what is essentially a white interpretation of blues. Perhaps it was even conceivable that I'd come to celebrate its appropriation amidst the backdrop of the appropriated. Garon, one of the founders of *Living Blues* magazine, quotes in his conclusion Thelonious Monk's comments about white dance bands: '(They) carried off the healthiest child of Negro music and starved it of its spirit until its parents no longer recognised it.'[17]

We wandered along Cherry Street and across Elm Street, which by now was full of local youngsters who had come out for the evening to enjoy the carnival atmosphere. Richard and I climbed onto the loading platform of what, from the faded lettering on the wall below the broken windows, had once been a warehouse owned by the Helena Wholesale Grocer Company.[18]

Despite being seated, Big George Brock's large frame, dressed in a deep red suit and matching fedora, dominated the stage. Now in his 80s, Brock originally hailed from Grenada, Mississippi, a town about 60 miles south-east of Clarksdale, and has been a sharecropper, musician, boxer and club owner. He met the likes of Memphis Minnie at house parties when he moved up to the Walls area, and has recalled how he met Howlin' Wolf through hanging around a theatre when he had a job putting the gas line along Highway 61. At the theatre he would help set up equipment or do anything just to be around musicians. It was during this time that he got friendly with Wolf, who eventually let him play. Like so many others around him, Brock moved north in the 1950s; he settled in St Louis and formed Big George and the Houserockers. One of his blues clubs was the Club Caravan on Garrison and Franklin Street, which he ran until he tragically lost his wife in a shooting one night.[19]

Leaving one Mississippi harmonica legend, I wandered back to the levee because another was due on the main stage. We'd first come across James Cotton's name in Chicago, as he had once been a resident in Muddy Waters's South Lake Park Avenue and one in a line of famous harmonica players with Waters's band until he got shot five times.

Like Brock, James Cotton was born in the mid 1930s in Mississippi, the son of a family of sharecroppers. He was given his first harmonica as a Christmas

James Cotton, King Biscuit Blues
Festival, Helena, Arkansas.

present by his mother, who played the harmonica herself, although religious music was played in the home and blues was strictly forbidden. His Damascene moment came when he discovered the King Biscuit show and heard Sonny Boy Williamson playing harp. By the age of 9 Cotton had lost both parents; his Uncle Wiley, who'd recognised the youngster's talent for the harp, took him to Helena, where they sought out Sonny Boy Williamson. Cotton spent the next six years living under the same roof as him. When Cotton was 15, Williamson left the band to find his wife, who had left and gone to Milwaukie, and Cotton found himself as a band leader, but he did not have the maturity to make things work. He ended up moving to Memphis, where he worked on the shoe shine box on Beale Street and in Handy Park. However, he never gave up on music and by the early 1950s was prominent on the Memphis and West Memphis music scene and had had a period playing with Howlin' Wolf's band, the House Rockers. Cotton's big break came in 1954 when Muddy Waters invited him to the Memphis Hippodrome on Beale Street to step into the shoes previously filled by Little Walter and Junior Wells.[20]

I watched the crowd part at the gates as Cotton's stretch limousine pulled up by the edge of the main stage. A conspicuous show of wealth seemed all part of the show and I'd noticed that the grandeur of the stretched limos and tour buses became more impressive throughout the day. I remembered that this was someone who'd rented a room in Muddy Waters's house for near on six years and whose uncle had brought him from a sharecroppers' shack to live with Sonny Boy Williamson when not yet a teenager.

A line of state troopers marched past as we crossed Cherry Street on our way back to our car. By now the wind was gusting stronger and I was becoming a little concerned about crossing the half-mile expanse of bridge back into Mississippi. As we left we drove past the pot-holed streets behind Cherry Street, which had become a car park for police vehicles, the occupants of which were standing round chatting, and a mind-bending whirl of red and blue light strobed across the neighbourhood.

The wind whipped the rain against the windscreen as we made the crossing back into Mississippi and my fears about the bridge being closed proved groundless. The dark line of the levee stretched out ahead of us as we crossed the flood plain on the Mississippi side. Every so often sheet lightning momentarily broke the blackness over the surrounding fields as rain drove tangentially across the beams of the car lights. As we reached Tunica, the rain subsided and a series of lights rose up way off in the distance, lighting up the low clouds hanging over the Delta. We were driving through the heart of the Tunica Resorts and somewhere out in the darkness of the cotton fields, between the illuminated casino complexes, was the little town of Robinsonville.

Notes

1. *Living Blues* 224:44, No. 2, pp.76–91. For a detailed listing of blues festivals held in the United States and Canada see www.livingblues.com.
2. For the purpose of describing a journey that progresses from north to south, the account of the King Biscuit Festival precedes the Highway 61 Festival; however, in 2012, the year of our roadtrip, the Highway 61 Festival was held the week prior to King Biscuit Festival. Likewise other events described are not necessarily in the order that they occurred.
3. Murray, Charles Shaar, *Boogie Man: The Adventures of John Lee Hooker in the American Twentieth Century*, Canongate, 2011, p.27.
4. Lawson, R.A., *Jim Crow's Counterculture: The Blues and Black Southerners*, Louisiana State University Press, 2010, p.137.
5. Lomax, Alan, *The Land Where the Blues Began*, The New Press, 1993, p.221.
6. Gordon, Robert and Nemerov, Bruce (eds), *Lost Delta Found: Rediscovering the Fisk University–Library of Congress Coahoma County Study, 1941–1942*, Vanderbilt University Press, 2005, p.29; for Lewis W. Jones introduction see p.39.
7. Palmer, Robert, *Deep Blues*, Penguin, 1982, p.173.
8. Twain, Mark, *Life on the Mississippi*, Wordsworth, 2012, pp.209–10.
9. 'Helena, Arkansas', www.city-data.com/city/Helena-Arkansas.html.
10. Palmer, *Deep Blues*, pp.187–8. The story was recounted to Robert Palmer in an interview with Robert Lockwood in Cleveland, Ohio, in 1979, where Robert Lockwood had lived since 1960 or '61; Ibid., p.176.
11. Guralnick, Peter, *Searching for Robert Johnson*, Dutton, 1992, pp.18–19.
12. Palmer, *Deep Blues*, p.179.
13. Segrest, James and Hoffman, Mark, *Moanin' at Midnight: The Life and Times of Howlin' Wolf*, Thunder's Mouth Press, p.42.
14. Guralnick, *Searching for Robert Johnson*, p.19.
15. Guralnick, Peter, *Feel Like Going Home*, Omnibus Press, 1978, p.96.

16. Palmer, *Deep Blues*, pp.173–4. Palmer discusses areas in Helena where Johnny Shines, Robert Johnson, Robert Lockwood Jr and Howlin' Wolf would have played.

17. Garon, Paul, *Blues and the Poetic Spirit*, City Lights, 1996, p.204.

18. Silva, Rachel, 'Walks Through History: Cherry Street Historic District', 13 April 2013, www.arkansaspreservation.com.

19. Stolle, Roger, *Hidden History of Mississippi Blues*, The History Press, 2011, pp.115–17. See also Stolle, Roger, 'The Big George Brock Story', *Blues and Rhythm* No. 205, Christmas 2005, pp.16–19.

20. Whiteis, David, 'James Cotton: I'm All Right with the Blues', *Living Blues* 224:44, April 2013, pp.8–17.

7
Juke Joints, Shacks and BBQ:
CLARKSDALE

Fifty miles south of Robinsonville is Clarksdale, the city many argue is the epicentre of the blues. Blues historian Bill Ferris said of the city, 'if there is a musical navel or crossroads for Mississippi Delta blues, it must be on the streets of Clarksdale, a city that lies in the heart of the region known for the blues.'[1] Clarksdale resident, barrelhouse pianist and hired farmhand Jasper Love recalled when interviewed by Ferris in 1968 how in the early 1960s he was scared to death when the English blues researcher Paul Oliver came to meet him accompanied by a white woman. He was particularly afraid because they shook hands with him in the street; even in the 1960s it was still strictly forbidden for a black man to shake the hand of a white woman. Oliver had come to Clarksdale in the summer of 1960, with his wife Valerie, to record Jasper Love as part of a selection of field recordings to illustrate his book *Conversation with the Blues*.[2]

That summer other things were happening in Clarksdale that, as Francoise N. Hamlin's recently published research suggests, are the stories that made the blues. At the same time as Jasper Love was feeling threatened by the handshake of a white woman, two African American women, Irene and Myra Jones, arrived in the city to attend their grandmother's funeral. While they were in Clarksdale they went to Woolworths and sat at the lunch counter. The waitress, under orders from her manager, ignored the women and eventually the manager asked them to leave. The two women complained and then left the store but were later apprehended by police and taken into custody, where they remained until appearing in court the following morning. The judge ordered that after the women had attended their grandmother's funeral they should report back to the City Hall. Thereafter they were followed by a patrolman until their car reached the Mississippi state line.[3]

A few months later Mary Jane Pigee, the daughter of Clarksdale civil rights activist Vera Pigee, sang with the white folksinger Guy Carawan in what has been described as the city's first interracial concert.[4] Carawan stayed in Clarksdale with the Pigees, having met both Mary Jane and her mother at a workshop at the Highlander Folk School. However, Carawan soon attracted the attention of the authorities, and he and his pregnant wife, Candi, found themselves falling foul of the Clarksdale police department, supposedly for committing a traffic offence, which led to them being taken to the police station. Carawan was active in the Highlander Folk School, an organisation that ran workshops based around community and trade union issues and viewed folk music as a central tool in its activities. In 1959 Carawan, in his role as Highlander's co-ordinator of music, had been instrumental in reintroducing spirituals, including 'We Shall Overcome' at workshops for civil rights organisations.[5] Dr Martin Luther King Jr had been a student at the Highlander Folk School at Monteagle, Tennessee, and the song was seen on the nation's televisions as King led the Montgomery, Alabama, bus boycott.[6] The Highlander Folk School at Monteagle was also where Rosa Parks had attended civil rights training courses, prior to her refusal to give up her bus seat to a white man.

Perhaps less well known is the fact that in 1955, when the Highlander Folk School first tried developing links with African American community organisations in Tuskegee, Alabama, it was Lewis Wade Jones (who had worked with Alan Lomax on the Coahoma Study at Clarksdale) who introduced Henry Shipherd, the Highlander leader, to leaders of the African American community in Tuskegee.[7] By this time Lomax – having been listed in *Red Channels*, which named so-called communist influences in the media – had fled the United States to live in Europe so as to avoid Joseph McCarthy's anti-communist witch-hunt, which was being conducted under the auspices of the House Committee on Un-American Activities.[8]

Ten years later, Dr Martin Luther King Jr led a march from Selma to Montgomery in support of voter registration. The Selma marchers had been viciously attacked with clubs and electric cattle prods and hundreds of protesters were jailed, which prompted King to write an open letter to the American people from his cell highlighting that there were more protesters in jail with him than on the voting rolls for Selma.[9] Marching with the protesters over a period of three days was the campaigning white folk singer Pete Seeger, who had been signed by John Hammond to Columbia Records in 1961.

The same John Hammond had publicised Robert Johnson to a white audience and, if it had not been for Johnson's murder, would have brought the 'King of the Delta Blues' to Carnegie Hall. Furthermore, this is the same John Hammond who was so outraged by segregation in the South that he wrote a report for *Down Beat* magazine of Bessie Smith's tragic death in a road accident just outside of Clarksdale. Hammond's report effectively secured into folklore accounts that Smith had bled to death because she'd been refused access to Clarksdale's white hospital.[10] Irrespective of whether this was or was not the actual course of events, and later research suggests it probably wasn't, Hammond's story highlights the reality that the Jim Crow laws conditioned social relations between people, even at the point of death.

What Lomax and the researchers from Fisk found in Clarksdale was music that was the product of a changing society. As Marybeth Hamilton suggests, 'they heard Delta Blues as, in essence, politicised, rife with the tensions bred by wage labour and by the sexual volatility that migration brought in its wake'.[11] Elijah Wald makes the point that one of the reasons why Lomax chose to record music in the Mississippi, rather than other regions that had also been considered, was to record the musicians around Robert Johnson. This in part was due to John Hammond's influence, who had introduced Lomax to Johnson's music.[12] Moreover, Wald also recognises how important the views of Hammond and Lomax were upon liberal opinion when he says that, 'While their influence would virtually reach around the globe, Lomax and Hammond were to a great extent operating within the small bubble of New York liberal intellectual society, and in this world virtually everyone accepted their opinions as definitive when it came to "country blues".'[13]

Much of what we know about Clarksdale and the environment in which the Delta blues flourished in the early 1940s comes from the Coahoma Study. Its field trips not only captured on disc for the first time the music of Muddy Waters, David 'Honeyboy' Edwards and Son House, they also provided documentary evidence of life in Clarksdale's African American community. A few lines in Chapter VI of John Work's summation succinctly captures the state of guitar music in the Delta when the study was undertaken:

The playing of 'Son' House represents the pinnacle of guitar performance. The style he plays elevates the guitar to an equal importance with the voice ... 'Son' House belongs to the generation of Robert Johnson and 'Blind Lemon' Jefferson, who won the attention of the recording companies and created a mild vogue for guitar records in the twenties.

David Edwards and McKinley 'Muddy Water' Morganfield, already referred to several times, are able representatives of the current virtuosic style of performance.

For over twenty years, guitar music in the Delta has been mainly blues.[14]

John Work states that Muddy Waters started playing harmonica after having heard Son House play the guitar. He copied the styles of guitarists by listening endlessly to phonograph records and told the interviewers that a particular favourite of his was Robert Johnson. Waters is also on record as saying that he was in great demand among both Negro and white plantation folk; Work reported that 'for coloured dancers, Morganfield must play blues and music which stems from them, such as "Number Thirteen Highway" and "I'm Goin' Down Slow" – his current favourite piece.'[15]

The Coahoma Study is also important because it gives us a historical snapshot of Clarksdale, as opposed to personal reminiscences by artists at a later date or the product of music business hyperbole. As such it tells us about Honeyboy Edwards, Muddy Waters and Son House at a time when they were all essentially popular or regional musicians, but not nationally well known. Moreover, they had all played with, influenced or been influenced by Robert Johnson, who himself, despite having travelled beyond the Delta, had only experienced limited recording success.

Lomax, in his own account of the study, admits he first heard Johnson's work 'in 1939, when only a handful of us appreciated him'. He adds, 'it is clear that Johnson's recordings stood out as the finest example of the blues along with those of the great Blind Lemon Jefferson in the twenties'.[16] Given that the Coahoma Study had also considered Natchez, Adams County, Mississippi; Ripley, Tennessee, and Carthage, Mississippi, as locations, perhaps it was the hope of locating the pinnacle of Jim Crow blues within an emerging rural proletariat that appealed to the New York opinion maker. As Marybeth Hamilton suggests:

In the blues of the Delta, the Fisk team heard not the voice of folk, but of the black proletariat – secular, urban, flouting tradition. Their stress on the music's modernity echoed Sterling Brown, Langston Hughes and other African-American intellectuals who like Charles Johnson had come of age in the New Negro movement. And in describing it as proletarian music they evoked a rallying point for some of the American left: a vision of African Americans as a revolutionary vanguard. Like Richard Wright, like Langston Hughes, they sought the radical potential of African American culture.[17]

When Lomax and Work arrived in Clarksdale, they drove into a city that had a population of 12,000, of whom 10,000 were African Americans.[18] Today the population is just under 18,000 and the countryside around has undergone massive depopulation. Just over 40 per cent of those living in the city survive below the poverty line and this figure increases to nearly 47 per cent for African Americans.

Samuel C. Adams described how in the 1940s plantation 'negros' would come into the city and frequent the areas of the New World District around

Bridge over Highway 61, Clarksdale.

Three-guitar sculpture marking the junction of Highway 49 and 61 at The Crossroads, Clarksdale, Mississippi.

Fourth, Issaquena and Sunflower Street. Of Sunflower Street, Adams noted this 'is the "roughest" of all places. The major attraction on this street is "Tommy's Place", since this is the only place in Clarksdale where Negro youth are allowed to dance.'[19] However, today's Clarksdale doesn't boast the nine juke joints that Adams recorded.

When we arrived in Clarksdale, it was just over seventy years since Lomax had described the bustle of the New World District. It was mid-week and I had a feeling things would be fairly quiet, although I'd heard that the King Biscuit festival at Helena and the Highway 61 Blues Festival at Leland had been arranged back-to-back so as to encourage blues pilgrims to stay in the Delta. That being the case, there was a good chance there'd be some music going on somewhere close by. We came into town and made the obligatory stop at the junction of Highways 61 and 49, which in blues pilgrimage mythology is of course The Crossroads, and is marked by a large, blue steel sign with three guitars pointing in three directions.

An equally iconic sign at The Crossroads announces 'Abe's BBQ Drive-in', a diner tucked along North State Street within a few metres of the crossroads. It's complemented by another sign that tells you that you've arrived at 'Abe's at the Legendary Crossroads'. I pulled the car onto the forecourt and thought there was no better way for a blues pilgrim to pay respects to Robert Johnson than to pop in and sample Abe's hot tamales, which of course I had with chillies in accordance with Johnson's red-hot tamales.

Abraham Davis, the father of Pat Davis, the present owner, came to the Mississippi from Lebanon in 1913 and opened a barbeque called the Bungalow Inn in 1924. In 1936 the restaurant moved to its crossroads location and Davis jokes that Robert Johnson would sit where the sycamore trees stand today, strumming his guitar, having a drink while eating one of his barbeques. Like The Crossroads, maybe this is just another apocryphal story, but it is symbolic of the history that begot the blues, because Abe's was one of only two restaurants on the highway that would serve all races. Davis has recalled how in 1947 his father defended the right of two black customers to eat in the restaurant and be left alone when four white men dealt them a tirade of racist abuse and threatened his father's livelihood if he served black customers.[20]

In 1965 the restaurants along the highway were visited by young African Americans to test whether or not they would serve black customers. Of all the restaurants visited only Abe's BBQ and the Chamoun's Rest Haven, another Lebanese restaurant on Highway 61, would serve the youngsters.[21]

I left Abe's forecourt and the crossroads with a new image of Robert Johnson in my mind's eye: a young man sitting by the sycamore trees playing his guitar, eating one of Abe's tamales, with a copy of *New Masses* secreted in the inside pocket of his pin-striped suit. Far-fetched maybe, but more real than a midnight liaison with Lucifer.

The rusting freight train that lined the rail tracks on the bridge over Highway 61 appeared not to have moved since my last visit to Clarksdale. In the rear view mirror I caught a glimpse of the blue and white graffiti across the railroad bridge that seemed to proudly spell out the city's name, as if to declare to passing motorists that this wasn't just any old community.

Reaching the bridge over the Sunflower River, we turned into Sunflower Avenue and drove past rows of blue-painted timbered houses on one side and the banks of the Sunflower River on the other.

When Lomax crossed the tracks and entered the African American New World District for the first time he was unprepared for the experience. In *The Land Where the Blues Began* he describes the bustle and excitement on the streets, the slick young sheiks in Harlem drape-shape coats and women in poor dresses as well as the latest fashions. He talks about how every make and vintage of car lined the curbs and of the people drinking in the bars with the sound of the juke boxes blasting out. Lomax's portrayal of the revelry in the New World District includes a guitarist with a black felt hat who sucked and blew on a harmonica on a rack whilst a blowsy woman in house slippers danced seductively before flinging herself around the young Honeyboy Edwards.[22] This was the same guitarist who John Work refers to in the Coahoma Study as maintaining a devoted following, despite pressure from audiences to perform the popular songs heard on the juke box.[23] Lomax admits that when Edwards finished playing, however much he wanted to, he was too timid to follow him into one of the juke joints.

I pulled over and parked by the footway outside the Riverside Hotel, just as I had five years earlier when I'd arrived for Clarksdale's annual Juke Joint Festival. An event at which I was fortunate enough to see a very senior Honeyboy Edwards perform.

The building served as the G.T. Thomas African American Hospital prior to 1940, and in 1944 became Clarksdale's Riverside Hotel, run by Mrs Z.L. Hill, where African Americans could stay when visiting Clarksdale.

Hill's son, Frank Ratliff, the current proprietor of the Riverside, has been running tours of the hotel for guests and visitors since his mother's death in 1997. We followed him through the long corridor of the hotel that juts out over the bank of the Sunflower River as he tapped on the door of each room pointing out where Robert Nighthawk, Sonny Boy Williamson, Howlin' Wolf and Ike Turner and his band would stay. (Ike Turner lived at the Riverside for a period when he was a youngster.) Frank's tours always finished back at room 2, the room to which Bessie Smith was brought following the car accident. This is the room where she died and it is maintained as a shrine to the singer.

It appeared that Frank's health had deteriorated since my last visit, yet he still gave us the tour of the hotel. Due to an error on my part our room had been double booked, so Frank made us up a room in the basement and explained that at the end of the corridor Ike Turner, Jackie Brenston and the band had rehearsed 'Rocket 88' and recorded the demo before driving up to Sun Studios. Apparently, Frank's mother had sewn the badges on the band's ties.

Abe's BBQ at The Crossroads, Clarksdale, Mississippi.

In the evening Richard and I walked along the bank of the Sunflower River, passing the mix of clapboard houses that border the edge of the New World District, until we reached Red's Lounge. Red Paden sat by the door, next to old crates and the tamale oven, collecting $5 cover charges as we entered. Red's Lounge, which even *Here's Clarksdale*, the monthly magazine of Clarksdale culture, described as looking closed and scary, still bears the name Lavine's Music Center above its tattered canopy: the music store where Ike Turner once bought his instruments.

My eyes took a bit of time to grow accustomed to the gloom inside Red's Lounge. Fittingly, it does have an ambient red glow, but there was just enough light to make out the plastic sheeting fixed to the ceiling, exposing the joint's general state of disrepair. Of course, the combination of the juke joint's decor

and the Delta blues artists who perform there is exactly why Red's attracts blue pilgrims from all around the world. As Roger Stolle says of the juke joint experience, 'An evening spent in a crowded, sweaty, Delta juke with live music, dancers and drink is as close as you can get to time travel. It's history with one foot in the grave.'[24]

The bartender leant into a long chest fridge and used a car inspection lamp to locate the beers I'd ordered and then rummaged round in a bucket for change. As the juke filled up, many of the faces were familiar from the Helena Festival and other Delta towns we'd visited. People started swapping stories about the places they'd found and everyone seemed to be searching for that one last authentic juke joint that was not to be missed.

We walked back along the river to the hotel; Frank was still up and invited us into the lounge. We chatted about our journey as Frank drew on a cigarette and regaled us with memories of the legendary artists that had stayed in the rooms further down the corridor. Some months later, while I was writing the account of our time in Clarksdale, I heard the news that Frank had died. The news felt like another link with the past had been broken and I knew that

Riverside Hotel, Clarksdale, Mississippi.

Red's Lounge, Clarksdale, Mississippi.

Frank's death would touch people across the world who had been privileged enough to hear his insights into the city's blues history at first hand. Frank's daughter, Zelena, continues to run the hotel and make blues pilgrims from around the world welcome.

Morning sun streamed down Sunflower Avenue and we found Frank, along with a handful of tenants and guests, sitting out front. Someone was sorting laundry and others were just passing the time of day. I asked Frank how to get to the building which had once housed Aaron Henry's Fourth Street pharmacy, as I had read it was just round the corner from the Riverside. Henry, born on the Flowers Plantation, Clarksdale, had fought in the Second World War and been president of the Mississippi National Association for the Advancement of Colored People (NAACP). He'd been one of the most prominent civil rights activists in Mississippi and at the heart of the African American community's struggle through the 1960s and '70s.

Frank explained that the pharmacy had burnt down in 1993, which I found slightly ironic, considering that it had survived two attacks in 1963 at the height of the voter registration drive, including being bombed. This period saw an increase in support from both black and white civil rights campaigners outside of the community, as well as the organisation of food shipments following the withdrawal of community winter relief from African American families who had participated in civil rights campaigns. This was at a time when less than 10 per cent of those who tried to register to vote were successful. It wasn't only the pharmacy that was bombed; a month earlier US Congressman Charles Diggs was at Henry's home on Page Avenue, a few blocks away from the pharmacy, when a bottle filled with gasoline or kerosene was thrown through the window at 3 a.m., while the occupants of the house, including Henry's 11-year-old daughter slept.[25] Congressman Diggs had witnessed the trial of the murderers of Emmett Till and it probably came as little surprise to Henry or Diggs when the two fire-bombers, who had explained their actions as a prank, were released soon after the incident.

The first time I crossed the tracks and explored Fourth Street had been to find the New Roxy Theater on Issaquena Avenue. At the time the theatre was in a state of disrepair, although its marquee was being used as a cover and backdrop for blues artists playing in the New World District throughout the weekend. The theatre had served as the picture house for the New World District and has recently been restored to an open-air theatre. Today a Blues Trail marker outside the New Roxy commemorates the singer Sam Cooke, born a few blocks away on Seventh Street, who wrote and recorded 'A Change is Gonna Come'.

On this occasion, some five years following my first visit, as we made our way from Red's Lounge to the New Roxy, we passed the surviving buildings between the vacant lots along Fourth Street. Through the work of Françoise Hamlin, from her time living in Coahoma State and her extensive research undertaken thereafter, the story of ordinary Clarksdale women and men and their roles in the black freedom struggle has been pieced together. Hamlin doesn't dismiss blues history or those who travel thousands of miles to come to Clarksdale to feel closer to it, but instead she challenges those of us who do to consider it in the wider historical context of the communities out of which it rose. She argues that:

> Clarksdale's African American history resonates much deeper than the musical melodies emanating from the juke joints and the fields. The fact that the blues, a musical form documenting hard life and harder knocks, found a fertile home here speaks to the stories of struggle and survival on the ground where it matured.[26]

It's difficult not to read these streets and buildings through the narrative that Hamlin constructs. In 1962 Dr Martin Luther King Jr made a two-day tour of Coahoma County where he made contact with more than 5,000 people at country stores, plantations, cotton gins and schools. King had come to Clarksdale to address a meeting of 1,000 people at the First Baptist Church in support of voter registration for African Americans and expressed the determination 'to send the first member of that race to congress since Reconstruction'.[27] Further along Fourth, on the opposite side of the street, stood the Haven Methodist Church, where a great proportion of Clarksdale's civil rights meetings were held and where Dr Martin Luther King Jr also spoke and met many of the city's young men. The Haven Methodist Church was used as a storage centre for the provisions of clothes and food sent by supporters of the civil rights struggle during the 1960s. Just as the homes and shops of local people active in the civil rights struggle were at risk of attack, so too were the churches. On 3 April 1963 a gas bomb was thrown into a crowd of 800 people attending a voter registration rally at the Centennial Baptist Church, situated a block away.[28]

Leaving the New World District, we made our way under the bridge over Issaquena Avenue and stopped at the Clarksdale passenger depot. Here, on a summer's day in 1943, just a couple of years after being recorded for the Coahoma Study, Muddy Waters walked off his job as a tractor driver on the Stovall plantation following an argument with a new overseer, Ellis Rhett, regarding wages and caught the train to Chicago, becoming another statistic in the Great Migration northwards.[29] That same year Mary Jane Pigee was born. Eighteen years later she, along with two other teenage members of the NAACP youth council, would be arrested for attempting to buy train tickets from the white ticket counter at the station.[30]

Slightly overwhelmed by the historical significance attached to the buildings we'd visited that morning, I decided to pay a visit to the Delta Blues Museum, which is housed in the old ICR freight depot building next to the old station. At the far end of the museum stands Muddy Waters's shotgun shack, which features in the historic photograph of Waters sitting outside playing guitar, with

New Roxy Theater, Clarksdale, Mississippi.

Son Sims on fiddle, in the summer of 1943, just prior to Waters's departure for Chicago. It has been rescued from its original site because it had fallen prey to overzealous blues pilgrims, who over the years had removed splinters of it as a form of relic. As I sat on the floor of the museum and leaned back on the wall of Waters's cabin, I let the sound of blues music waft over me.

Blues tourism has moved on since I first visited Clarksdale. Roger Stolle, the owner of the Cat Head Delta Blues and Folk Art store on Delta Avenue, still tells the story of how, only a few years ago, downtown Clarksdale would simply evacuate at 5.15 p.m. and it was a question of who would be the last person out of downtown. There was very little for any visitor to do after the shops had closed. Stolle's enthusiasm for what the town has to offer is always apparent and he's proud that today there are at least three restaurants open most nights of the week. In many respects Stolle serves as the linchpin when it comes to what's happening in blues and tourism, which isn't surprising, as he's combined the store's activities with raising the profile of surviving Delta blues artists; has produced blues artists such as Big George Brock; and has co-directed and co-produced the films *We Juke Up in Here!* and *M for Mississippi*. For his efforts he was awarded a 2009 Blues Music Award. When I visited Cat Head, Stolle told me he was working on a new film – *Moonshine and Mojo Hands*, with his past collaborator Jeff Konkel – about travelling Mississippi's back roads looking for the blues. He explained that there is now blues on somewhere in Clarksdale virtually seven nights a week throughout the year; yet when he first came to Mississippi, many of the old musicians weren't working simply because the venues and the publicity opportunities had ceased to exist.

Red Top Lounge juke joint, Clarksdale, Mississippi.

A year before Stolle arrived in Clarksdale, Morgan Freeman and Bill Luckett opened the Ground Zero Blues Club next to the Delta Blues Museum, offering local food and live music as well as accommodation for visitors in its Delta Cotton apartments above the club. The club has a juke joint feel to it and can accommodate large audiences and high-profile bands, yet still feels homely on evenings when just a few people are in town. When we spoke to Bill Luckett at his club, he rightly pointed out that none of the juke joints in Clarksdale are original. Indeed, it's completely unrealistic to expect joints like the Dipsie Doodle, referred to in the Coahoma Study, or the Red Top Lounge, established around 1947, to still be functioning. I can't think of many clubs, taverns or theatres in which I saw some of the best music of my generation that still survive today, yet for some reason we expect a small town that has experienced huge demographic shifts and economic change, to remain just as it was. For me, what's so amazing about Clarksdale is the extent of the historic blues archaeology that's still here to be seen. That you can also spend the evening listening to local Mississippi blues artists in a juke joint that's run by the likes of Red Paden, who's been running joints in the area for more than forty years, is a bonus. It's the synergy of all the businesses and the combined efforts of local entrepreneurs that are keeping a blues flame burning in Clarksdale.

That night we were booked into the Shack Up Inn, Clarksdale's fastest-growing accommodation provider aimed specifically at blues pilgrims, which is situated on the Hopson plantation, off of old Highway 49 just on the edge of Clarksdale. We parked by the plantation office, booked in at the Cotton Gin and took possession of the keys to a sharecropper's shack, which was original on the outside but came with air-conditioning and plumbing on the inside. The Cotton Gin doubled as office, bar and breakfast room and had a stage set up with instruments for anyone in the mood to play a little impromptu blues. Other blues pilgrims were relaxing after a day on the road. The evening breeze lowered the outside temperature a little as we sat on the benches in the yard outside the Cotton Gin and swapped information with one another over beers. The talk was of the small rural towns we'd found which still had juke joints and the down-home restaurants off the beaten track that sold the best fried catfish or the most succulent pulled pork. Many of the those staying at the Shack Up Inn that night, like us, were exploring the Delta mid-week between the Helena and Leland blues festivals and expressed opinions about the artists they'd seen so far and which ones they hoped to see during the coming days.

After a couple of beers I left and wandered around the plantation buildings, intrigued as to which structures had survived from a time before mechanisation, when shacks similar to the ones here now would have housed the sharecroppers. Looking at pictures taken as part of the New Deal's Farm Security Administration in 1939 and 1940 it appears that the outer structures of the Cotton Gin and the Hopson Commissary and office have changed little.

The extent to which the Delta was changing at the time of Waters's departure from Clarksdale is captured in an April 1944 letter from Richard Howell, the manager of the Hopson plantation office, to the local cotton industry association. In it he urges the cotton plantations of the Delta to introduce mechanised cotton production for two reasons: first, that it would overcome the growing problem of African American flight from the Mississippi in search of better life, and second because of what he described as 'the serious racial problem which confronts us at this time' and suggested that mechanisation would help 'equalise the white and black population'.[31] Nicholas Lemann quotes Aaron Henry as saying, 'They wished we'd go back to Africa, but Chicago was close enough.' Six months after Howell sent his letter, the Hopson plantation put on the first demonstration of a cotton field being harvested by eight mechanical cotton pickers. They replaced the work of 400 pickers and the system of sharecropping would soon be replaced by the use of casual day labour.[32]

The following morning I walked back to the plantation office to take a closer look at the vintage cotton picking machines that stand rusting by the side of the railroad track opposite the plantation office. The early morning sun sent shafts of light across the fields, reflecting off the chrome work on the trucks heading south down Highway 49. Visitors were emerging from the sharecroppers' shacks, some sitting out reading papers on the verandas, reading and drinking coffee as the sun rose over Mississippi.

After breakfast we drove back through Clarksdale for the final time and followed the swampy bayous and the Cyprus trees of Deer Creek that border the Stovall plantation. I slowed the car down as three Delta dogs out for a morning's scavenge wandered into the road in no great rush; I recalled on my first visit to Clarksdale coming across Maude Schuyler Clay's photographs of these dog that wander the roads across the Delta.

A lone Blues Trail marker stood under the trees that bordered the edge of the Stovall cotton fields. From the road, a gravel track led off and cut a line through the cotton until it seemed to meet the horizon. The only clue as to where Waters's wooden shack once stood is a small mound on the grass. Only the cypress trees on the bank of the creek opposite broke the monotony of the Delta's interminable flatness. Not surprising then that the young McKinley Morganfield would play in the swampy waters of Deer Creek, attracting the name Muddy.

The Delta dogs caught up with us and one broke from the others, sidled up to my leg and sniffed my pocket for food. As soon as you are outside the towns, these dogs are as much part of the landscape as the cotton fields and the bayous. Maybe on that hot last day of August when Alan Lomax and John Work had driven alongside the creek on their way to meet Waters they too had met lazy Delta dogs.

There was just one last place I needed to visit before departing Clarksdale and heading south to Greenville and Leland. Friars Point, once a busy cotton port and one of the ferry crossings over to Helena, was another couple of miles north of Stovall. The port fell outside of the jurisdiction of Clarksdale, which despite the boisterous reputation of its New World District enforced a midnight curfew on its African American residents. As a result revellers would disperse to the plantations or Friars Point, where late-night partying could continue without hindrance from the law. And it was here that Robert Johnson and Robert Nighthawk would play. The town even gets a mention (along with Rosedale and Vicksburg) in Robert Johnson's 'Travelling Riverside Blues', and he alludes to the fact that the riverside towns can party all night without restrictions when he sings 'best come back to Friars Point, Mama, where we can barrelhouse all night long'.[33]

Between Clarksdale and Friars Point there's very little apart from farmland, broken only by the occasional timber shack and a few solitary trees at the perimeter of the fields. The line of telegraph poles offers the only clue that the road doesn't simply stop at the Mississippi River. Just before the road reached the levee, we passed a mixture of well-kept bungalows with lawns, small enclaves of mobile homes, a few boarded-up shops and groups of ageing wooden shacks. Friar's Point, a town with a 95 per cent African American population, like so many Delta towns, has the outward appearance of a community that combines the reasonably off alongside substantial numbers of those who have very little; this is reflected in the fact that just under 40 per cent of the town's 1,200 residents have an income below the poverty level.[34] I aimed for the water tower, which I guessed was close to the centre of town, and parked by a rusting military tank and tractor on the lawn outside the small North Delta Museum. The town has the feel of a forgotten rural outpost, except that very few work the land anymore. In fact, of those in work, only

4.1 per cent have agricultural jobs and nearly half of Friars Point's residents fortunate enough to have employment work in service industries, which no doubt included the riverside casinos.

The town's most notable past resident is blues slide guitarist Robert Nighthawk, who, although born across the river in Arkansas, often used Friars Point as a base for his drifting lifestyle. Francis Davis argues that one of Nighthawk's weaknesses was that he was forever returning to the Delta and never stayed in cities long enough to establish himself as one the greats alongside his contemporaries like Howlin' Wolf, Muddy Waters and Sonny Boy Williamson II. Only a year before his death he could still be found playing at Maxwell Street Market.[35] Nighthawk went back to Friars Point so often that he even recorded a song that included the lyric 'going back to Friars Point'.

Even before Waters had played a note on a guitar he knew Nighthawk from around Clarksdale and Nighthawk played at Waters's first wedding.[36] Waters told Jim O'Neal and Amy van Singel that Nighthawk 'definitely knew Robert Johnson, because they all grew up around Friars Point way'.[37]

Richard had wandered over the road from the museum and sat on one of the bench seats outside of Hirsberg's drugstore, keen to sit where, according to Muddy Waters, Johnson had busked to a large group; Waters had gone to peek over the crowd, but he was so overwhelmed by the guitarist's virtuosity that he turned and left.[38] Waters would say later that he never saw Johnson that day, just heard him through the crowd. This amused me, as I often tell people how from the roof of an open-top double-decker bus positioned to overlook the Capital Blues Festival at Alexandra Palace I got to hear Muddy Waters but never got to see him.

Notes

1. Ferris, Bill, *Give My Poor Heart Ease*, University of North Carolina Press, 2009, p.143.
2. Oliver, Paul, (liner notes), *Conversation with the Blues*, Paul Oliver, Decca, Mono LK 4664, 1965.
3. Hamlin, Françoise N., *Crossroads at Clarksdale: The Black Freedom Struggle in the Mississippi Delta after World War II*, University of North Carolina Press, 2012, p.78.
4. Ibid., p.80. This volume provides a detailed history of the role of local Clarksdale activists in the civil rights struggle.
5. Roy, William G., *Reds, Whites, and Blues*, Princeton University Press, 2010, p.167.
6. Noebel, David A., *The Marxist Minstrels*, American Christian College Press, 1974, p.176.
7. Roy, *Reds, Whites, and Blues*, p.159.
8. Filene, Benjamin, *Romancing the Folk – Public Memory and American Roots Music*, University of North Carolina Press, 2000, p.163.
9. Wilkinson, Brenda, *The Civil Rights Movement*, Crescent Books, 1997, pp.136–7.
10. Davis, Francis, *The History of the Blues: The Roots Music and the People*, Da Capo, 2003, pp.78–9.
11. Hamilton, Marybeth, 'The Blues, the folk, and African American history', *Transactions of the Royal Historical Society* 11:17–35, 2001, pp.29–30.

12. Wald, Elijah, *Escaping the Delta: Robert Johnson and the Invention of the Blues*, Amistad, 2004, p.231.
13. Ibid.
14. Work III, John W., Coahoma Study – untitled manuscript, in Gordon, Robert and Nemerov, Bruce (eds), *Lost Delta Found: Rediscovering the Fisk University–Library of Congress Coahoma County Study, 1941–1942*, Vanderbilt University Press, 2005, p.88.
15. Ibid., pp.118–20.
16. Lomax, Alan, *The Land Where the Blues Began*, The New Press, 1993, p.13.
17. Hamilton, 'The Blues, the Folk and African-American history', p.29.
18. Adams, Samuel C., 'Changing Negro life in the Delta', in Gordon and Nemerov, *Lost Delta Found*, p.229.
19. Ibid., p.231.
20. Drash, Wayne, 'Barbecue, Bible and Abe chase racism from Mississippi rib joint', CNN, edition.cnn.com.2009/TRAVEL/09/04/Mississippi.
21. Montagne, Renee, 'Kibbe at the crossroads – A Lebanese kitchen story', NPR News, 2008, www.npr.org/2008/01/31/18547399/kibbe-at-the-crossroads-a-lebanese-kitchen-story.
22. Lomax, *Land Where the Blues Began*, pp.30–1.
23. Work, Coahoma Study, in Gordon and Nemerov, *Lost Delta Found*, p.86.
24. Stolle, Roger, *Hidden History of Mississippi Blues*, The History Press, 2011, p.67.
25. *Chicago Defender*, daily edition, 15 April 1963, p.2. *ProQuest Historical Newspapers: The Chicago Defender (1910–1975)*.
26. Hamlin, *Crossroads at Clarksdale*, p.1.
27. 'King says Mississippi can elect five negro congressmen', Southern Christian Leadership Conference press release, 8 February 1962. Accessed at *The King Center Archive* www.thekingCenter.org/archive/document/sclc-press-release-about-mississippi-political-rally.
28. Hamlin, *Crossroads at Clarksdale*, p.109.
29. Gordon, Robert, *Can't Be Satisfied: The Life and Times of Muddy Waters*, Pimlico, 2003, pp.63–4.
30. *Chicago Defender*, daily edition, 29 August 1961.
31. Lemann, Nicholas, *The Promised Land: The Great Black Migration and How It Changed America*, Vintage Books, 1992, pp.49–50.
32. Ibid., see pp.3–7 for discussion of the impact of mechanised picking and the role of the Hopson plantation.
33. Wald, *Escaping the Delta*, see pp.180–1 for discussion of the lyrics of 'Travelling Riverside Blues' and references to Friars Point.
34. *United States Census Bureau*, US Department of Commerce, factfinder2.census.gov/faces/nav/jsf/pages/community_facts.xhtml.
35. Davis, *The History of the Blues*, p.190.
36. Gordon, *Can't Be Satisfied*, p.28.
37. Ibid., pp.26–7.
38. Ibid., p.31.

1. Chuck Berry statue, by sculptor Harry Weber, Chuck Berry Plaza, Delmar Boulevard, St Louis.

2. W.C. Handy's house, Beale Street, Memphis, Tennessee.

3. Beale Street, Memphis, Tennessee.

4. The Arcade Restaurant, Main Street, Memphis, Tennessee.

5. Ground Zero Blues Club, Clarksdale, Mississippi.

6. Ground Zero Blues Club, Clarksdale, Mississippi.

7. Blues mural where W.C. Handy first heard the blues in 1903, Tutwiler, Mississippi.

8. Triple B Tires and Carwash, Highway 61, Baton Rouge.

9. Burgundy Street, the French Quarter, New Orleans, Louisiana.

10. Houses in the French Quarter, New Orleans, Louisiana.

11. Twin bridges, Interstate 55.

12. Stax Museum, McLemore Avenue, Memphis, Tennessee.

13. 'The Great Migration' mural, by Marcus Akinlana, at Elliott Donnelly Youth Center, South Side, Chicago, Illinois.

14. Bronze statue at the site of Maxwell Street Market.

15. Derelict gas station, Money Road, Mississippi.

16. The grave of Howlin' Wolf (Chester A. Burnett), Oakridge cemetery, Cook County, Illinois.

17. School buses.

18. Beale Street takes a rest, Memphis, Tennessee.

19. Sun Studio, 706 Union Avenue, Memphis, Tennessee.

20. Lorraine Motel, site of Dr Martin Luther King Jr's assassination, Memphis, Tennessee.

21. Jimmy Reed mural, Leland, Mississippi, honouring the life and music of Mathis James Reed.

22. Po' Monkey's Lounge, Merigold, established by Willie Seaberry (pictured) in 1963.

23. The New Roxy Theater, Issaquena Avenue, New World District, Clarksdale, Mississippi.

24. Greyhound bus station, Clarksdale, Mississippi.

25. Highway 61, Mississippi.

26. Vasti Jackson, King Biscuit Blues Festival, Helena, Arkansas.

27. Cherry Street, Historic District, King Biscuit Blues Festival, Helena, Arkansas.

28. Robert Johnson's headstone, Little Zion Missionary Baptist Church, Money Road, near Greenwood, Mississippi.

29. Voodoo shop in the French Quarter, New Orleans, Louisiana.

30. Classic Diner, Missouri.

32. Miss Del's General Store, Clarksdale, Mississippi.

33. James Cotton at the King Biscuit Blues Festival, Helena, Arkansas.

8

The Ghosts of Emmett Till:
TUTWILER TO GREENVILLE

As we left Clarksdale along Highway 49, a feeling of the Delta's emptiness grew on me, along with a sense of its abandonment. We'd only driven a few miles out of Clarksdale when the endless panorama of soya and cotton fields was broken by a forest of cypress trees with buttressed trunks which rose out of the swampy water by the side of the highway. It was an elemental, almost prehistoric scene, which contrasted with the mile upon mile of flat, cultivated land we'd seen thus far. Was this how the Delta looked a mere century or so ago? In an interview for the Coahoma Study, Phineas MacClain spoke of a frontier land, of going all over by boat and of the places he fished, where there was later cotton and corn.[1] Pioneers like MacClain described a land that was mysterious; a land where ex-slaves could make a future. The pioneers who came here to clear the forest and the swamps came as free men, albeit poor ones. Plantation capital and small-holders acquired the land while African Americans brought the skills they had acquired under slavery. New forms of tenure relationships emerged between those who owned and those who worked the land, of which one, sharecropping, would gain ascendency.

In the half century between the clearance of these seemingly primordial swamps and the great migration to the urban landscapes of the mid-western cities, blues began in the Delta. By the late 1920s the blues guitarists from the Delta were being recorded, but by and large their popularity was minor in comparison to the women vaudeville singers like Mamie Smith, Ma Rainey, Bessie Smith, Clara Smith, Ida Cox and Ethel Waters. Such women had attracted the attention of the record companies from 1920, after Mamie Smith's 'Crazy Blues' sold 75,000 copies.[2] Although companies continued to record male blues guitarists through and after the Depression, their sales tended to be local and relatively small in comparison with pre-Depression sales of the women blues singers. For instance, it's believed that Robert Johnson's most successful hit, 'Terraplane Blues', sold no more than 4,000 records. During the height of vaudeville in the 1920s, the women blues singers mentioned above could attract weekly earnings in the region of $2,000 to $4,000, which puts the record sales of the male blues guitarist into context.

After a couple of miles, a sign on the side of a water tower informed us we were approaching Tutwiler and proudly proclaimed the town as the birthplace of the blues. A highway patrol car sat on the grass close to the gas station at the edge of town, watching those that drove in and out of town and across the bridge that runs through the centre of Tutwiler. Cypress trees grew along the middle of the river, like a line of markers pointing to the heart of the town. It had been five years since I'd first driven there and asked as to the whereabouts of Sonny Boy Williamson's grave. I thought then that it was odd that the two local people we spoke to seemed unaware of the existence of the grave in such a small rural town. Tutwiler still looked as lazy as it had on my first visit. A few youngsters hung around a boarded-up store by the side of a square and in the distance a couple holding hands walked under the canopy of trees shading the old railroad. Our car bumped over the railway crossing; the buckled rail tracks run past the crumbling remnants of the platform of a railroad depot. Only the murals painted on the walls of Front Street's surviving buildings and a solitary Mississippi Blues Trail marker, hint at Tutwiler's place in blues history.

Today the couple of shops by the station square look closed, as they no doubt did in the early hours of the morning in 1903 when W.C. Handy was stranded on the platform waiting for a train that had been delayed for nine hours. A mural on the wall opposite the platform depicts the scene as Handy described it:

> a lean loose-jointed Negro … commenced plunking a guitar beside me while I slept. His clothes were rags; his feet peeped out of his shoes. His face had on it some of the sadness of the ages. As he played, he pressed a knife on the strings of the guitar in a manner popularised by Hawaiian guitarists who used steel bars.[3]

Handy, fascinated by the sound, which he described as the weirdest music he had ever heard, asked the singer the meaning of his lyrics of 'Goin' where the Southern cross' the Dog'. The singer said he was on his way to Moorhead,

Blues mural, Front Street, Tutwiler, Mississippi.

where the Yazoo and Mississippi Valley Railroad crossed the tracks of the Southern Railroad.

There has been much speculation as to whether Handy's account was true or an allegory which conveyed that he and his band 'were all musicians who bowed strictly to the authority of the printed notes' and had adapted a vernacular music 'that did not come from books'; rather, 'suffering and hard luck were the midwives that birthed these songs. The blues was conceived in aching hearts.'[4] Handy's account, as Marybeth Hamilton suggests, can be seen as a foundation myth that communicates something about the essence of the blues and a truth inherent within it.[5]

However, Hamilton draws attention to the fact that the Handy story locates the birth of the blues in its discovery rather than its invention.[6] And yet, it is in 1941, the same year that Handy's story is published, that Lomax and the Fisk University academics locate the blues in a modernising Clarksdale, emerging from a world where the old order was rapidly changing, in a period of urbanisation, electrification and on the cusp of rural mechanisation. Unlike Handy's bluesman at the station, a product of the old plantation order, the Coahoma Study found that it was the younger generation that had a greater preference for blues. As Fisk scholar Samuel C. Adams noted in his thesis 'Changing Negro Life in the Delta', when Clarksdale residents were asked to name their favourite songs, 'the younger generation listed more than twice the number of blues as given by the older generation'.[7]

Ma Rainey, when interviewed by John Work, told of a girl who came to the tent of the troupe she was travelling with one morning in 1902. Rainey recalled the girl creating a sound that was so strange and poignant it attracted much attention, and so she incorporated the song into her act. Not only did Rainey use the song, she claimed that when she was asked what sort of music it was, she responded by saying, in what she described as her moment of inspiration, 'it's the Blues'.[8]

Interestingly though, Rainey doesn't discover the young blues singer in the Mississippi, but much further north, in Missouri. Neither did the first of the blues singer guitarists (scouted by record companies seeking songs for the new African American record market) originate from the Delta. These included down-home blues singer guitarists of the likes of Sylvester Weaver from Georgia, with 'Guitar Rag' and 'Guitar Blues', in 1923; Papa Charlie Jackson, from New Orleans and living in Chicago, with 'Lawdy Lawdy Blues', in 1924. One of the most successful of the lone blues singer guitarists was Blind Lemon Jefferson from Dallas, Texas, whose first release was 'Booster Blues' in April 1926. The more sophisticated sound of Lonnie Johnson, from New Orleans, with 'Mr Johnson's Blues' was released in 1925. It wasn't until the summer of 1926 that the first of the recordings of Mississippi Delta blues were made (by the Okeh record company); Tommy Johnson was recorded in 1928, and Charley Patton in 1929.

As I sat on the concrete platform conjuring up images of Handy's mythical lean, loose-jointed guitarist, the lyrics, 'I feel so sad and lonesome and I could not help but cry' came to mind. Richard paced the length of the murals on the wall across from the tracks, looking at them through various camera lenses. Sitting on the platform at Tutwiler it occurred to me just how powerful a few songs heard at a formative age had been. Forty years later I'd come thousands of miles to a deprived town in one of America's poorest states because of a few tunes on a live album that had got under my skin. The title of that album tipped a nod to a Blind Boy Fuller record; Fuller, as it happened, was another guitarist John Hammond wanted to feature at Carnegie Hall. Like Robert Johnson, Fuller didn't make it – he was serving a prison sentence for shooting his wife.[9]

Our trip to Tutwiler had brought us some 40 miles east of Highway 61 and over to the Tallahatchie River side of the Delta. The Delta is so littered with blues pilgrimage sites it made sense to stray from Highway 61 for a day or so and rejoin it a little further south, when we reached Leland and the Highway 61 Blues Festival.

Highway 49 took us south towards Mississippi's State Penitentiary, better known as Parchman Farm, a working prison farm extending over 46 square miles. The farm's notoriety was dealt with as a subject of irony by white jazz pianist Mose Allison, who was born just 10 miles away. Covers by Georgie Fame and John Mayall of 'Parchman Farm' increased awareness of the song, which appropriately draws on the words of a work song.[10] Not long after Mayall recorded the song, an investigating committee recommended an end to what they termed 'farming for profit' at the expense of rehabilitation. Parchman's security was run with the 'trusty guard' system, whereby selected inmates were armed and charged with keeping guard over the others. At the time, the prison's superintendent was a plantation owner and the prison psychologist had just resigned, saying that he didn't want to work for a plantation.[11]

On the approach to Parchman Farm there is nothing to see but wide open fields, with a few mobile homes and shacks to break the monotony. Mississippi State Penitentiary is so vast that there are designated roads running across the farm. What attracted musicologists like John and Alan Lomax, who recorded work songs in the Southern prisons between 1933 and 1947, was

the belief they could locate pure musical traditions, untarnished by the external influences of a changing world, such as commercial music and new patterns of work organisation. By the 1940s Alan Lomax's approach was an acceptance of functionalism, which approached folklore as a response to the conditions of the society from which it emanated. As Benjamin Filene noted, Lomax's new approach moved away from the sole study of isolated communities and looked towards ones that were in the process of rapid change, which is how Lomax and the Coahoma Study academics saw the city of Clarksdale.[12]

Nevertheless, Alan Lomax couldn't resist the search for pure work songs, untarnished by the outside world, and in 1959 he returned to Parchman Farm with his girlfriend, English folk singer Shirley Collins. What Lomax found, as Collins explains in her account of the trip, was a music that 'in the intervening years since he'd first recorded there, had lost something of its grandeur and despair … perhaps it was that the younger prisoners didn't want to keep up the old way of singing and the old songs.'[13]

Set back from the side of the road was a cluster of trees, and as the car drew closer we could see a complex of buildings under the shade of the foliage. The grass border between the trees and the edge of the highway had been mowed short and had that velvety look as though it was regularly watered. From the outward appearance of respectability we could have been approaching an out-of-town sports club or a private aerodrome. Only the sign instructing motorists not to stop gave any clue as to what lay beyond the cluster of buildings amongst the trees.

The gravelly voice of Bukka White singing 'Parchman Farm Blues' played from the car stereo as we drove over the crossroads of Highway 49 and Highway 32. Across the top of the farm gates stands a canopy bearing a sign that simply reads 'Mississippi State Penitentiary'. The heartfelt spiritual struggle of White's songs, like 'I Am in the Heavenly Way' or 'Promise True and Grand', both recorded in 1930 with Memphis Minnie, is made more poignant by the knowledge that in 1937 he was sentenced to 'the term of the balance of his natural life' in Parchman Farm for shooting and killing a man. However, he was released within three years to pursue a recording contract with Vocalion.[14]

Charley Patton also sung about Parchman Farm, but didn't serve time there; Son House claimed to have served time on the farm for the killing of Leroy Lee, but according to Gayle Dean Wardlow no court records have been discovered to show that this was the case. Furthermore, Daniel Beaumont in his biography of House noted that his own searches for court dockets had not come up with any documentary evidence.[15]

On 15 June 1961 another group of inmates started arriving at the gates of the farm. Forty-five Freedom Riders locked in darkened trucks headed into the penitentiary. The group, which comprised twenty-nine African Americans and sixteen whites, were stripped, humiliated and some were shocked with an electric cattle prod before being taken to the maximum security wing. By the end of June more Freedom Riders were being arrested and brought from the county jails. It was a new song, 'You Don't Have to Ride Jim Crow', which was disconcerting the authorities at Parchman that summer.

The Freedom Riders had set off on Greyhound buses from Washington to New Orleans in May, with the purpose of challenging segregation on interstate travel. The first two buses were met by Dr Martin Luther King Jr, who told the riders that they would never make it across Alabama. They didn't, and mobs of segregationists set the first bus ablaze in Aniston, while the occupants of the second bus were dragged out and beaten when they arrived in Birmingham. Despite the attacks on the first buses, the outrage provoked by the violence brought forth more than 400 American citizens who bravely embarked on Freedom Rides that year, irrespective of the very real threat of severe violence and intimidation. Over 40 per cent of the African American activists who took part in the Freedom Rides were born in the South.

We obeyed the signs by the side of the highway and didn't stop at the gates to Parchman Farm, though of course we took the obligatory photos at the gates as we drove past. Richard, clutching Steve Cheseborough's *Traveling Blues* asked me if I knew that Elvis's dad, Vernon, had served eight months on the farm in 1938, apparently for forging a cheque, which got us singing *Jailhouse Rock* as we accelerated away from Parchman and headed east.[16]

Highway 49 gradually worked a long lonely arc round the bend of Swan Lake. Occasionally the odd northbound four-by-four passed, and then it was just local traffic. Only the cypress swamps bordering the edge of Swan Lake offered any relief from the relentless brown earth of the ploughed fields. Yet there is something about the vastness and predictability of the Delta landscape that is captivating: the shacks and the one-storey timbered homes; trucker's cabs parked next to a mobile home plot and the mud-spattered station wagons. Everything is there for a purpose and there is nothing superfluous. In the Delta there's very little that's aesthetic for its own sake, yet in its totality it lives in the moment, albeit a long, slow moment with the appearance that it's been there for going on for half a century or more.

The oxbow lakes, with their enclaves of cypress groves, and the bayous are the only interruption in the vast monotony of the Delta, hinting at how the landscape must have looked when it was home to the Choctaws.

At the side of the road I glimpsed a hand-painted sign that read 'Emmett Till Museum', with an arrow pointing down a narrow lane towards the Tallahatchie River. Just before the river, the lane crossed a single railroad track and turned onto Main Street in Glendora, which was more of a village than a town. Main Street soon gave way to potholes before petering out into a dirt track. A line of shabby cabins ran parallel to the edge of the railroad track and backed onto the banks of the Tallahatchie River. Five or six middle-aged African American men gathered under a porch outside what appeared to be a ramshackle bar, drinking beer from cans. The windows of the adjacent building were boarded up and the sense of abandonment increased the further we drove down Main Street. At the end of the row of buildings was a vacant lot with a shell of a caravan parked at the rear; around the doorway sat a few youngsters.

The only building that could have been a museum was shut that day. I wanted to ask where the Emmett Till Museum was, but the youngsters seemed to look right through us. There was no eye contact and their stares threw me somewhat. Reluctantly, I turned the car round and drove back along Main Street. That night, still troubled by our detour into Glendora, a quick internet search showed that nearly 80 per cent of the town's residents had an income below the poverty level and 46.4 per cent had an income below half of the poverty level.[17] A list of places ranked by per capita income in Mississippi (compiled from 2010 United States Census Data) ranked Glendora the thirteenth poorest in a list of 329 places. When we got back to England I rang the Emmett Till Museum at Glendora and they told me it was located in a new building at 33 Thomas Street, a continuation of Main Street. I promised myself I would return. The town also boasts a Sonny Boy Williamson II Bed and Breakfast Cyber Café, the town's tribute to the harmonica player who was born on a plantation at Glendora.

As we drove back slowly over Main Street's pot holes a memorial marker just before the railroad crossing caught my attention. The memorial was to Clinton Melton and his wife, Beulah, who had been killed within a few days of each other in Glendora in December 1955. Their deaths came only a month after Roy Bryant and J.W. Milam had been acquitted for the murder of Emmett Till by an all-white jury at Sumner, just a few miles back up Highway 49.

Elmer Kimball, a friend of Milam, drove into a gas station in Glendora in a car he'd borrowed from Milam and shot Clinton Melton, the black gas attendant, whom Kimball accused of having mistakenly filled his tank rather than just putting in a dollar's worth of petrol. White witnesses, including the owner of the gas station, testified that the murder had been unprovoked. Just days prior to Kimball's trial for the murder, Melton's wife, Beulah, who had been gathering information to be used at the trial, drowned in Black Bayou after her car came off the road. Two of her children were rescued from the car but Beulah Melton was unable to escape. Many believed that the official explanation of faulty driving was incorrect and that Beulah's car had been forced off the road. Kimball was acquitted of Clinton Melton's murder by an all-male white jury.[18]

Two weeks and 700 miles after we first came across the tragedy of the young Emmett Till, in the Burr Oak cemetery, his story had confronted us again as we drove through the communities where his murder had taken place.

Our plan was to head east at the crossroads with Highway 8, cross the Tallahatchie River and then pick up the Money Road that would take us to Greenwood, where we'd find Robert Johnson's final resting place. We also wanted to visit the site of the Three Forks store, where many people believed he'd been poisoned at the age of 26 by a jealous lover or her husband, but there remains much speculation about the cause and even the place of

Derelict gas station, Money Road, Mississippi.

Bryant's grocery store, Money Road, Money, Mississippi.

Johnson's death.[19] Richard dug out the Robert Johnson CD we'd brought for this occasion.

The Money Road winds a course between the backwaters and bayous of the Tallahatchie. But after Glendora, I sensed an overwhelming sadness, which felt as hopeless as the immobile iron-red marooned agricultural machinery that littered the dusty yards we passed at the side of the highway. Between Glendora and Greenwood, the community of Money, which was little more than a few houses and mobile homes, lies by the roadside, sandwiched between the river and the railroad track. If it wasn't for the events that occurred there in the summer of 1955, probably nobody outside of Leflore County would have ever heard of it. Yet, because of what happened at Money and the national outrage it caused, many see the events of that summer as the start of the Civil Rights Movement.

Set back from the road was a derelict gas station, with peeling paint and petrol pumps long gone, although a canopy still hung in front of the station's office. Next door stood the ruins of a store, a buckled shell of a building enveloped in ivy, the ground floor of which was boarded up; its upper floor was exposed to the sky. In front of the store was a Mississippi Freedom Trail marker:

Bryant's Grocery
Fourteen-year-old Emmett Till came to this site to buy candy in August 1955. White shopkeeper Carolyn Bryant accused the black youth of flirting with her, and shortly thereafter, Till was abducted by Bryant's husband and his half-brother. Till's tortured body was later found in the Tallahatchie River. The two men were tried and acquitted but later sold their murder confession to *Look* magazine. Till's death received international attention and is widely credited with sparking the American Civil Rights Movement.
Placed during the 50th anniversary of the freedom rides – 1961–2011

A truck slowed down as Richard took a photograph of Bryant's Grocery and pulled up next to the building at the rear of the store. The occupants got out and went into the building. A few tears welled up, as they had the day we searched for Emmett Till's grave, and a little of the hopelessness I'd felt as we left Glendora lifted.

We drove in silence for the next few miles as we headed towards the city of Greenwood, the county seat of Leflore County. The Tallahatchie snaked back and forth across the flat fields and every so often would reappear by the side of the highway before once again arcing away. Every so often the road offers a glimpse into a Cyprus grove or a bayou of a stranded oxbow lake, and it's easy to believe that the ghosts of the Money Road would lurk here. But of course ghosts can't be found along the Money Road. It's the fear that the ghosts of the Money Road may lurk within ourselves that's so disturbing.

A small, white clapboard church stood in a graveyard a little way back from the long sweeping bend on the Money Road, a mile or so before Greenwood. A hand-painted sign on the lawn at the front of the church read 'Little Zion Missionary Baptist Church – Pastor McArthur McKinley'. This was the original reason we'd taken the detour towards the Greenwood area. Johnson's death certificate merely states that he was buried at Zion church on 17 August 1938 and that he died the previous day. It doesn't give any clues as to which Zion church near Greenwood it refers to and subsequent research presents the blues pilgrim with the possibility of three graves. Interestingly, Johnson's death certificate states that he'd been a musician for ten years and that the last time he worked in his occupation was July 1938 and also that his death occurred outside of Greenwood.[20]

Visiting blues pilgrims had left a Bacardi bottle, some cigarettes, a half-smoked cigar, some dipping snuff, an ample selection of plectrums and a few necklaces. All these gifts for a guy whose pain was so severe before he died he was 'crawling along the ground on all fours, barking and snapping like a wild beast'.[21] They'd also left a collection of empty beer cans under the large tree next to the grave, which I thought a little discourteous given that the church had been gracious enough to allow a gravestone celebrating a man who some believe sold his soul to the devil.

During the course of his research, music historian Steve LaVere spoke to Mrs Rosetta Eskridge, a local woman who claimed that her husband had dug Johnson's grave. Eskridge recalled this as being near to the big tree in the Little Zion graveyard and LaVere suggests that this is the most likely place where Johnson was buried.[22] The Delta Media Project's *Blues & Abstract Truths* documentary features an interview with Mrs Eskridge in which she explains how the owner of the Star of the West Plantation, Luther Wade, asked her husband to dig the Johnson grave.[23]

The publication of the 1940 Census led to new research by Bob Eagle, published in *Blues and Rhythm* magazine in 2013; it raises new queries about Jim Moore, the informant on Johnson's death certificate, and the possibility that Rosie Eskridge is the person named as Rosie Leeks, a lodger with Tom Eskridge, at the time of the 1940 Census.

Just before reaching the Little Zion Baptist Church, we'd noticed a collection of sharecroppers' dwellings set back off the Money Road. After leaving Johnson's grave, we drove back up the road to take a closer look at the shacks and found that they were all restored sharecroppers' homes (albeit with plumbing and air conditioning) and went under the name the Tallahatchie Flats. The set-up looked very similar to the Shack Up Inn, where we had stayed the night before. The Tallahatchie Flats are owned by Steve LaVere.[24]

Within a couple of miles of the Little Zion Church, the Money Road becomes Grand Boulevard and enters the leafier suburbs of the city of Greenwood. The pockets of rural poverty in evidence throughout the morning were conspicuously absent along Greenwood's tree-lined boulevard, bordered by

Robert Johnson's gravestone, Little Zion Baptist Church, Money Road, near Greenwood, Mississippi.

manicured lawns and curved driveways leading to smart columnated homes that alluded to their antebellum forebears. Greenwood looks cared for, even down to the vacant lots, which look as though someone tends them.

Heading over the river, we made for the Crystal Grill, a restaurant that was recommended in Tom Downs' *Blues and BBQ*. It wasn't the first time I'd been to the Crystal Grill. On the previous occasion it was a Sunday and the maître d' led us through a number of ornate dining rooms with high corniced ceilings and polished furniture to a table at the rear of the restaurant. On this occasion, Richard and I arrived mid-week and I sensed a more secular feel about the Crystal Grill, with people taking a break after their morning's work. We chose grilled catfish, straight out of one of countless catfish ponds in this part of Mississippi.

On each place setting was a table mat with a picture of hands clasped in prayer accompanied by the message, 'Let us give thanks for the many blessings we, as Americans, enjoy.' I wasn't sure if this could be applied equally to the people of Glendora as it did the residents of Grand Boulevard. This wasn't

the only thought that crossed my mind, as it dawned on me that, by the look of the clothes people were wearing, many had probably come straight from church. Despite a tinge of guilt at the knowledge that we were probably the only ones in the restaurant on the trail of Robert Johnson, we were treated to the usual Southern hospitality and a superb lunch. When I felt sure that neither of us was being observed by the smart women at the next table, I folded up a table mat and slipped it into the pocket of my jeans.

Before we left Greenwood, there was one other site connected with Robert Johnson that we wanted to check out: the possible site of Johnson's last gig and his poisoning. All there is to see today is a church and small cemetery on the spot where the Three Forks juke joint had been until it was destroyed by a tornado in the 1940s. According to Steve Cheseborough this is one of the possible places where Johnson played at a dance and was poisoned by the owner because he'd been having an affair with his wife. It's believed that Johnson suffered an agonising death within a few days, maybe finally dying not far from the Little Zion Church, where we'd been that morning.

Much of the Three Forks theory is based upon an interview Honeyboy Edwards gave to Pete Welding in 1967, in which Edwards named the Three Forks juke joint and stated that Johnson was poisoned 3 miles from Greenwood. This ties up neatly with the Highway 49/82 intersection site. But, as Cheseborough points out in his *Blues Traveling* guidebook, there are other possible sites, and he notes that one needs to take account of the fact that the highways have been realigned and the exact location of the intersection has changed.

The more Richard and I threw maps and blues guidebooks around the car's dashboard in an effort to locate sites, based upon little more than the vague and conflicting recollections of other musicians, the more I wondered if it really mattered. It was the overall feel and sense of the Delta that was important, from the clues to be found about it, of what it had once been and how it had changed over time. It is out of this that we had to construct our sense of Robert Johnson.

Leaving Johnson behind, we decided to head over to the Dockery Farm plantation, which by the 1920s had become home to a number of blues singers, one of whom was Charley Patton, who would later be influential in the development of the blues. On the way we had planned to call in at the small town of Indianola, home town of B.B. King, and visit the museum that has been established there. It is a half an hour's drive west along Highway 82 to get to the museum. About 8 miles before Indianola we passed a sign to the town of Moorhead, at the crossroads with Highway 3. Moorhead is the town that the 'lean, loose-jointed Negro (who) had commenced plunking a guitar' and 'pressed a knife across the strings in a manner popularised by Hawaiian guitarists who used steel bars' had sung about and awoke W.C. Handy on the night his train was delayed for nine hours as Tutwiler.[25] We'd heard from other blues pilgrims at the Shack Up Inn that sections of old rusting railroad track remained in each direction at the crossing point where once 'the Southern cross' the Dog'. Unfortunately we needed to press on to Indianola because we'd been tipped off there would be live blues in a juke joint out in the cotton fields a few miles north of Cleveland. The guidebooks mention Po' Monkey's as a juke joint not to be missed, but also note that the owner, Willie Seaberry, rarely hosts live blues. However, because people were in the Delta for the Helena and Leland festivals, on this occasion there was to be live music.

With time getting tight we pulled into Indianola, drove through downtown Church Street, where the juke joints with live music had been located. It was through listening outside the clubs on Church Street as a youngster that Riley B. King got his first taste of the blues. Today one of the few joints left in Church Street, Mary Price's Key Hole Inn, can be found a little way down on the left-hand side, although it no longer has live music.[26] The few restaurants and bars surviving on Church Street soon give way to housing as one moves away from the downtown area, so we turned around and went back to the crossroads with Church Street and Second Street, which is where the young

King made his early professional appearances playing for tips. Here we found King's handprints, footprints and signature imprinted in the concrete on the footway, marking the spot where he played to the downtown passers-by.

Every year King returns to Indianola to play at the Club Ebony on Hanna Avenue, which he owned for a period, and which is now owned by the Delta Blues Museum. King ties this event in with an afternoon homecoming event in memory of Medgar Evers, field secretary for NAACP, who was assassinated outside his home in Jackson in 1963. King has headlined this event annually since the mid 1960s and co-sponsors it with Medgar Evers's brother, Major Charles Evers, who was himself a blues club owner.[27] Medgar Evers had been instrumental in finding witnesses who would testify against Emmett Till's killers.[28]

A short drive along Second Avenue brought us to one of the newest blues attractions in the Delta, the B.B. King Museum. It hadn't yet been built when I last visited Indianola, in 2007. It's an example of what Mississippi is trying to do in a very positive way with the history it has on its doorstep, both in terms of the music and placing it in the wider context of the history of the Delta's local communities.

The museum took up much of the afternoon, so we decided to put Dockery Farm and Charley Patton on hold till the morning. We drove across one of the minor back country roads to join Highway 61 just south of Cleveland and after another few miles saw a small motel set back from the highway. Motels, like people, can be deceptive from outward appearances and on closer inspection one often finds the result of decades of neglect lurking behind the facade. The receptionist looked up from the Bible that was open next to the motel reservations book. I peered over the desk and noticed she'd marked two or three verses in yellow highlighter. This wasn't the first time while travelling in the Southern states that I'd come across someone studying their Bible whilst engaged in a customer-facing occupation.

The receptionist asked us where we were from, then requested our passports and studied each one closely before reluctantly sliding them back across the reception desk together with one room key, attached to something more akin to a doorstop than a keyring. As we walked to the stairs at the far end of the accommodation block, two young children pulled back greying curtains and pressed inquisitive noses against the window of their room. We noticed as we trundled our luggage along the upper walkway that most of the locks had been forced at one time or another; they had been repositioned over the years and their splintered doors repaired with metal plates. Within half an hour we'd had enough of the motel room and decided to take a drive towards Merigold, where Charley Patton had lived for about five years from 1924, and look for Po' Monkey's. The two children reappeared at the window and their eyes followed us to the car, no doubt intrigued by the men who had unloaded laptops and cameras a few minutes earlier and were now loading everything back into the boot of their car.

B.B. King mural, Indianola, Mississippi.

The instructions we'd been given were to head north to the Merigold junction on Highway 61 until we saw a yellow 'Dollar Store' sign on our right, and then turn left onto a narrow road. After passing some mobile homes on the right, we took a left fork down a gravel track. I could see the rear lights of a car in the distance and then caught the flash of another car's headlights as it pulled onto the track some distance behind us. Our headlights picked out a line of cars and trucks parked at the side of the cotton fields, and out in the field a single illuminated shack stood surrounded by the blackness of the Delta night.

A naked bulb lit the hand-painted signs on what appeared to a be at least two or even three shacks held together by shuttering board and corrugated iron sheets. Christmas lighting strung under the eaves hinted at good times to be had on the other side of the rickety door, which had a 'caution' notice nailed to it. A large sign facing the track informed us that this was 'Poor Monkey Lounge – Doctor Tissue DJ $5 on Thursday Night – No Drug Products' and a sign below instructed patrons, 'NO Loud Music; Dope Smoking; Rap Music; Beer Brought Inside'.

On the other side of the door someone asked for a $5 cover charge. Hundreds of fairy lights and paper lanterns lit up the juke joint, and black plastic sheets concealed the hotchpotch of shack architecture. The first room had a pool table, and a small hatch across a doorway, from which the joint's owner, Willie Seaberry, known to the locals as Po' Monkey, was serving wine-bottle-sized beers that were too cold to hold for any length of time.

Long bench tables ran alongside the wall in the bar where a band was playing. A few local people came and sat down next to us and enquired if we'd come far; they laughed when we explained we'd come from England.

'You sure don't look like you come from India,' replied a young white woman as she took a second glance at the two of us.

'No, not India; we've come from England, near Canterbury,' I repeated.

'You've come all the way from England and you've come here!' she shouted across the table and then seemed to slip a little as her elbow lost its grip on the polythene tablecloth.

'We were told there was blues on here tonight and that Terry "Harmonica" Bean would be playing, who we saw up at Clarksdale,' I replied, trying to ensure that I didn't give reason for any offense.

'There's blues here tonight? Oh, I didn't know. We only come here because there's nowhere else to go round here.' Then she turned and gave her boyfriend a hard tap on his shoulder and told him that we'd come all the way from England.

During the evening Willie Seaberry appeared on the dance floor dressed in a series of different long, flowing women's wigs and did a twirl in front of the band before returning to the bar with a camp gait while maintaining an eye on his revellers.

Harmonica Bean got up and joined the band in what was little more than an alcove next to the dance floor. He started playing harmonica seriously nearly

twenty-five years ago, having gone to Greenville to see Robert Lockwood Jr because he'd been the last person to play with Little Walter. He ended up playing with T-Model Ford for a few years before branching out on his own.[29] Today, as well as playing the Delta festivals and juke joints, he tours abroad and has recently toured in Europe and Africa. He's also featured in the two Roger Stolle and Jeff Konkel films, *M for Mississippi* and *We Juke Up in Here*. The month before we commenced our blues pilgrimage he'd had a four-page interview in *Living Blues* magazine. Bean is one of the Delta Mississippi musicians who still plays his style of hill country and Delta blues in the surviving juke joints. Later in the evening Bean was joined by Deak Harp, who we kept crossing on our travels – we'd seen him earlier in the week when he was playing Red's Lounge at Clarksdale. When Harp gets going, his music packs a punch and it feels as though a freight train is coming through the joint.

A big Mississippi moon lit up the cotton fields as we emerged from Po' Monkey's. Waiting at the foot of the steps was the tamale man and his oven, with irresistible offerings of six or twelve tamales to soak up the evening's beer. Standing at the edge of a cotton field unwrapping steaming hot tamales wrapped in corn husks after a night in a Delta juke joint is extremely difficult to improve upon.

In the morning the Bible-reading receptionist was topping up the coffee for the buffet breakfast and refilling the hot shelf with the smallest burgers I'd ever seen. Thinking about the joys of hot tamales, my mind wandered onto great Southern breakfasts of wafer-thin crisp bacon with grits, cornbread and eggs whichever way you wanted them, but this wasn't to be.

The plan for the morning was to drive down to Cleveland and find Dockery Farm, which, largely owing to a one-time tenant Charley Patton, is a pivotal site in the history of Delta blues. Today we revere the bluesman as a significant figure in a chain of influence that passes to Son House, Robert Johnson and through to Muddy Waters.

Some would also add Tommy Johnson to that list, another guitarist who arrived on the Dockery plantation during the time Patton was there. Like Patton, he arrived at Dockery a couple of years after having taken up the guitar, and claimed to have acquired his guitar skills from a visit to the crossroads at midnight, some ten years or so before Robert Johnson. It is worth considering that when blues musician and music historian Elijah Wald visited the Delta in 1991, to play at the dedication of one of Robert Johnson's grave markers, he was surprised to find that the names of neither Robert Johnson nor Charley Patton were familiar to local people.

While it is has not been the aim of my journey to champion the merits of any one construction of the blues narrative over another, I endeavoured to be mindful of the fact that the importance the blues pilgrim ascribes to the places, people and events encountered along the journey is to a great extent predetermined by our received 'story of the blues'. As Francis Davis reminds readers, 'what is evidence but things arranged in such a way as to mean what

Po' Monkey's Lounge, Merigold, Mississippi.

we want them to mean'.[30] And that's what I bore in mind as we pulled up in front of the Dockery Farm buildings.

The last time I'd been here, this first building, set just back from the highway, had been an old, disused gas station. I remember peering through its broken windows at the scattered remains of office furniture on a floor strewn with the debris of a building that had served no useful purpose for many years. Now it was transformed into a pristine retro 1950s gas station, complete with Coca Cola signs and period petrol pumps, although I doubt the original Dockery service station ever looked this spick and span. Pressing a button close to the Mississippi Blues Trail marker resurrects the sound of Charley Patton, whose gravel voice haunts the Dockery Farm's buildings from twelve hidden speakers. I spoke to William Lester, the executive director of the Dockery Farms Foundation and he sees the restoration of Dockery Farm as complementing the other developments in the mid-Delta, such as the B.B. King Museum. Lester talked about how these initiatives would link with the new GRAMMY Museum at Cleveland, due to open in 2015.

Patton's parents epitomised the newness of the Delta, as they were one of the families that moved to Dockery in 1897, within a year or so of Will Dockery starting a lumber business and clearing the land for farming. Dockery's was viewed by many African Americans moving to the area as a relatively fair employer.

Patton had already got a liking for the guitar and had been playing with the members of the Chatmon family, the nucleus of the Mississippi Sheiks, which would became the most well-known of the recording Mississippi string bands. At Dockery, Patton came under the influence of Henry Sloan, a guitarist whom Robert Palmer describes as playing a 'rough rhythmic sort of music' and someone who 'was playing blues in 1897, making him one of the first blues musicians anywhere'.[31] Some commentators have even suggested that Sloan may have been the guitarist Handy saw at Tutwiler. It's believed that by 1918 Sloan had migrated to Chicago while Patton remained in the area of the mid-Delta, gaining a reputation as one of the most popular local guitarists, renowned for his showmanship, which included playing the guitar behind his head, between his legs and throwing and spinning the guitar in the air. Similarly to Son House, who talked about Patton's influence, for Howlin' Wolf seeing Patton play was a life-changing event; Wolf has said that he'd hang around Patton and ask him for lessons.[32] Likewise Roebuck 'Pops' Staples, who lived at Dockery, is on record as saying how Patton inspired him to play guitar.[33]

Just like countless other blues pilgrims who turn up at Dockery Farms, I wandered over to the surviving wooden buildings beyond the gas station and pondered the history of the site as I stared up at the Dockery Farms sign. It has taken on almost iconic status in blues mythology, appearing in films, documentaries and books about the music's origins, its red and black lettering simply stating that it was established in 1895 by Will Dockery 1865–1936, like a bold declaration that history will continue to judge it kindly. The cotton gin,

mule shed and fertiliser sheds are the same buildings that Patton would have been familiar with. A Mississippi Blues Trail marker declares this place to be the 'birthplace of the blues', but then adds a question mark.

Like many, we'd set out on this journey with a notion that there was a lineage of guitar heroes that would lead from our generation's popular interpreters of blues and bring us somewhere deep in the Delta and Charley Patton. Indeed, that's what's so attractive about Highway 61, the 'blues highway': it can, if one wants it to, fit neatly with this particular historical narrative of blues. Yet unlike highways, designed to take us to a given destination, history has an infinite number of starting points and end points. It's what we select from the past that to a great extent determines which destination our route takes us to.

As I walked between the buildings on the Dockery complex, it occurred to me that three weeks ago our journey had started visiting recording studios, theatres and the clubs. However, the further south we'd driven down the blues highway the more such sites had been supplanted by street corners where busking musicians once performed, dilapidated juke joints that had once reflected the common brutality of everyday conditions experienced by musicians and their audiences alike, and finally, here at Dockery, a plantation where people lived, worked and took leisure in a single location.

That is why Dockery is so important, because it is here that history locates Charley Patton. Yet history also tells us that despite Patton's popularity in the Delta, as Wald has noted, only half a dozen of Patton's earliest records sold well and his 'records appeared at the tail end of the country blues period and attracted relatively little attention outside of the Delta, but on his home turf he inspired a school of similar players'.[34] In comparison with the sales of the women blues singers, or guitarists such as Blind Lemon Jefferson, whose records had been bestsellers, Patton and his acolytes were minor players with African American consumers.

When Samuel Charters wrote his seminal history of country blues, in part a political act, he described 'black music and black culture in a way that would immediately involve a certain kind of younger, middle class white American',[35] he was not, as Marybeth Hamilton aptly put it, 'interested in rarities'. Referring to Charters's *Country Blues*, Hamilton states:

> The book that resulted barely mentioned Charley Patton, gave a bit more attention to Robert Johnson, but put the spotlight on Lonnie Johnson, Leroy Carr and Big Bill Broonzy, the musicians whose recordings black Americans of the 1930s had bought.[36]

Neither the album *The Country Blues*, nor *The Rural Blues*, brought out around the time of the publication of Charters' book, included a track by Charley Patton. However, as Hamilton points out, in 1944 James McKune, a heavy-drinking record collector who lived in a single room at the Williamsburg YMCA, New York, found a copy of 'Some These Days I'll Be Gone', which Patton had recorded in 1929. To McKune, and a small group of record collectors, who were to be dubbed the Blues Mafia, Patton represented the epitome of a great country blues singer. Nevertheless, as Stephen Calt suggests:

> None of them venerated records that were easy to come by and thus lacking value as items to trade or sell. The surpassing vocals of Blind Lemon Jefferson, who was avidly (but not artfully) copied by the same bluesmen they collected, held no charm for them: his works had been best-sellers.[37]

As a result, Calt suggests, awareness of the records that this group collected remained known only within a small circle of collectors, which consisted of a mere twenty people.[38] This is the same number of people that McKune refers to in an article he wrote in response to Charters' *Country Blues* for *VJM-Palaver*, a British jazz collector's magazine. In the first of a series of essays entitled 'The Great Country Blues Singers', McKune states 'I know twenty men who collect the Negro country blues. All of us have been interested in knowing who the great country blues singers are, not in who sold best.'[39]

In 1960 Pete Whelan, one of the collectors associated with McKune, established the Origin Jazz Library, an independent record label, whose first issue was *Charlie Patton! 1929–32*. The stated aim of the label was to bring original recordings of blues artist to the blues enthusiast based on 'their musical merit alone'.[40] By the 1960s a new narrative of the blues had emerged, reflected in the folk-blues revival, which sought to locate authenticity within rural obscurity. Sharp-suited Chicago bluesmen who had pioneered the electrification of urban blues would be ringing their tailors to be fitted out in the dungarees of their youth. By the end of the 1960s Charley Patton has been elevated to a new pivotal position in the story of the blues; Paul Oliver describes him as 'one of the most important figures in the whole story of the blues'.[41] In this revised history some even located Patton as being the lean, loose-jointed Negro whom W.C. Handy met in the early hours of the morning at Tutwiler, while others have him as one of the three local musicians who were asked to play in the interval at one of Handy's engagements in Cleveland.[42]

I drove out of Dockery Farms and headed back towards Cleveland and Highway 61, still thinking about the inclusion of the question mark on the Blues Trail marker. We'd pick up Highway 61 in a few minutes and after another 25 miles south we would reach Leland, the Highway 61 Blues Festival and the home town of someone who for me represented one of the most obvious links between the music of my youth and the Delta: Jimmy Reed.

Storm clouds darkened the flatland of the mid-Delta as we turned off the main highway onto old Highway 61, which becomes Broad Street as it approaches the edge of Leland. Drizzle turned to heavy rain and we pulled into one of the angled parking bays that line either side of the few businesses in downtown Leland. The appearance of the flat-roofed, red-brick Victorian buildings implied that the town's prosperity was long past. The wind buffeted the car doors as we made a rain-soaked dash towards the double doors of what had once been the Montgomery Hotel, built in the 1920s. In better times the hotel had been three storeys high and an impressive stopover for travellers using Highway 61. Today the building stands one-storey short, but despite its reduced stature serves a useful purpose as the new home of Leland's Highway 61 Museum. An impressive double staircase still graces the foyer and leads to an upper landing, under which sat James Moss, one of the museum's curators. We'd arranged to pick up tickets for the festival from the Highway 61 Museum and James's enthusiasm for both the local music and the social history came across as he chatted to us and other blues pilgrims who dropped in. James explained that the museum would get five or six Europeans visiting a week and, like others involved with blues tourism in the region, he added that he'd noticed a gradual increase, helped by the fact the museum has networked with other blues museums across the state.

Leland has had a good number of contemporary musicians working in the Greenville and Leland area and James mentioned Eddy Cusic and the late Lil' Dave Thompson. Pat Thomas, the son of James Thomas, who is featured in the Bill Ferris film, is producing both art and albums as well working closely with the museum.

The festival would prove to be one of the last appearances of local Greenville bluesman James Ford, known as T-Model Ford, who died in the summer of 2013. I had been fortunate enough to also see T-Model Ford perform his freeform boogie style of north Mississippi hill music at the Clarksdale juke joint festival in 2007. He had been a regular performer in Greenville's Nelson Street juke joints and he went on to record with Fat Possum throughout his last twenty years.

The lights above the main stage lit up the fine rain, which whipped back and forth across the audience, as the Cedric Burnside Project determinedly made the best of the deteriorating weather. Cedric Burnside's extensive percussive style and vocals complemented 26-year-old Trenton Ayer's attacking lead and slide. Their music tipped a nod towards north Mississippi hill country blues. Both Ayers and Burnside had grown up in Mississippi musical families, with Cedric having played with his grandfather Robert Lee 'R.L.' Burnside, who was renowned for his style of raw, Mississippi hill country blues.

Earlier in the afternoon Mickey Rogers and the Soulmasters treated the festival to some versatile blues and soul/blues. Rogers, who originally hailed from Mississippi, has toured widely over a long career, travelling to England in 1964 with Howlin' Wolf and Hubert Sumlin and then playing with Tyrone Davis and Bobby Rush for many years.

Trenton Ayers with the Cedric Burnside Project, Highway 61 Festival, Leland, Mississippi.

The bad weather set in for the evening, and Richard and I left Leland and drove the 10 miles to find the motel we'd booked in Greenville, which turned out to be a nondescript roadside chain motel, set alongside garage forecourts lined with trucks, fast-food restaurants and liquor stores.

It was here in Greenville that the worst of the Mississippi levee failures occurred, on 21 April 1927, when the Mississippi broke through at Mound's Landing, some 20 miles upstream. In total the levee failed in forty-two places and wreaked death and disaster along the downstream states of Mississippi, Arkansas and Louisiana.

Like much in the Delta, the levee system was relatively new. With increased settlement and logging, drainage of water into the Mississippi increased. In addition a new threat emerged, as those living along the river developed strategies to deal with its annual flooding. The tactics have been compared to a poker game in which:

> men attempted to alter the natural cycle of the river in flood. More and more settlers built dikes, but the longer the line they built, the more pressure the river exerted, for the surging water to break through. Each planter attempted to make his levee stronger than his neighbour's, but, finally tiring of this competition, planters united in organizations that worked to strengthen entire lines of levees. Then the battle was directed not against neighbours, but, against the settlers on their side of the river; as in a poker game, one side would raise and the other would call. The stakes were high, for if the levee on one bank caved in the other side would be relieved of the river's pressure. Occasionally people cheated at the game: men would destroy a levee across the river or downstream from their own farms in order to protect their crops.[43]

For some time, as the waters rose, people had become used to seeing boats passing, as if floating by along the tops of the levee. When the levee at Mound Landing collapsed, the river poured through the crevasse at a rate equal to the Niagara Falls, but then slowed to a terrifying crawl that crept across the countryside at a rate of 14 miles a day, until it engulfed more than 2 million acres.[44] Within two days of the breach, the towns we'd driven through during the course of the last few days had flooded, including Helena, Greenwood, Indianola and Leland.[45] Two years after the event Charley Patton recorded 'High Water Everywhere', considered by many to be the greatest song he recorded, a first-hand account of the power and devastation of the flood, which had a particularly catastrophic effect on Mississippi's African American population.

The following morning, in the motel's communal laundry, I met a farmer who told me he commuted to the area from Ohio. He'd bought cheap land to farm in Mississippi, which was why he was staying in the motel. We got chatting about Greenville and I explained we planned to visit the levee and take a look at Nelson Street, once renowned as one of liveliest streets in the Delta for live music and entertainment. He warned me about the risks associated with Nelson Street, which reinforced the words of caution I'd gleaned from guidebooks, from 'even long-time residents of Greenville, even some blues musicians, might caution against it' to 'Nelson St has also long been notoriously crime-ridden, and although it's true that drugs and sex are bought and sold along the street, it's generally safe enough in the afternoon to drive or walk through to have a look at the dilapidated remains of the old district'.[46] Thinking it best to move the subject on, I asked if he could suggest the best place to eat in Greenville, whereupon he told me that I should go to Doe's. I was somewhat surprised by his answer as I'd already read that Doe's was on Nelson Street.

'But that's on Nelson Street – and you've just advised me not to go down there.'

'No, you go down and park opposite and they've got a guy that can shoot anyone from 200 yards and he'll see you in there and even look after your car while you eat.'

Of course this did little to alleviate any concerns I had, but, as Steve Cheseborough quipped in *Blues Traveling*, 'after all those warnings, how could you *not* want to visit Nelson Street?'[47] And, of course, we did.

From Walnut Street, which nestles under the levee and still has a few bars and restaurants, a road ascends up onto the top of the levee. Tucked away on the river side of the levee on the edge of town, the city has allowed a number of pontoon floating casinos. Looking down from the levee across the rooftops of Walnut Street and the city beyond, it's not so hard to imagine the devastation of the 1927 flood, and that's exactly what Patton does in 'High Water Everywhere' – he's overwhelmed by the extent of the devastation. In his cry, he describes how the water crept through his town and what Patton sees as the whole country. The water drives him down from Sumner and he hears that at Leland the water is high; then, as he thinks of moving to Greenville, the levee breaks. Patton's protagonist is not a hero, he's someone conveying the anguish of a situation that he can't control. Nowhere he thinks of turning – Rosedale, Sharkey County, Tallahatchie and Stovall – can offer escape.

Patton talks of another reason that prevents him from escaping the flood when he sings of going to the hill country but can't because 'they got him barred'. R.A. Lawson suggests that 'they' is referring not to the rising water but a 'human adversary'.

Patton may have been referring to the more than 150 refugee camps established after the flood, which housed more than 300,000 flood victims in the Lower Mississippi Valley, many of which effectively became forced labour camps.[48] Before the waters had even subsided, letters and articles in the *Chicago Defender* were drawing attention to conditions in 'colored' camps being maintained in Greenville and Natchez. An article by Ida Wells-Barnett carried the headline 'Flood Refugees are held as Slaves in Mississippi Camp', and asked the question why only African American people were being forced at gunpoint to work on the levees for $1 a day before they were given relief rations. The article interviewed an African American who had escaped from a government camp in Louisiana, where he'd been separated from his wife and children and forced to work on the levee and was shot in the leg when he attempted to leave. At night he escaped and walked to Arkansas City, where he hitched a lift to Helena. From there he rode a train to Memphis and then made it to Springfield. At Springfield he described how a kind-hearted white man gave him a lift to Chicago.[49]

Rain beat down on the hardstanding, which sloped from the top of the levee to the casinos at the water's edge. If Charley Patton had walked along here he would have known this expanse of water as the Bachelor Bend. Surprisingly, what today appears to be the Mississippi when we look down from the Greenville levee is actually Lake Ferguson, a long sweep of artificially created oxbow lake named after General Harley Ferguson, who realigned the run of the Mississippi through three new channels known as the Ashbrook, Tarpley and Leland cut-offs.[50]

A rainy squall blew in from Lake Ferguson and beat across the top of the levee as we looked down onto Nelson Street. Pianist Willie Love – who played on Nelson Street with Sonny Boy Williamson II and accompanied him on his first release, 'Eyesight to the Blind' – immortalised life in Greenville's African American centre of entertainment in 'Nelson Street Blues'. Love would also team up with Elmore James and play in Greenville.[51] Love's 1951 recording invited anyone who 'ever go to Greenville to please go down on Nelson Street, where you can laugh and have a lot of fun with almost everyone you meet'. Looking down on a windswept and rainy Nelson Street, I saw little evidence of fun. The Flowing Fountain club still had murals of blues artists who had played on the street and a little way further down, just after the railway crossing, is a Blues Trail marker that recalls the time when a young Louis Jordan performed on the street in 1928. Jimmy Reed's face stared out from the array of murals that adorned the wall of 828 Nelson Street, sandwiched in between a mural of Honeyboy Edwards and Roosevelt 'Booba' Barnes.

Despite the colourful hand-painted signs and murals, the weather, which had got steadily worse, cast a depressing hue over some of the street's more distressed buildings.

After leaving Greenville, we headed into the country towards Dunleith to find the Shady Dell plantation, where Jimmy Reed was born in 1925. While living near Leland as a youngster, Reed met Eddie Taylor, who lived at Benoit, a small rural community a few miles to the north of Greenville. Taylor's mother had been a friend of Memphis Minnie and had a few musical boyfriends, so

Taylor was surrounded by musicians as he grew up. He played guitar on the same streets as the likes of Honeyboy Edwards and saw both Charley Patton and Son House play in towns around the Delta.

Reed became reacquainted with Taylor when he moved to Chicago in the late 1940s and they started playing together with Kansas City Red on drums. Maxwell Street, where Taylor had busked when he first arrived in Chicago, had featured at the start of our journey and now our journey brought us to where he had started out. Mike Rowe argues that Reed, who was a comparative newcomer to the music scene, was to a great extent dependent upon Eddie Taylor's accompaniment and his timing: they always sat facing one another so that Reed could watch Taylor's changes.[52]

A gravel track, Colliers Road, named after the owner of the Shady Dell planation, led down to where a Blues Trail marker denotes Jimmy Reed's birthplace. Puddles collected in the fields either side of the rough track. The Delta's baked earth, which only two days ago had signified long languid summers, suddenly appeared heavy and claggy as it soaked up the unremitting rain.

Leaving Jimmy Reed's birthplace, we made our way back to Leland and the Highway 61 Museum. At the museum we learned that one of the best-known blues clubs in the Delta still stands in Leland, although some doubted it would last much longer. McGee Street is across the tracks in downtown Leland. Around Railroad Avenue the town has a somewhat desolate appearance but it soon runs into a residential enclave of small clapboard houses. A couple of blocks down, on McGee Street, stands a Blues Trail marker, next to what's left of Ruby's Nightspot. The trail marker may well outlast the twisted structure that was once one of Ruby Edwards' two big Delta blues clubs; its buckled roof was pushing down onto the front of the club, distorting the clapboard sides of the building. Edwards had arrangements with the 'powers that be' which enabled Ruby's to gain a reputation for liquor and gambling, despite Mississippi's prohibition laws, which were not repealed until 1966. Ruby's was big enough to attract national touring acts such as Bobby Bland, Ray Charles, Junior Parker, Big Joe Turner and Eddie 'Cleanhead' Vinson. The club also hosted some of the most well-known Delta blues acts including Sonny Boy Williamson II and Elmore James, as well as up-and-coming acts like Ike Turner.

The very existence of Ruby's, albeit as a site of historic interest, owed as much to the region's impoverishment, which mitigated against development and renewal, as it did to investment in restoration. Somewhere other than the Delta capital would have swept the old aside and rebuilt, or else would have removed, restored and rebranded under the guise of regeneration. But therein lies the appeal of Leland, itself a historical curiosity that invites you to believe that time stopped around the period depicted in the murals that adorn the walls of its Victorian buildings.

The storm that had been brewing all day had now set in for the evening. We wanted to get up to Holly Ridge and find Charley Patton's grave, and having seen the mural of Boog-a-loo Aimes preforming at Lillo's restaurant we'd thought we'd give it a try on the way back, even though we'd heard it was rare for them to have blues these days. Coming out of Leland, the police flagged us down and warned us that flooding under the old railroad bridge had made the highway impassable. Rain and the spray from trucks lashed the windscreen as we joined a convoy of trucks that, like ourselves, had been diverted onto old Highway 61 and through downtown Leland. Despite it being well into the evening, members of the local community had turned out on street corners in the torrential rain to direct out-of-town truckers through the back streets.

At Holly Ridge the cotton fields were holding water and started to resemble lakes rather than cultivated land. Weather reports on the radio announced that in some parts of the Delta 4in of rain had fallen in the last few hours. Gusts of wind whipped the cotton that had been picked and wrapped in bales the size of shotgun shacks, which lined the roadside.

Holly Ridge is a small hamlet that Patton came to in 1933 and where he spent the last couple of years of his life with his last wife and blues singer Bertha Lee. For a period Patton lived at the grocery store at the Holly Ridge junction and would often play at the back of the store, although it wasn't the store that stands at Holmes Road and Holly Ridge today. In 1934 the economy was starting to pick up again after the Depression and record companies were looking for artists once again. The American Record Company sent W.R. Callaway to the Delta to seek out Patton, whom he tracked down to the jail in Belzoni, where Patton and Bertha Lee had been locked up for drunken behaviour. In spite of suffering from a mitral valve prolapse and the rigours of his lifestyle, Patton and Lee were whisked to New York for a three-day recording session.[53] The couple travelled back to the Delta in February but within a matter of weeks Patton died in Bertha Lee's arms; he was 45.

The first time I'd visited Patton's grave it was under a midday sun and the whistle of a freight train sounded in the distance. I remember waiting as the train slowly came into view. The driver looked across at me standing by the gravestone and the train whistled again. I wondered if the driver knew that every time he did this trip he was passing the grave of Charley Patton, the man whose gravestone attributes him as 'the foremost performer of early Mississippi blues, whose songs became cornerstones of American music'.

This evening was different. Fork lightning cut the night sky and hit the horizon somewhere over Leland. By the time we reached Patton's grave our trousers and shoes were soaked and the cemetery, like the fields, was turning to pools of mud. Driving back towards Greenville, fields had become lakes extended away into the darkness on either side of the highway. This seemed particularly poignant as we'd started the day at the Greenville levee and ended up at the grave of the man whose song had captured the ever-present fear of the river's capacity to wreak havoc. Wind ripped under the sheets covering the cotton bales and cotton fell in sodden heaps in the mud, only to be blown back into the fields.

Ruby's Nite Spot, Leland, Mississippi.

Charley Patton's grave, Holly Ridge.

Notes

1. Gordon, Robert and Nemerov, Bruce, (eds), *Lost Delta Found: Rediscovering the Fisk University–Library of Congress Coahoma County Study, 1941–1942*, Vanderbilt University Press, 2005, p.33.
2. Davis, Francis, *The History of the Blues: The Roots, Music and the People*, Da Capo, 2003. For further discussion regarding the women who 'dominated the first few years of blues recording, after the success of Crazy Blues' see pp.80–5. For sales figures see p.62.
3. Handy, W.C., *Father of the Blues: An Autobiography*, Da Capo, 1991, p.74.
4. Ibid., p.76.
5. Hamilton, Marybeth, 'The blues, the folk and African-American history', *Transactions of the Royal Historical Society* 11, 2001, p.23.
6. Ibid., p.23.
7. Adams, Samuel C., 'Changing Negro Life in the Delta' in Gordon and Nemerov (eds), *Lost Delta Found*, p.267.
8. Wald, Elijah, *Escaping the Delta: Robert Johnson and the Invention of the Blues*, Amistad, 2004, p.11; Wald quotes from John W. Work III, *American Negro Songs and Spirituals*, Crown, 1940, pp.32–3.
9. Driggs, Frank and Haddix, Chuck, *Kansas City Jazz: From Ragtime to Bebop*, Oxford University Press, 2005, p.180.
10. Cheseborough, Steve, *Blues Traveling: The Holy Sites of Delta Blues*, University Press of Mississippi, 2009, pp.109–12.
11. *Chicago Defender*, daily edition, 8 November 1972, p.1. *ProQuest Historical Newspapers, The Chicago Defender (1910–1975)*.
12. Filene, Benjamin, *Romancing the Folk: Public Memory and American Roots Music*, University of North Carolina Press, 2000, p.142. For discussion of B.A. Botkin and the New Deal folklorists' adoption of functionalism see pp.137–82.
13. Collins, Shirley, *America Over the Water*, SAF, 2007, p.127.
14. Wardlow, Gayle Dean, *Chasin' That Devil Music: Searching for the Blues*, Backbeat Books, 1998, pp.102–3.
15. Beaumont, Daniel, *Preachin' the Blues*, Oxford University Press, 2011, p.47.
16. Cheseborough, *Blues Traveling*, p.110.
17. 'Glendora, Mississippi', www.city-data.com.
18. Orr-Klopfer, M. Susan, *Where Rebels Roost: Mississippi Civil Rights Revisited*, M. Susan Orr-Klopfer, 2005, pp.280–3. For detailed discussion regarding the death of Clinton and Beulah Melton. See also Tallahatchie Civil Rights Driving Tour, Tallahatchie County Mississippi, for details of locations connected with the deaths of Clinton and Beulah Melton and Emmett Till.

19. For discussion regarding the cause of Johnson's death see Wald, Elijah, *Escaping the Delta: Robert Johnson and the Invention of the Blues*, Amistad, 2005, pp.123–4; Wardlow, *Chasin' That Devil Music*, pp.86–93; and Eagle, Bob, 'The 1940 Sequel: Revisiting Robert Johnson's Death Certificate', *Blues and Rhythm 278*, April 2013.
20. Wardlow, *Chasin' That Devil Music*, p.87. Information obtained from copy of death certificate reproduced on p.87.
21. Ibid., p.91. Wardlow refers to the recollections of David 'Honeyboy' Edwards and Johnny Shines.
22. Cheseborough, *Blues Traveling*, p.137.
23. *Blues & Abstract Truths*, Ed Silvera, Mississippi Valley State University, Delta Research and Cultural Institute.
24. The Tallahatchie Flats are located at 58458 County Road 518 Greenwood, MS 38930. Phone (662) 453-1854.
25. Handy, *Father of the Blues*, p.74.
26. Knight, Richard, *The Blues Highway*, Trailblazer Publications, 2001, pp.110–11.
27. Delta Blues Commission, Charles Evers, Mississippi Blues Trail marker.
28. Wilkinson, Brenda, *The Civil Rights Movement*, Crescent Books, 1997, p.85.
29. Watson, Erik and Bonner, J. Brett, 'Terry "Harmonica" Bean' (interview), *Living Blues* 220:43, No. 4, August 2012, pp.32–5.
30. Davis, *The History of the Blues*, p.28.
31. Palmer, Robert, *Deep Blues*, Penguin, 1982, pp.51, 57.
32. Segrest, James and Hoffman, Mark, *Moanin' at Midnight: The Life and Times of Howlin' Wolf*, Avalon, 2004, pp.19–20.
33. Palmer, *Deep Blues*, p.61.
34. Wald, Elijah, *The Blues: A Very Short Introduction*, Oxford, 2010, p.36; and 'Charley Patton: Folksinger', *Sing Out!*, 2002, Elijah Wald Archive www.elijahwald.com.
35. Charters, Samuel B., *The Country Blues*, Da Capo, 1974, p.x.
36. Hamilton, Marybeth, *In Search of the Blues: Black Voices White Visions*, Jonathan Cape, 2007, p.182.
37. Calt, Stephen, *I'd Rather Be the Devil: Skip James and the Blues*, Chicago Review Press, 2008, p.217.
38. Ibid., p.217.
39. McKune, James, 'The Great Country Blues Singers' (1), 3–4, reproduced in Hamilton, *In Search of the Blues*, pp.182–3.
40. 'By way of Introducing the Origin Jazz Library' (liner notes), *Charlie Patton! 1929–32*, The Origin Jazz Library OJL-1, 1960. Scans of the original liner notes were accessed at 'Origin Jazz Library', www.wirz.de.
41. Oliver, Paul, *The Story of the Blues: The Making of Black Music*, Pimlico, 1997, p.34.

42. Davis, *The History of the Blues*, p.97.

43. Daniel, Pete, *Deep'n As it Come: The 1927 Mississippi River Flood*, Oxford University Press, 1977, pp.2–3.

44. Lawson, R.A., *Jim Crow's Counterculture: The Blues and Black Southerners*, Louisiana State University Press, 2010, pp.136–7. Quoted by Barry, John, *Rising Tide*, Simon and Schuster, 1997, p.192; and Daniel, *Deep'n as it Come*, p.9.

45. Palmer, *Deep Blues*, p.73.

46. Cheseborough, *Blues Traveling*, p.155; and Downs, Tom, *Blues and BBQ*, Lonely Planet, 2005, p.37.

47. Cheseborough, *Blues Traveling*, p.155.

48. Lawson, *Jim Crow's Counterculture*, pp.141–2.

49. Wells-Barnett, Ida B., 'Flood Refugees Are Held as Slaves in Mississippi Camp', *Chicago Defender* national edition, 30 July 1927.

50. Middleton, Pat, *America's Great River Road, Volume 4*, Heritage Press, 2005.

51. Rowe, Mike, *Chicago Blues: The City and the Music*, Da Capo, 1975, p.200. Originally published in 1973 as *Chicago Breakdown*.

52. Ibid., pp.155, 159.

53. Palmer, *Deep Blues*, pp.77–89.

9
Beyond Catfish Row:
VICKSBURG TO NATCHEZ

The route from Leland to Vicksburg is 90 miles of classic road-trip country through the Deep South, and passes through Hollandale, home town of Sam Chatmon, as well as Rolling Fork, the birthplace of Muddy Waters. Marc and Luc Borm, Belgian musicians who were travelling round the Delta playing clubs, recommended that Richard and I follow Old Highway 61. We picked up the old highway on Broad Street, where it runs through downtown Leland, past the Highway 61 Museum, and stuck with it along the banks of Deer Creek, all the way to Hollandale. Maybe because the scene from Walter Hill's movie *Crossroads* in which Willie Brown, Eugene and Martone take shelter from the storm in the abandoned house was filmed not far from Hollandale, this stretch of country is extremely evocative of the South.

A few shotgun shacks survive way out in the cotton fields. On a clapboard chapel white paint curls away from the wood, and every so often there is another forgotten hamlet, with a gas station, post office and a row of shops frozen in time. These small communities were bypassed the day the new highway came and cut them off from the rest of America. Stumps of trees protrude from the swampy waters of Deer Creek and modest avenues of oak-lined drives led to houses built with lazy riverside views in mind.

After Hollandale the old highway joins its newer namesake, although little changes. It's still two lanes, just a little better maintained, and for most of the journey never goes far from the banks of Deer Creek. As we approached Vicksburg, vegetation turned to a lush green and the ever-present invasive Kudzu envelops everything in its path, creeping round trees and derelict buildings. The Delta National Forest to the north of Vicksburg has some of the largest tracts of swamp forest still to found in the United States, yet I was still somewhat perturbed to see my first 'beware of alligators' sign by the side of the highway. Considering Mississippi is said to have an alligator population of between 32,000 and 38,000, this shouldn't have been a surprise. The previous year, when the waters of the Mississippi were running high, local residents reported seeing dozens of alligators basking in the sun on the Vicksburg levee.[1]

Nine days ago we'd been standing in the lobby of the Peabody Hotel, Memphis, the place that in 1935 David L. Cohn, a Southern writer from Greenville, wrote was where 'the Mississippi Delta begins'. Now we'd arrived in Vicksburg and were looking for Catfish Row, the place where Cohn said the Delta ends. Steve Cheseborough notes that the locations used by Cohn to define geographic limits of the Delta also contrasted the extremes in lifestyle of those who frequented the Peabody and those who had lived on Catfish Row.[2] To the lobby of the Peabody came 'the businessmen of the Delta to make loans, sell cotton, buy merchandise, and attend conventions'; whereas down on Catfish Row 'tumble-down shacks lean crazily over the Mississippi River far below. Inside them are dice games and "Georgia skin"; the music of guitars. The aroma of love, and the soul-satisfying scent of catfish frying to luscious golden-brown in sizzling skillets. In Vicksburg Negros eat catfish as catfish at fifteen cents a plate. In the cities white folk eat it as fillet of sole at a dollar a portion.'[3]

Like Memphis, Vicksburg developed on bluff land above a bend in the Mississippi. A ladder of streets descends down from the high ground onto Catfish Row, past warehouses situated on Levee Street, which runs alongside the river's edge and the rusting rail tracks that once carried cargo to and from the port side. Today the tumbledown shacks have been replaced by a row of thirty-two murals, and parents with young children are more in evidence than people playing dice or 'Georgia skin', a high-stakes poker game.

Crossing the tracks from the park, I walked over to get a closer look at Dafford's depiction of Willie Dixon, which shows him in Vicksburg's famous nightspot the Blue Room. In Chicago, Dixon's grandson, Keith, had shown us round Chess Studios. There Leonard Chess had appointed Dixon chief house producer, a position from which he would exercise immense influence over the direction of Chicago blues. In the foreground of the mural a pink-suited Dixon is playing upright bass. To one side of him are sheet music stands depicting some of the 500 songs he either wrote or collaborated on with artists such as Chuck Berry, Howlin' Wolf and Muddy Waters. To the other side of him, the sheet music depicts the numerous artists that have covered Dixon's songs, such as the Stones, Led Zeppelin and Eric Clapton.

Willie Dixon's early years were spent in Vicksburg until his family moved to Chicago in 1935. Dixon's childhood home is no longer standing, but the small, timbered homes in the street convey a reasonable idea of what it would have been like. It was as a youngster in Vicksburg that Dixon, like a number of others with an enthusiasm for music, came under the influence of blues pianist Little Brother Montgomery. Montgomery, an artist whom Robert Palmer described as a seminal Deep South blues pianist of the 1920s and '30s, had developed a barrelhouse blues known as the 'Forty-Fours' as well as boogie-woogie styles, which he put to use in the saw mills and lumber camps around Louisiana and Mississippi.[4] Blues historian Paul Oliver suggests that in Vicksburg, Montgomery's collaboration also included the pianists Robert Johnson and Ernest 'Forty-Four' Johnson, and that 'together they developed the most widespread of blues themes, the "Forty-Four Blues"'.[5] According to Oliver, Montgomery taught the theme to pianist Lee Green, who likewise introduced it to Roosevelt Sykes.

All these pianists would be in Chicago by 1930, as would Willie Dixon, although Dixon would pursue a career in boxing until 1937, when he won the amateur Golden Glove tournament. However, following a subsequent ban from the sport, Dixon returned to music as a street musician and by the mid 1940s started playing jump blues with The Big Three Trio.

We walked through the Catfish Row Art Park and ascended the steep hill up Clay Street from the river. It reminded me of Beale Street, the way streets from the old town suddenly descend at a steep angle from the bluff down to the river. Halfway up the hill we found a vacant lot next to the wall of one of Vicksburg's old riverside warehouses, where the Blue Room had stood until it was demolished during a programme of urban renewal.[6]

The club's owner, Tom Wince, who appears in the background of Dafford's mural, was a major player on the chitlin' circuit and of all the black promoters in the 1940s he was considered to be the top man in Mississippi.[7] As well as running the Blues Room, Wince booked bands in a number of joints around the South including Ruby's Nite Spot at Leland, where we'd been the previous day.

Also in the background of the mural is the Skyline, the upstairs ballroom in Wince's club. Despite segregation, the Blue Room had a policy whereby whites could watch the acts from the balcony but were not allowed on the dance floor.

We had one more day before we had to get down to New Orleans and complete our journey. This meant we only had time for a stopover in one more city before hitting the last stretch of Highway 61. At the King Biscuit Festival we'd been given the telephone number of Peggy Brown, who organises the Central Mississippi Blues Society's Blue Monday nights in Jackson, so I gave her a call to find out if and where this was happening. We were in luck as there was blues at Hal & Mal's that evening, on Commerce Street, in the heart of the old capital.[8]

Three Delta dogs came down to the grass shoulder and were making a collective effort to pull a deer up the grass bank at the side of the highway and

into the woods. The southern end of the Delta is far more wooded than the north and mid-Delta and the change of landscape came as a relief.

Sunnyland Slim played on the radio, a musician who had been influenced by the pianist Little Brother Montgomery. Most of the sites we had visited in the upper and mid-Delta primarily had connections with the history of lone singer guitarists. Now, as we were in the lower Delta and close to the bigger cities, similar to the piano towns of St Louis and Memphis, the influence of the blues pianists was again becoming apparent. Yet the influence of blues pianists must have penetrated the guitar country of the cotton-growing Delta flatlands, as Paul Oliver argues:

There is much evidence, from the reminiscences of these men, from Roosevelt Sykes and Little Brother Montgomery among others that a pattern of piano blues existed as an underlay to the more striking guitar blues in the Mississippi Delta. Willie Love, who was born in Greenville in 1906, was part of this.[9]

Nevertheless, beyond the logging camps there were impediments that kept the country guitarists and pianists apart, partly based on class. Robert Palmer has made the argument that many of the blues pianists came from upwardly mobile families and found their entry into circles where city slickers and ambitious country boys met much easier. Palmer describes these audiences as being 'oblivious to the charms of the country blues' and 'would have considered Charley Patton and Son House primitive and déclassé'.[10]

Interstate 20 took us into Jackson, the capital city of Mississippi, and we worked our way round towards Farish Street. The street had once been the main African American business and entertainment centre and we managed to find a chain motel near the Amtrak station, a couple of blocks down from Farish Street.

Our first stop was to visit the site of the assassination of Medgar Evers, Field Secretary of the NAACP in Mississippi, who had taken a leading role in gathering evidence and persuading witnesses to testify against Emmett Till's murderers. Evers had also worked closely with James H. Meredith's campaign to gain entrance into Mississippi State University, which was backed by the NAACP's Legal Defense and Educational Fund. Meredith became the first African American graduate of 'Ole Miss', but three years after graduating, Meredith himself was shot.

Evers had also been involved with the case of Clyde Kennard, a University of Chicago student who had to return to Mississippi to look after the family farm, having completed three years of study. Kennard made the mistake of applying to transfer to the University of Southern Mississippi to complete his degree. Immediately after his interview with the university, he was arrested for reckless driving. Over the course of the next few months Kennard was charged with a number of doubtful crimes and was finally found guilty of stealing $25 worth

Medgar Evers's home and the site of his murder, in Jackson, Mississippi.

of chicken feed by an all-white jury and sentenced to seven years in Parchman Farm. The *Chicago Defender* reported that 'none of this would have happened if Kennard hadn't wanted to enrol at Mississippi Southern University'.[11]

Following a number of threats, including a firebombing of his family home and an attempt to run him down in the street, Medgar Evers was shot outside his home on 12 June 1963 as he carried a bundle of NAACP T-shirts that bore the words 'Jim Crow Must Go'. He was only 37 years old. It was not until thirty years after Evers's murder that Byron De La Beckwith was successfully convicted of his murder and spent the last three years of his life in prison. Maybe it is not so surprising therefore that at the time of Beckwith's arrest, in 1963, an article in the *Chicago Defender* warned that 'any effort on the part of the press or the authorities to depict the deliberate and traditionally biased Beckwith as "extremist" or "lunatic fringe" or anything at variance from the mind of say, Governor Wallace of Alabama, would be digression from the facts and from history'.[12]

Today, however, it's along Dr Martin Luther King Jr Drive and Medgar Evers Boulevard that one drives to get from the centre of Jackson to the house that was once the Evers family's home. Named after the African American poet, Margaret Walker Alexander Drive is a respectable middle-class residential road on the outer fringes of the city, with shady, tree-lined drives and well-kept lawns. The house is now a museum to Evers' memory. Standing outside the house, I saw the road as reflecting the aspirations of a person who, similar to Clyde Kennard, had been denied entrance to the university of his choice due to segregation; someone who would posthumously have an airport, a college and even a US naval ship named after him.

After leaving the museum, we retraced the journey that Evers made most days to get to the NAACP Field Secretary's office on North Farish Street. On first appearances Farish Street appears to be in the middle of a transformation, until you speak to some local people who tell you that transformation has been going on for over thirty years.

A brown-brick Victorian building, with metal-framed windows broken and a boarded-up shop on the ground floor, is what we found as we pulled up outside 507–509 North Farish Street. Jackson is hoping to restore this site but it is still awaiting the care and attention it deserves.

Standing on the opposite side of the road taking in the history of this building filled me with conflicting emotions. It was here, having taken on the field secretary position in 1954, that Medgar Evers campaigned for a future that he could be equally part of. Around this time Sonny Boy Williamson and his wife, Mattie, had an apartment in the same building. Williamson was recording with Trumpet Records, who released eleven of his records between 1951 and 1955. According to Cheseborough, Williamson's associates Elmore James and Willie Love also stayed in the apartment.[13] I thought of Evers hunched over correspondence, trying to work on a campaign, then imagined a bunch of musicians drinking whiskey somewhere in the building as they came down from the night before. Perhaps their paths never crossed; maybe they did, but each was oblivious of the other. Then again, it could be that the graduate from Alcorn, denied access to study law, was thinking of a world far removed from the one frequented by the down-home blues artists who turned up around the offices on Farish Street.

We walked one block down, the same walk that Sonny Boy Williamson and Elmore James would have taken to the office of Trumpet Records. The first place they would have passed was the Alamo Theater, which has been at the present site since 1949. During the 1940s and '50s the theatre hosted blues and jazz acts including Cab Calloway, Nat 'King' Cole, Elmore James and Louis Jordan. Otis Spann showed his potential at the age of 8, when he won a talent show. Another artist who found success and a recording contract after winning the Alamo's talent nights was Dorothy Moore, who had a big hit with 'Misty Blue'.[14]

On the next block stands the building that once housed Lillian McMurry's Trumpet Records. By the time Sonny Boy Williamson II got to record 'Eyesight for the Blind' for Trumpet, in March 1951, he'd already achieved a decade of regional recognition through his performances on King Biscuit Time. He spent five years with Trumpet and made eleven records before moving on to Checker (a subsidiary of Chess) in 1955, where he worked with Muddy Waters, Otis Span, Jimmy Rogers and Fred Below.[15] The McMurrys bought the premises in 1949 intending to run a furniture store, but Lillian started selling blues records from the shop, aided by speakers put outside the store to draw in customers. They soon realised they had found a ready market. McMurry and her husband, Willard, transformed the store into the Record Mart and established their own record company. Elmore James recorded his first record, 'Dust My Broom', with Trumpet. Other Trumpet artists included Big Joe Williams and Arthur Crudup.

The last historic site on our list was one of the final links in a chain of influence that led from Henry Sloan (the guitarist who blues scholar David Evans argues helped shape Charley Patton's music on the Dockery plantation) via Son House and Robert Johnson on to the Chicago blues.[16] Historian Gayle Dean Wardlow says that 'no other legend stands out as indelibly across the grooves of recorded music in the memoirs of Mississippi blues and sanctified music as does Henry C. Speir.'[17] Speir sold records to Jackson's African Americans from his stores on Farish Street and searched the South for blues talent for record companies such as Paramount, Okeh, Vocalion and Victor. His search spanned more than two decades, during which he discovered Charley Patton, Ishman Bracey and Skip James, and was indirectly responsible for Willie Brown, Son House and Louis Johnson recording for Paramount. It was through the doors of his store that Robert Johnson came one day in 1936 to audition.

Wardlow tracked Speir down in 1964 and between then and Speir's death in 1972 maintained an association that provided an insight into his relationship with the Delta bluesman of the 1920s and '30s. Wardlow has said that Speir could not remember recording a demo for Robert Johnson but did recall him coming into the store and singing 'Kindhearted Woman'. Speir liked

The building that once housed the NAACP office where Medgar Evers worked, Farish Street, Jackson.

Site of Trumpet Records, Farish Street, Jackson.

what he heard and recommended him to Ernie Oertle, an agent for ARC, who arranged for Johnson to record three sessions at the Gunter Hotel on 23, 26 and 27 November 1936, during which sixteen of Johnson's twenty-nine songs were recorded.

The Central Mississippi Blues Society's Blue Monday was well under way by the time we got over to Hal & Mal's restaurant in Jackson's old capital. A taxi dropped us off outside what appeared to be an industrial premises. In fact it was an old train depot, transformed into one of Jackson's most important music venues. Only the lettering painted on the side of a loading ramp leading up to the doors suggested that this was the place we were looking for. Inside we found familiar faces from our travels who had also made it to Jackson.

Mike Stephenson, from the UK-based *Blues and Rhythm* magazine, was one such person. In common with many of the blues travellers we'd met, he was over from England for the Highway 61 and King Biscuit festivals. As Mike had been visiting the Southern states for a number of years I was interested to talk to him about the forms of blues he thought still held significant appeal for African Americans. Mike suggested that it was a combination of blues and soul and mentioned artists such as Sir Charles Jones, Vick Allen, O.B. Buchana, Ms Jody, Bobby Rush, Denise LaSalle and Willie Clayton. These are the artists who were getting airplay on the blues shows of the regional radio stations and attracting African American audiences. He added that probably the three most prolific labels covering these artists were Malaco Records, based in Jackson; ECKO Records, at the other end of the Delta, a Memphis-based label; and CDS Records up in Ohio.

As far as the Delta region was concerned, Mike saw Clarksdale as a centre for visiting blues fans, and mentioned the venues we'd been to on our journey. Clarksdale had local Delta musicians and with the help of tutoring through the Delta Blues Museum there's a generation of younger musicians coming through.

The house band at Blue Mondays has Rick Lewis on drums; Johnny Sharpe on keyboards and saxophone; King Edward on guitar; Abdul Rasheed, Pat Brown and Dennis Fountain on vocals; and Malcolm Shepherd on congas, so even before any of the evening's guests had got up to join them we were treated to some outstanding musicianship. Mickey Rogers, who we'd seen at the Highway 61 Festival, joined the band with his own particular brand of soulful blues. During the course of the evening I was fortunate enough to chat with Rogers about his schedule of overseas tours and the artists he has played with over the years. His first trip out of the country was with Howlin' Wolf, and he was mentored by Hubert Sumlin. Rogers even has a Walk of Fame Stone to honour him at Greenville.

Then during the course of the conversation Rogers happened to mention a personal story, which brought home how the chequered history of a segregated society was never far below the surface in the history of the blues. He told me that when he was about 8 or 9, his mother had put him on a bus back to Mississippi from Chicago and that another boy on the bus was Emmett Till, whom he knew well, as their families had been neighbours. Putting someone on a bus at that age was not unusual in those days, he explained. When his parents heard about Emmett's murder they sent word to the people Mickey was staying with and had him return home.

Emmett Till's story had found us again. Not once had we gone looking for it. It didn't leave me angry, but with an underlying sadness, which seemed to seep gradually into my own narrative of the blues.

On the penultimate day of the road trip, we made the 100-mile drive down to Natchez; the forest was broken only by the columnated antebellum mansions as we passed through Port Gibson. If we'd had time to spare we would have taken the Natchez Trace Parkway, originally a trail used by the Choctaw and Chickasaw Native Americans, and which is marked on French maps from 1733 as 'The Path to the Choctaw Nation'.[18] The Trace runs mostly parallel with Highway 61, crossing it on a number of occasions, and makes for a scenic drive from Port Gibson all the way into Natchez. Unfortunately time was scarce, as we wanted to explore Natchez, one of the areas where the cotton industry took off, which explains the 600 opulent mansions to be found around the town.

In recent years the city has started to explore the history of the ancestors of its African American citizens, upon whose forced labour so much of the wealth of the city was built. Following the Louisiana Purchase in 1803, which opened up the Mississippi as an avenue for international trade, Natchez grew immensely wealthy from the slaves who worked the land. Before the Civil War the city became the first cotton capital, boasting that half the millionaires in the United States lived in Natchez.

We stopped the car at a triangular patch of grass sandwiched between the carriageways of Highway 61. The holding pens of one of the biggest distribution points for slaves were situated on the high ground here on the outskirts to ensure that cholera wasn't brought into the city.[19] It wasn't the importation of slaves that made the city such a lucrative cog in the sale of human beings, as that had been banned by Congress on 1 January 1808. Instead the Natchez slave market met the increasing demand for forced labour from new expanding western states through the reproduction of the existing slave population.

The level of human traffic is estimated to have been worth $20 million dollars annually.[20] Slaves were transported from Virginia and Maryland and later from the Carolinas and Kentucky; some were marched along the Natchez Trace. Most slaves were brought by boat to New Orleans and then shipped up the Mississippi.

We stayed at the Eola Hotel in historic downtown, a couple of blocks back from the river front. The Eola's interior today is a 1982 makeover, undertaken when the hotel reopened, having been closed for nearly a decade.

Mickey Rogers at Hal & Mals, Blue Monday, Central Mississippi Blues Society, Jackson, Mississippi.

The extravagant lobby's high ceilings are supported on grandiose stucco marbled. pillars topped with rolled capitols in faux gold-leaf. The flag that was draped over General Ulysses Grant's coffin now hangs framed in the hotel's reception under dimmed lights. Maybe the choice of the Union flag reflects the fact that this Confederate city, which surrendered to Union forces on 13 May 1862, remained relatively unscathed from the Civil War. Natchez's welcome guide informs visitors that the town survived the Civil War with little or no loss to property; it suffered only one civilian death and was quietly occupied by federal forces in the summer of 1863.

Walking two blocks along Main Street brought us down to neat public gardens with a small bandstand by the river's edge. From here one can stare out across the mile-wide flow of the Mississippi, which served as a reminder that we were nearly at our journey's end. I'd come down to the gardens on Broadway to find the memorial to the 209 young African Americans who'd lost their lives in the Natchez Rhythm Club fire on 23 April 1940. As I walked across the freshly mowed lawn where the memorial stood, the enormity of the two spans of the impressive Natchez–Vidalia Bridge, linking Mississippi with Louisiana, came into view. No doubt many of the young people that were trapped inside the Rhythm Club that night had watched the construction of such a massive feat of engineering with fascination over the previous months. They would likely have had friends or relatives employed in its construction or may have even worked on it themselves.

The Rhythm Club was constructed of wood and corrugated tin; Spanish moss had been draped from the ceiling and over the beams under the tin roof. As a precaution against bugs dropping from the moss onto the dancers, it had been sprayed with Flit, a petroleum-based insect repellent. Walter Barnes and his orchestra, The Royal Creolians, played on as the fire caught, telling people to keep calm. Within seconds the fire whipped through the Spanish moss and the wooden structure caught too. The windows of the club had been nailed shut and all doors apart from the main entrance had been barricaded. The band played on until the roof collapsed on those who had not been able make their escape or had already succumbed to the smoke. Of the nine band members only Barnes' drummer, Oscar Brown, escaped. He had brought a hammer to nail his drums down to the stage and used it to batter his way out of the inferno through a boarded-up window.[21]

Two months following the horrific fire at the Rhythm Club, John Wesley Work wrote to Thomas Elsa Jones, the president of Fisk University, proposing that a study be undertaken at Natchez because he predicted that 'to the abundance of folklore natural to the community, a new body of lore is about to be added. It is the ballads and music arising out of the holocaust of last April … the impact of this terrible fire with its religious implications on the minds and imagination of the unlettered Negroes of that region must of necessity be of such weight as to stimulate the creation of a tremendous amount of folk expression.'[22] A few days later Work wrote to Jones again, suggesting that Fisk consider tying up with Alan Lomax and the American folklore collectors at the Library of Congress.

Within a year Work's original plans had become subsumed into what became the Coahoma Study. From his initial proposal arose the first academic African American study of black folk music. The study resulted, as Robert Gordon and Bruce Nemerov note, in 'the first recordings of blues musicians Muddy Waters, David "Honeyboy" Edwards and Son House; recordings by several other musical greats including Sid Hemphill; and detailed documentation of a society'.[23]

Notes

1. 'Mississippi flooding: Residents warned as snakes and alligators seek dry land', *Telegraph* (website), 9 May 2011, www.telegraph.co.uk/news/worldnews/northamerica/usa/8503838/Mississippi-flooding-Residents-warned-as-snakes-and-alligators-seek-dry-land.html.

2. Cheseborough, Steve, *Blues Traveling: The Holy Sites of Delta Blues*, University Press of Mississippi, 2009, p.178.

3. Abbott, Dorothy (ed.), *Mississippi Writers: Reflections of Childhood and Youth: Volume 2 non-fiction*, University of Mississippi, 1986, pp.126, 127; excerpt from Cohn, David L., 'Where I was born and raised', David L. Cohn, 1935, 1947 and 1948, and University of Notre Dame Press, 1967.

4. Palmer, Robert, *Deep Blues*, Penguin, 1982, p.150.

5. Oliver, Paul, *The Story of the Blues: The Making of Black Music*, Pimlico, 1997, p.91.

6. Mississippi Blues Trail marker, The Blue Room, Vicksburg, Mississippi Blues Trail Commission.

7. Lauterbach, Preston, *The Chitlin' Circuit*, Norton, 2012, p.10.

8. Hal & Mal's, 200 Commerce Street; Peggy Brown, Hit the Road Entertainment, (601) 613-7377, prblues22@gmail.com.

9. Oliver, *The Story of the Blues*, p.173.

10. Palmer, *Deep Blues*, p.150.

11. *Chicago Defender*, national edition, 24 November 1962, p.9. *ProQuest Historical Newspapers: The Chicago Defender (1910–1975)*.

12. *Chicago Defender*, national edition, 27 June 1963, p.12.

13. Cheseborough, *Blues Traveling*, p.195.

14. Mississippi Blues Trail marker, Dorothy Moore/Alamo Theater, Mississippi Blues Trail Commission.

15. Wyman, Bill with Havers, Richard, *Blues Odyssey*, Dorling Kindersley, 2001, p.265.

16. Oliver, *Story of the Blues*, p.34. However, as David Evans has stated, 'although the Delta and Chicago were enormously important blues centres and this line of historical development is indeed on the big stories of the blues, it is not the only way the story can and should be told'. Evans, David, Philips Barry Lecture, Annual Meeting of the American Folklore Society, Memphis, TN, 22 October 1999, *ISAM Newsletter* 29:1 at depthome.brooklyn.cuny.edu.

17. Wardlow, Gayle Dean, *Chasin' That Devil Music*, Backbeat Books, 1998, p.126.

18. Middleton, Pat, *America's Great River Road*, Heritage Press, 2005, p.86.

19. Barnett, Jim and Burkett, H. Clark, 'The forks of the road slave market at Natchez', *Journal of Mississippi History* 63:3, 2001 at mshistory.k12.ms.us.

20. Cooper, William J. and Terrill, Thomas E., *The American South – A History, Volume 1*, McGraw-Hill, 1991. For discussion of the westward movement and the interstate slave trade see pp.216–21.

21. Lauterbach, *The Chitlin' Circuit*, pp.66–70. Provides an account of the Rhythm Club fire.

22. Work III, John W., Jones, Lewis Wade, Adams, Samuel C., in Gordon, Robert and Nemerov, Bruce (eds), *Lost Delta Found: Rediscovering the Fisk University–Library of Congress Coahoma County Study, 1941–1942*, Vanderbilt University Press, 2005, p.9, quoting from Work III, John W., *John Work III Collection*, Special Collections, Franklin Library, Fisk University.

23. Ibid., pp.8–9.

10 Carry Me Down on Rampart Street:
NEW ORLEANS

Now 170 miles of Highway 61 was all that separated us from New Orleans and the end of our journey. Our tight schedule would only allow us one night in the city, which is accepted by many as the place where jazz began and, for some as the birthplace of blues. This didn't feel like enough time, but then there never is enough time. Known as the Crescent City, a name derived from its location on a long horseshoe bend in the Mississippi, New Orleans is the city that Jelly Roll Morton called the 'cradle of jazz'.[1]

Between Natchez and Baton Rouge one is conscious that the Mississippi is always there, but you hardly see it. The clues are in the lush green of the vegetation: the swamps, the Spanish Moss hanging from the oaks and the kudzu that cloaks almost everything by the side of the highway. Through Baton Rouge, Louisiana's state capital, the traffic slowed to a crawl. After an hour or so we broke out of the suburbs and thereafter it was mile after mile of forest, broken only by the occasional bayou. At Laplace we turned onto Highway 51 to get over to Interstate 10 for the final run into New Orleans.

Concrete stilts support Interstate 10 as it cuts through the roof of the forest and the swampy land below. A weird landscape of contrasts opened up, different from anything we'd seen thus far. To our right was swamp stretching to the horizon, and to our left the dark, watery expanse of Lake Pontchartrain extended for 40 miles. Far away in the distance, immense constructions of steel appeared, as did industrial plants the size of towns, whose cooling towers, distilleries and silos rose out of the swampy water.

Beneath the concrete highway, boardwalks led precariously between the trunks of cypress trees to swamp boats moored at the side of bayous. Wooden homes built on small pockets of land staked a place amidst the swamp. Their occupants went about their daily business, seemingly oblivious to the incessant rumble of the interstate above. There are cabins on the side of Lake Pontchartrain, like the one to which Buddy Bolden (the musician whom Jelly Roll Morton called the first great powerful cornetist) is brought to by his friend Webb, in Michael Ondaatje's novel *Coming through Slaughter*, to escape the pressure of music and encroaching insanity.[2]

Approaching New Orleans, we dropped down from the interstate onto Highway 61. I'd booked a hotel opposite Congo Square, now part of Armstrong Park. The Place Congo is the square where in the nineteenth century slaves were allowed to congregate when it was too hot to work. Here they were allowed to make music with other slaves and 'free people of colour' whose origins were in Africa or the Indies. An official New Orleans proclamation in 1817 recognised slave dancing in the square.[3]

Benjamin Latrobe's journal recorded the instruments he saw being played in the Place Congo in 1819, which included drums and stringed instruments.[4] As blues historian Paul Oliver notes, 'some slaves did attain skill as musicians and if the drums were banned in Mississippi, the drumming in Congo Square, New Orleans was long a tourist attraction.'[5] Outside of French Louisiana, slaves were generally forbidden to use loud or percussive instruments for fear that they might communicate uprisings (although Robert Palmer notes that there is evidence to suggest that accounts of slaves using forms of percussion in some other Southern states were not unheard of).[6]

The hotel's reception staff greeted us and handed out notices from the City Authority informing visitors that it was unsafe to drink the water, bathe or shower. Someone had opened the wrong valves, resulting in the temporary contamination of the New Orleans' water supply. The all-pervasive odour of sewage wafted through the French Quarter, which added a degree of authenticity to our stay; this reinforces the myth that it is below sea-level (it isn't), and it meant that we would have to forsake salads and stick to alcohol for the next twenty-four hours.

The city was still suffering from the aftermath of Hurricane Katrina, nearly a decade after the event. A news report highlighted local complaints about a new type of poverty tourism: bus-loads of sightseers were being taken on tours of the Lower Ninth Quarter to gawp at people in the poorest section of the city, who were still struggling with the devastation caused by the collapse of the levee walls.

Entrance to Armstrong Park and Congo Sqaure, Rampart Street, New Orleans, Louisiana.

Not only is Rampart Street, where we were staying, conveniently situated on the edge of the historic French Quarter, but I just happen to love Freddie King's cover of J.B. Lenoir's 'Mojo Boogie', the lyrics of which informed me that on Rampart Street I would sure have a wonderful time. According to the song, the 'mojo hand' or 'mojo charm' that J.B.'s aunt introduces him to on Rampart Street knocks him off his feet.

Perhaps the real reason J.B. Lenoir got knocked off his feet was that on the day he travelled to Rampart Street from his home in Mississippi, in 1944, he got to sit in with Sonny Boy Williamson II and Elmore James at a gig in the New York Inn. Mike Rowe suggests that the memory of this may well have inspired Lenoir's song 'The Mojo'.[7]

Symbolically, this was a great place to end our journey, because it is here that many musicologists argue the polyrhythmic patterns, blue notes and vocalisation found in West African music were expressed by slaves and free people of colour to accompany their dances in Congo Square. However, that music was neither blues nor jazz. Blues musician and writer Robert Palmer states that 'Black American Music as it was sung and played in the rural South was a continuation of deep and tenacious African traditions and a creative response to a brutal, desperate situation.'[8] Nevertheless, he qualifies this by arguing:

Over the nearly three centuries between the first accounts of slave music in North America and the earliest recordings of black folk music in the South, blending of innumerable kinds and degrees took place. By the period of the Civil War, almost every conceivable hue of musical spectrum must have been present to some degree in black folk culture, from an almost purely African to the almost purely white American.[9]

Certainly by the nineteenth century many black musicians had learnt to play styles of European music and were members of slave orchestras and plantation house bands. As such these musicians would have assimilated European scales and rhythms and incorporated these into African styles. Blues would have evolved from these multiple influences, but whether this evolution occurred in a number of places across the South or in one location, such as New Orleans, remains unknown. As Elijah Wald suggests, 'the first music to be called the blues seems to have been slow, but not necessarily sad – it was a sexy rhythm, popular with African American working class dancers in New Orleans and other parts of the Deep South.'[10]

A police car was parked in front of the illuminated arched entrance to Armstrong Park, the gates of which were locked, although that in itself wasn't unusual as dusk had fallen a couple of hours previously. Many guidebooks suggest that visitors should be careful, adding that the park could be dangerous even in the daytime. However, earlier in the year the park had reopened following a complete redesign and we were told it is well used by both locals and visitors. Statues that celebrate the city's musical heritage include Buddy Bolden, Louis Armstrong and Mahalia Jackson. Inside the gardens is the Perseverance Hall (not to be confused with the Preservation Hall on St Peter Street in the French Quarter), where some of the great jazz musicians of New Orleans played, including cornetist Buddy Bolden. Also here is the Mahalia Jackson Theater for the Performing Arts.

We crossed Rampart Street, which as the name suggests was originally the outer limit of the French city, and proceeded into the warren of streets that make up the French Quarter, or the *Vieux Carré*, to find Jackson Square, the central plaza. The architecture met my expectations with wooden shotgun houses, richly painted, alongside brick and stucco terraces and balconies overhanging the street, one above another, with intricately ornate iron-work balustrades. Stairs spiralled down into small, secluded courtyards, separated by iron gates from the bustle of the streets.

We turned onto Royal Street, which once had been the route of the streetcar line named Desire. On evenings when Louisiana's oppressive humidity weighs heavily upon the neighbourhood, it's easy to imagine characters with the fragile desperation of Blanche DuBois and the visceral anger of Stanley Kowalski. The maze of back streets opened onto Jackson Square, its plaza lit by the soft glow of imitation gas lamps around the edge of the gardens under the shadow of St Louis Cathedral. Michael the Realistic Mystic offered tarot card readings from a table set with a flock tablecloth and crystal ball just a few metres away from the cathedral steps. The gentle sound of a saxophonist and, a little further on, a lone guitarist playing jazz hung on the warm air of the evening, offering a serene contrast to the neon-lit clubs and bars along Bourbon Street.

Richard and I negotiated our way through the evening crowds around Bourbon Street and stopped for a couple of cold beers at an open-air courtyard bar. People on the tables around us were fuelling up for the night ahead. On Bourbon Street people come to party, visit the strip joints and clubs, and drift uninhibited through the blaze of neon and noise that assaults the senses. Stag parties, office outings and middle-aged men sporting casual attire, who no doubt would sit full of regret in business conventions the following morning, all gravitated to Bourbon Street.

As we made our way further along Bourbon Street, a pedicab – a cross between a rickshaw and a tricycle – pulled up. I explained that we only had a few hours in New Orleans and I wanted to see where Storyville, the old red-light district, had been, although it was now late and we had concerns about going beyond the boundaries of the French Quarter. We also wanted to

French Quarter, New Orleans, Louisiana.

find some jazz on Frenchman Street, on the opposite side of the quarter, and find a restaurant.

I'd read that one or two buildings had survived the ordinance to close down the red-light district's activities in 1917 and Storyville's eventual demolition in the 1930s. I mentioned to Mark, the pedicab driver, that one of my older guidebooks had cautioned about this part of town, stating that it was ill-advised to visit after dark. Mark said that he hadn't encountered any problems himself and while he wouldn't recommend us walking at night, he thought we'd be okay with him. So, putting our trust in a man with a one-geared tricycle with practically no acceleration and carrying a combined human load of 250kg, the three of us set off to find Storyville. We passed lines of tourists queuing for the clubs on Bourbon Street and Mark picked up a little speed as we zipped through the narrow residential streets on the outer fringe of the French Quarter. Mark brought the tricycle to a halt outside a red-painted brick building on the corner of Bienville Street. It had the appearance of a fast-food takeaway, and metal shutters were pulled over the front windows. Only the heavy steel door tied open with a piece of string and the white glow of fluorescent light indicated that the 'Basin Supermarket, Seafood & Grill' was open for business. A group of young men smoking and drinking sat on the steps of a boarded-up building nearby.

This, explained Mark, was one of the last surviving buildings from Storyville, an area which once stretched from Iberville Street to St Louis Street and from Basin Street to Robertson Street. We were looking at what had once been a side building of Lulu White's Mahogany Hall, one of Storyville's most well-known brothels. Louis Armstrong is on record as saying that Jelly Roll Morton played in one of the rooms there.[11] The building had merely been an annex to a much grander four-storey house that sported a castle turret. The red-brick 'Basin Supermarket' once had an additional two floors, and on what had been the third floor Tom Anderson published his 'Blue Book', a guide to the services provided by the prostitutes of Storyville.[12]

Today Storyville's place in the history of New Orleans, blues and the birth of jazz owes as much to myth as it does fact. The myth locates the emergence of jazz in Storyville, sometime after 1884 following the enactment of Code 111, which imposed restrictive race segregation on coloured Creoles, effectively denying them many white occupations. This, it is argued, brought Creole musicians familiar with ragtime closer together with black musicians more familiar with blues styles. This consequently led to musical collaboration in the brass and dance bands of New Orleans. For Alan Lomax it was in the barrelhouses and brothels of Storyville that this collaboration of the oppressed

French Quarter, New Orleans, Louisiana.

One of the last buildings from Storyville. The annex to Lulu White's
Mahogany Hall, Basin Street, New Orleans, Louisiana.

culminated in jazz. Describing his recorded interviews with Jelly Roll Morton in 1938, Lomax suggests that Morton 'perceived that jazz was the product and resolution of painful class tensions between "lower" class American blacks and "upper" French speaking mulattos'.[13]

Charles Edward Smith pointed Lomax in the direction of Jelly Roll Morton, who by the late 1930s was reduced to playing in a small club, the Jungle Inn in Washington, largely forgotten about since his heyday in the early 1920s. Just over a year after Lomax had made his recording of Morton's account of New Orleans jazz, which included tales of Storyville, Charles Edward Smith and Frederic Ramsey's book Jazzmen was published.[14]

According to this narrative, jazz came out of Storyville, the product of musicians such as Jelly Roll Morton, Joe 'King' Oliver and Bunk Johnson, who built upon ragtime and the variations around melodies that the New Orleans's brass bands had introduced. As Elijah Wald says:

> The music of Buddy Bolden, the New Orleans trumpeter who is generally credited with leading the first true jazz band, is usually described as a fusion of blues – the main African American style brought to the city after emancipation – and the Caribbean Creole style of the city's earlier colored residents.[15]

The subsequent 'New Orleans Revival' of the 1940s now had a narrative with biblical parallels. Storyville was not only the setting for jazz's 'foundation myth', but its closure in 1917 provided jazz with a symbolic diaspora, as musicians were evicted and took their music with them. Philip Larkin, when writing about Jazzmen, referred to the underlying suggestion of ancestral expulsion from Eden. Similarly, Norman K. Risjord refers tonthis symbolic jazz diaspora when he states:[16]

> With Negro boys pushing their belongings in two-wheeled carts, the 'Red Light Queens' made their way out of Storyville, accompanied by their brass bands playing a jazzed up version of 'Nearer My God to Thee'. The closing of Storyville was symbolic of the jazz diaspora, as the musicians of New Orleans and Memphis joined thousands of other blacks who moved north during the war.[17]

We stood on the crossroads of Basin Street and Bienville Street and photographed the remaining one-storey of 237 Basin Street. Looking at its shuttered windows and graffitied front door, I wondered for how much longer it could survive. The building stood as a monument to the ability of ordinary people to create exceptional and beautiful art out of appalling circumstances, because behind the glitzy façades of the Storyville brothels lay an ugliness, which Coming through Slaughter shows through the eyes of Buddy Bolden as

the cornetist makes his way past 'pox-ridden women who carry mattresses on their backs and charge a quarter a fuck'.[18]

Mark pointed beyond the first block on Bienville and explained that the other remaining Storyville building, Early's Saloon, stood on the next corner. This is where pianist Tony Jackson played, who many have said was the greatest of the Storyville professors and who Morton acclaimed as the one pianist better than himself.[19] Today the building houses the New Image Supermarket but still retains many of the outward characteristics of the French Quarter properties. Unfortunately Mark advised us that it would be unwise to venture further into the area until the morning.

But Storyville is as much about a story that tries to explain history as it is about the events themselves. Inseparable from that story are the people who helped shape it, such as Alan Lomax and the authors of Jazzmen.[20] Many recent histories have debunked the myth of Storyville, arguing that jazz developed outside of the red-light district and suggesting that the 'creation myth' of how jazz came about had very little to do with discriminatory legislation. Dr Lewis Porter argues that jazz wasn't born in the red-light district but in musicians' homes, and reminds us that it doesn't happen in a middle of a gig. He also suggests that it was the bars that hired bands, whereas the brothels hired solo pianists in little reception rooms. The view that jazz originated in the brothels of Storyville is, he says, 'misplaced bizarre sentimentality'.[21]

Nonetheless, the New Orleans revival emerged from the histories in Jazzmen. These stories resonated with English jazz musicians such as trumpeter Ken Colyer and trombonist Chris Barber, who were instrumental in bringing many of the Delta blues and Chicago blues musicians over to England in the 1960s. Colyer tells of how he met one of his great idols, trumpet player George Mitchell, at Muddy Waters's home on South Lake Park Avenue, the house on the South Side where our own journey had begun.[22]

Marybeth Hamilton says the authors of Jazzmen:

> (They) were the first blues historians. To dismiss them for finding the wrong story is to overlook the work such tales perform. … Eric Hobsbawn notes, for revivalists 'New Orleans' became a multiple myth and symbol: anti-commercial, anti-racist, proletarian populist, new Deal radical, or just anti-respectable and anti-parental depending on taste.[23]

We passed back along a deserted Basin Street squashed in the back of the pedicab. The absence of people on the footways beyond the French Quarter was at odds with the white light that bathed the vacant lots. I glanced back one last time at the last building in Storyville. I wondered if Jelly Roll Morton, who in a letter to Down Beat claimed to have created jazz in 1902, played at Lulu Whites. If he had, then this evening had made a fitting end to our journey.[24]

In Morton's letter he refers to the first blues players he heard as a youngster, and states that when he first started going to school he'd heard a number of blues players who could play nothing else: 'Buddie Carter, Josky Adams, Game Kid, Frank Richards, Sam Henry and many more too numerous to mention – what we call "ragmen" in New Orleans.'[25] Morton told Alan Lomax he'd also heard blues as a youngster, played by a Creole prostitute named Mamie Desdoumes, who lived next door to his godmother's house in the Garden District of New Orleans. She accompanied her singing on the piano, despite having two fingers missing from her right hand.[26] This is likely to have been towards the end of the 1890s, which would place Morton's first hearing of the blues around the same time as W.C. Handy in Mississippi and Ma Rainey in Missouri, or perhaps even a little before.

The pedicab came to a halt outside a dry cleaners. A sign hanging over the door read 'The Clothes Spin – Wash and Fold'. We were outside what looked like a French Creole building, in good repair, and through the window I could see an array of vending machines and a juke box. Appropriate, I thought, considering that when a young Cosimo Matassa first came here some seventy or so years ago, it was an old grocery store from which his father serviced juke boxes. When Cosimo started selling some of the old juke box records he found that there was a local demand them, and he renamed the store J&M Music Shop.

It wasn't long before Cosimo invested in a Duo-Press disc cutter and established a small recording studio in the rooms at the rear of the premises. The black-and-gold Rock and Roll Hall of Fame Museum plaque on the wall outside informs passers-by that here from 1947–56 was 'J&M Studios, owned and operated by Cosimo Matassa … along with producer and arranger Dave Bartholomew, Matassa recorded sessions by pioneers Fats Domino, Little Richard, Bartholomew, Professor Longhair, Smiley Lewis, Lloyd Price, Roy Brown, and Shirley and Lee, among many others'.

Little Richard had come through these doors, having been taken down to the Dew Drop Inn by Bumps Blackwell. Richard's morning session at J&M had been uninspiring, so everyone retired to the inn. It was while they were there that Richard walked up to an upright piano and belted out an impromptu 'Tutti Frutti' for the small lunchtime crowd. Bumps was so knocked out by what he heard that arrangements were made for Dorothy Labostrie to quickly tidy up the lyrics. The party returned to the studio and recorded 'Tutti Frutti' that afternoon.[27]

Dave Bartholomew had been a trumpeter on Bourbon Street; he'd been tutored by Peter Davis, who had also had taught a young Louis Armstrong.

J&M Records, Rampart Street, New Orleans.

Bartholomew's path crossed Matassa's when his band became the house band for the *Dr Daddy-O Show*, which was recorded and broadcast from the J & M Studio. Dr Daddy-O was a black DJ called Vernon Winslow; he'd had to move his broadcast from the New Orleans Hotel to the J & M Studio in 1949 because as a black man he was forced to ride the freight elevator. Not only did Winslow break new ground as a black DJ, but as Nelson George says: 'historians of New Orleans's fertile music scene credit Dr. Daddy-O with leading local radio away from swing jazz to the rocking sound of rhythm & blues that became the fifties, along with gumbo, the city's most popular local delicacy.'[28]

Dave Bartholomew's band went on to back Fats Domino on his first record a couple of years later and Bartholomew became the producer behind a string of Fats Domino's hits. As Adam Komorowski says, 'more than anyone else it was Bartholomew who put Cosimo Matassa's recording studios well and truly on the map.'[29]

The first historic site we visited on our trip was the 708, on Chicago's South Side, where a young, hungry Buddy Guy had got up and played Guitar Slim's 'The Things that I Used to Do'. And it was at the J & M Studio that Slim, backed by Ray Charles, recorded the song in 1953. Six years later Slim died of pneumonia at the age of 32 after collapsing on tour. His lifestyle had taken its toll. Yet according to Robert Palmer, Slim's short life and career had an incredible influence upon numerous artists, including Ike Turner, Earl King, Jimi Hendrix and Ray Charles.[30]

Back into the pedicab, Mark whisked us through to the other side of the French Quarter. As he left, he cautioned us not to wander away from the main streets this late in the evening.

We wanted to celebrate the end of the trip over a bottle of wine and some jazz on Frenchman Street. Music emanated from the bars and restaurants and we settled on a restaurant with a three-piece jazz band playing near the window. The maître d' sat us at a table on the street and fetched some drinks, assuring us a table inside would be free within a few minutes. I made my way to the wash rooms, and on my return discovered that Richard had found a new friend, although he hadn't caught her name. Leaving me with our new acquaintance, an attractive woman at least half my age, Richard departed for the wash rooms.

'What are you doing here,' she enquired, looking a shade tipsy.

'I'm writing a book about blues pilgrims and …'

'Have you been here all afternoon? I have.' She laughed loudly as she spoke, seemingly oblivious to my explanation of why I was in New Orleans.

'No, we've driven down from Chicago, down Highway 61 over the last three weeks. Are you waiting for some friends?'

'I was with some friends this afternoon, but they've gone now. What did you say you're doing?'

I looked across to the maître d', wondering if our table was ready yet and why he seemed oblivious to the slightly drunk young woman who had joined us.

'We've just come over here on a tricycle, from the last surviving building in Storyville,' I volunteered. 'Having come this far, it's a great to end here, in the French Quarter, and listen to some jazz.'

I was somewhat concerned about why our new friend was on her own and a little worse for wear. I started running through all the possibilities; why, of all the men on Frenchman Street, had she chosen two middle-aged blokes to sit next to. Was she after a drink, or maybe even a meal? Perhaps she had come down to the French Quarter with a group of work friends and had had a few too many.

'Do you work round here? Have you been working here all afternoon?' I enquired.

She threw her head back, laughing in mock embarrassment, before replying, 'Did you just ask me if I was a hooker?'

Notes

1. Morton, Jelly Roll, 'I created jazz in 1902', *Down Beat* 5:8, August 1938, p.3.
2. Ondaatje, Michael, *Coming through Slaughter*, Picador, 1984, p.21. Reference to Webb's cabin at Pontchartrain, Morton, Jelly Roll, 'I created jazz in 1902', p.3.
3. Ramsey, Frederic, Ramsey, Frederick Jr, *Been Here and Gone*, Cassell & Company Ltd, 1960, p.135.
4. Bultman, Bethany Ewald, *New Orleans*, Compass American Guides, 1996, p.186.
5. Oliver, Paul, *The Story of the Blues: The Making of Black Music*, Pimlico, 1997, p.10.
6. Palmer, Robert, *Deep Blues*, Penguin, 1982, p.33.
7. Rowe, Mike, *Chicago Blues: The City and the Music*, Da Capo, 1975, p.99. Originally published in 1973 as *Chicago Breakdown*.
8. Palmer, *Deep Blues*, p.39.
9. Ibid., p.40.
10. Wald, Elijah, *The Blues: A Very Short Introduction*, Oxford University Press, 2010, p.2.
11. Armstrong, Louis, *Satchmo: My Life in New Orleans*, Da Capo, 1971, p.104.
12. Bird, Christiane, *The Da Capo Jazz and Blues Lover's Guide to the US*, Da Capo, 2001, p.19.
13. Lomax, Alan, *Mr Jelly Roll*, University of California Press, 2001, p.xvi.
14. See Hamilton, Marybeth, *In Search of the Blues*, pp.125–60 for contribution of Alan Lomax and Frederic Ramsey, Charles Edward Smith and William Russell to the New Orleans revival.
15. Wald, Elijah, *The Blues*, p.82.
16. Palmer, Richard, *Such Deliberate Disguises: The Art of Philip Larkin*, Continuum, 2008, p.61. Quote from Larkin's article in *Truth*, 26 July 1957.
17. Risjord, Norman K., *Giants in their Time: Representative Americans from the Jazz Age to the Cold War*, Rowman & Littlefield Publishers, Inc., 2006, p.8.
18. Ondaatje, *Coming through Slaughter*, pp.118–19.
19. De la Croix, St Sukie, *Chicago Whispers: A History of LGBT Chicago before Stonewall*, University of Wisconsin Press, 2012, p.104.
20. Hamilton, Marybeth, *In Search of the Blues: Black Voices White Visions*, Jonathan Cape, 2007, pp.125–60. For discussion about the role of Alan Lomax, Frederic Ramsey, Charles Edward Smith and William Russell in the development of a jazz history see Chapter 5, 'Been Here and Gone'.
21. Porter, Lewis, 'Dr. Lewis Porter debunks the myth that jazz was born in Storyville', *WBGO Jazz 88.3 FM*, 9 June 2001, www.wbgo.org/internal/mediaplayer/?podcastID=1354 (podcast).
22. Colyer, Ken, 'Interview with Mike Pointon (Pt. 2)', *The Ken Colyer Website*, October 2002, www.kencolyer.org/BSMTwheelerint2.html.
23. Hamilton, *In Search of the Blues*, p.151.
24. Morton, 'I created jazz in 1902', p.3.
25. Ibid., p.4.
26. 'Jelly Roll Morton and Alan Lomax', *Library of Congress Narrative*, transcribed by Michael Hill, Roger Richard, Mike Meddings. Mamie Desmond's (sic) Blues, v/p June 12, 1938, www.doctorjazz.co.uk.
27. For account of the recording of 'Tutti Frutti' see Lauterbach, Preston, *The Chitlin' Circuit and the Road to Rock 'n' Roll*, Norton, 2011, pp.248–9; Komorowski, Adam, (liner notes, p.21), *The Cosimo Matassa Story*, Proper Records, 2007.
28. George, Nelson, *The Death of Rhythm and Blues*, Omnibus Press, 1988, p.53.
29. Komorowski, (liner notes, p.10) *The Cosimo Matassa Story*.
30. Palmer, *Deep Blues*, pp.249–50.

AFTERWORD

Frederick Ramsey Jr made his tape and photographic record of the South over the course of five trips between 1951 and 1957. In his account of these trips, he predicted that 'in twenty years or less, both music and artefacts will be forgotten, as they have been elsewhere in the United States', and concluded that 'from here on, the journey will have to be imagined'.[1]

When I undertook my first blues pilgrimage, I hadn't yet read Ramsey's *Been Here and Gone*. Despite the passage of time there is still much home-grown blues to be found in the South. Nevertheless, I was afraid that much of what I'd seen, certainly in terms of an archaeology of the blues, would have to be imagined within a couple of decades. In every town and city that Richard and I visited between Chicago and New Orleans there remains, albeit precariously, historic reminders of not only the music, but – more importantly – the lives and struggles of the people who made it.

I felt my heart a' beating, when I got up to Cotton Row
Still thinking about those memories of the old folks down home
I've come such a long way, and this is where I gotta be
I'm still searching, searching for that dream
I walked along some muddy river, up Louisiana way
Sailed up the Mississippi in that old steam boat, following the trail
Passed the old plantation, where the cotton used to grow
But the place was empty, there was nobody left, everyone had gone

Looking for the King of the Delta Blues
Gotta hear that bluesman play
Looking for the King of the Delta Blues
Wanna hear that bluesman play

Standin' by the roadside, as that Greyhound bus rolled by
All roads lead to Memphis, straight up that old highway
Y'know that this old town has sure seen better time
Like an Edward Hopper picture, it just sits there in your mind

Looking for the King of the Delta Blues
Gotta hear that bluesman play
Looking for the King of the Delta Blues
Wanna hear that bluesman play

So I walked along some backstreet, stepped into a bar
Yeah the vibes felt cool, the vibes felt good
Seemed it was the right place to be
The smell of stale tobacco was heavy lingering in the air
So I grabbed myself a table down the front
Poured myself a beer
Some old guy up on the stage was singing, playing his guitar
I could feel his soul, feel his music coming straight from the heart
The song he was playing, he was playing for me and you
Oh yeah I was listening to the King of the Delta Blues.[2]

Notes

1.   Ramsey, Frederick Jr, *Been Here and Gone*, Cassell & Company Ltd, 1960, p.xii.
2.   Lyrics by Davey Ralph, 'King of the Delta Blues', 2010. Used by kind permission of Popstopper Records, from the CD *Time Stealer* by Davey Ralph, 11 November 2010.

BIBLIOGRAPHY

Books

Adelt, U., *Blues Music in the Sixties: A Story in Black and White*, Rutgers University Press, 2011

Armstrong, L., *Satchmo: My Life in New Orleans*, Da Capo, 1986

Aswell, T., *Louisiana Rocks! The True Genesis of Rock and Roll*, Pelican, 2010

Barrett, R.J., 'The Heritage of Social Class and Class Conflict on Chicago's South Side', in Ruggles, D.F. (ed.), *On Location: Heritage Cities and Sites*, Springer, 2012

Beaumont, D., *Preachin' the Blues: The Life and Times of Son House*, OUP, 2011

Berendt, J.E. (ed.), *The Story of Jazz; from New Orleans to Rock Jazz*, Barrie & Jenkins, 1978

Berry, C., *The Autobiography*, Faber & Faber, 1988

Bird, C., *The Da Capo Jazz and Blues Lover's Guide to the US*, Da Capo, 2001

Calt, S., *I'd Rather be the Devil: Skip James and the Blues*, Chicago Review Press, 2008

Charters, S.B., *The Country Blues*, Da Capo, 1975

Cheseborough, S., *Blues Traveling: The Holy Sites of Delta Blues*, University Press of Mississippi, 2009

Cohn, D.L., 'Where I was Born and Raised', in Abbott, D. (ed.), *Mississippi Writers: Reflections of Childhood – Non-Fiction*, University of Mississippi, 1985

Collins, S., *America Over the Water*, SAF Publishing, 2007

Cooper, W.J., & Terrill, T.E., *The American South: A History, Volume 1*, McGraw-Hill, 1991

Danchin, S., *Earl Hooker: Blues Master*, University Press of Mississippi, 2001

Davis, F., *The History of the Blues: The Roots, the Music, the People*, Da Capo, 2003

De la Croix, St S., *Chicago Whispers: A History of LGBT Chicago before Stonewall*, University of Wisconsin Press, 2012

Downs, T., *Road Trip Blues & BBQ*, Lonely Planet, 2005

Driggs, F. & Haddix, C., *Kansas City Jazz: From Ragtime to Bebop – A History*, OUP, 2005

Ferris, W., *Give My Poor Heart Ease: Voices of the Mississippi Blues*, University of North Carolina Press, 2009

Filene, B., *Romancing the Folk: Public Memory and American Roots Music*, University of North Carolina Press, 2000

Franzen, J., *The Twenty-Seventh City*, Fourth Estate, 2010

Garon, P. & Tomko, G., *Black Hoboes & their Songs*, Charles H. Kerr, 2006

Garon, P., *Blues and the Poetic Spirit*, City Lights, 1996

Garon, P., *The Devil's Son-In-Law: The Story of Peetie Wheatstraw and His Songs*, Charles H. Kerr, 2003

Gennari, J., *Blowin' Hot and Cool: Jazz and its Critics*, University of Chicago Press, 2006

George, N., *The Death of Rhythm & Blues*, Omnibus Press, 1988

Glover, T., Dirks, S., & Gaines, W., *Blues with a Feeling: The Little Walter Story*, Routledge, 2002

Goldfield, R.D., *Black, White and Southern: Race Relations and Southern Culture 1940 to the Present*, Louisiana State University, 1991

Gordon, R. & Nemerov, B. (eds), *Lost Delta Found: Rediscovering The Fisk University Library of Congress Coahoma County Study 1941–1942*, Vanderbilt University Press, 2005

Gordon, R., *Can't Be Satisfied: The Life and Times of Muddy Waters*, Pimlico, 2003

Grazian, D., *Blue Chicago: The Search for Authenticity in Urban Blues Clubs*, University of Chicago Press, 2005

Guralnick, P., *Feel Like Going Home: Portraits in Blues & Rock 'n' Roll*, Omnibus Press, 1978

Guralnick, P., *Last Train to Memphis: The Rise of Elvis Presley*, Abacus, 1995

Guralnick, P., *Lost Highway: Journeys and Arrivals of American Musicians*, Penguin, 1992

Guralnick, P., *Searching for Robert Johnson*, Penguin, 1992

Guralnick, P., *Sweet Soul Music: Rhythm and Blues and the Southern Dream of Freedom*, Back Bay, 1999

Guy, B., with Ritz, D., *When I Left Home: My Story*, Da Capo, 2012

Halpern, R., *Down on the Killing Floor: Black and White Workers in Chicago's Packinghouses*, University of Illinois Press, 1997

Hamilton, M., *In Search of the Blues: Black Voices, White Visions*, Jonathan Cape, 2007

Hamilton, M., 'The Blues, the Folk, and African-American History' in *Transactions of the Royal Historical Society* 11, 2001

Hamlin, F.N., *Crossroads at Clarksdale: The Black Freedom Struggle in the Mississippi Delta After World War II*, University of North Carolina Press, 2012

Handy, W.C., *Father of the Blues: An Autobiography*, Da Capo, 1991

Hardy, P., & Laing, D., *The Faber Companion to 20th Century Popular Music*, Faber & Faber, 1992

Jones, F., *I Was There When the Blues Was Red Hot*, Borders Bookstore, 2009

Kerouac, J., *On the Road*, Penguin, 1991

Knight, R., *The Blues Highway: New Orleans to Chicago*, Trailblazer, 2001

Kozol, J., *Savage Inequalities: Children in America's Schools*, Crown, 1991

Lauterbach, P., *The Chitlin' Circuit and the Road to Rock'n'Roll*, W.W. Norton & Co., 2011

Lawson, R.A., *Jim Crow's Counterculture: The Blues and Black Southerners 1890–1945*, Louisiana State University Press, 2010

Lehmann, N., *The Promised Land: The Great Black Migration and How It Changed America*, Vintage Books, 1992

Lomax, A., *The Land Where the Blues Began*, The New Press, 1993

Mailer, N., *The White Negro*, City Light, 1957

Marcus, G., *Invisible Republic*, Picador, 1998

McKee, M. & Chisenhall, F., *Beale Black & Blue: Life and Music on Black America's Main Street*, Louisiana State University Press, 1993

Mercier, D., 'Memphis Minnie', in Smith, J.C. (ed.), *Notable Black Americans: Book II*, Gale Research Inc., 1996

Merrill, H., *The Blues Route*, William Morrow & Co., 1990

Middleton, P., *Discover America's Great River Road Vol. 2: The Middle Mississippi, Illinois, Iowa, Missouri*, Heritage Press, 1992

Middleton, P., *Discover America's Great River Road Vol. 3: The Lower Mississippi, St. Louis, Missouri, to Memphis, Tennessee*, Heritage Press, 1998

Middleton, P., *Discover America's Great River Road Vol. 4: Arkansas, Mississippi and Louisiana*, Great River Publishing, 2005

Murray, C.S., *Boogie Man: The Adventures of John Lee Hooker in the American Twentieth Century*, Canongate, 2011

Murray, C.S., *Cross Town Traffic: Jimi Hendrix and Post-War Pop*, Faber & Faber, 2001

Noebel, D.A., *The Marxist Minstrels*, American Christian College Press, 1974

Odum, H.W., *Rainbow Round My Shoulder: The Blue Trail of Black Ulysses*, The Bobbs-Merrill Company, 1928

Oliver, P., *The Story of the Blues*, Pimlico, 1997,

Ondaatje, M., *Coming Through Slaughter*, Pan Books, 1984

Orr-Klopfer, M.S., Klopfer, F. & Klopfer, B., *Where Rebels Roost: Mississippi Civil Rights Revisited*, M Susan Orr-Klopfer, 2005

Palmer, R., *Deep Blues*, Penguin, 1982

Pruter, R., *Doowop: The Chicago Scene*, Board of Trustees of the University of Illinois, 1996

Ramsey, F. Jr, *Been Here and Gone*, Cassell, 1960

Rowe, M., *Chicago Blues*, Da Capo, 1975

Rowley, H., *Richard Wright: The Life and Times*, John Macrae/Owl Books, 2002

Roy, W.G., *Reds, Whites and Blues: Social Movements, Folk Music, and Race in the United States*, Princeton University Press, 2010

Rudwick, E.M., *Race Riot at East St Louis, July 2, 1917*, Illini Books, 1982

Saikku, M., *This Delta, This Land: An Environmental History of the Yazoo-Mississippi Floodplain*, University of Georgia Press, 2005

Segrest, J. & Hoffman, M., *Moanin' at Midnight: The Life and Times of Howlin' Wolf*, Thunder Mouth Press, 2005

Sinclair, Upton, *The Jungle*, Prestwick House, 2005

Stolle, R., *Hidden History of Mississippi Blues*, The History Press, 2011

Twain, M., *Life on the Mississippi*, Wordsworth Editions, 2012

Twain, M., *The Adventures of Huckleberry Finn*, Puffin, 1977

Twain, M., *The Adventures of Tom Sawyer*, Oxford's World Classics, 1998

Wald, E., *Escaping the Delta: Robert Johnson and the Invention of the Blues*, Amistad, 2005

Wald, E., *The Blues: A Very Short Introduction*, OUP, 2010

Wardlow, G.D., *Chasin' that Devil Music: Searching for the Blues*, Backbeat Books, 1998

Wilkinson, B., *The Civil Rights Movement: An Illustrated History*, Crescent Books, 1997

Wolfe, C. & Lornell, K., *The Life and Legend of Leadbelly*, Da Capo, 1999

Wright, R., *Black Boy: A Record of Childhood and Youth*, Longman, 1984

Wright, R., *Native Son and How 'Bigger' Was Born*, Harper Perennial, 1993

Wyman, B., with Havers, R., *Bill Wyman's Blues Odyssey: A Journey to the Music's Heart and Soul*, Dorling Kindersley, 2001

Yalom, M., *The American Resting Place*, Houghton Mifflin, 2008

Articles

Chicago Defender articles and reports from Chicago Defender Archive online: pqasb. pqarchiver.com/chicagodefender/advancedsearch.html

New Masses archive: www.unz.org/Pub/NewMasses

Silva, R., 'Walks Through History, Cherry Street Historic District', 13 April 2013: www.arkansaspreservation.com/pdf/tour_scripts/Cherry%20Street%20HD%20 Helena%20Tour%20Script%202013.pdf

Wald, E., 'Charlie Patton: Folksinger': www.elijahwald.com/patton.html

Snyder, J.T., 'The Effects of Casino Gaming on Tunica County, Mississippi, A Case Study 1992–1997', Social Research Report Series 99-2, Mississippi State University, September 1999: jamesthomassnyder.files.wordpress.com/2011/11/effects-of-casino-gaming-social-science-research-Center.pdf

Evans, D., 'Demythologising the Blues', in ISAM Newsletter, Fall 1999, Vol. XXIX, No.1: depthome.brooklyn.cuny.edu/isam/evans.html

Magazines

Living Blues

Blues & Rhythm

Films

Chuck Berry, Hail! Hail! Rock 'n' Roll, 1987

M for Mississippi, A Road Trip through the Birthplace of the Blues, 2008

Mystery Train, 1989

We Juke Up in Here!, Mississippi's Juke Joint Culture at the Crossroads, 2012

INDEX